GLOBAL BUSINESS ASSOCIATIONS

Global business tends to be perceived as a number of individual but powerful multinational corporations, capable of controlling markets and influencing political decisions; in fact, global business is highly organized through a plethora of associations that bring together competing companies and conflicting national businesses. Indeed, global business associations have a long history and, with accelerated globalization, further opportunities emerge for unified business action.

This book fills a significant gap in the current literature, examining the pivotal role of global business associations and providing a concise and accessible overview of their different functions in a range of institutional contexts. Beginning by clarifying the concept of global business associations, the author puts their role into a historical and contemporary context in which their economic, social and political functions are sketched. Their historical origin is outlined, including the proliferation of global associations in the twentieth and twenty-first centuries. He then moves on to explore and analyze the different types of actors, explaining key categories and their place in the organization of global business with chapters on peak associations (e.g. ICC and WEF), industry associations, alliances, as well as clubs and think tanks, and facilitators.

Covering the history, current role and future evolution of this dynamic category of associations, this work will be essential reading for students and scholars of international political economy, international relations, international organizations and global governance.

Karsten Ronit is associate professor at the Department of Political Science, University of Copenhagen. He has studied the role of organized business and other interest groups in a range of domestic, regional and global contexts. He has published many articles and books on these subjects, most recently *Global Consumer Organizations* with Routledge.

GLOBAL INSTITUTIONS

Edited by Thomas G. Weiss
The CUNY Graduate Center, New York, USA
and Rorden Wilkinson
University of Sussex, Brighton, UK

The "Global Institutions Series" provides cutting-edge books about many aspects of what we know as "global governance." It emerges from our shared frustrations with the state of available knowledge—electronic and print-wise, for research and teaching—in the area. The series is designed as a resource for those interested in exploring issues of international organization and global governance. And since the first volumes appeared in 2005, we have taken significant strides toward filling conceptual gaps.

The series consists of three related "streams" distinguished by their blue, red, and green covers. The blue volumes, comprising the majority of the books in the series, provide user-friendly and short (usually no more than 50,000 words) but authoritative guides to major global and regional organizations, as well as key issues in the global governance of security, the environment, human rights, poverty, and humanitarian action among others. The books with red covers are designed to present original research and serve as extended and more specialized treatments of issues pertinent for advancing understanding about global governance. And the volumes with green covers—the most recent departure in the series—are comprehensive and accessible accounts of the major theoretical approaches to global governance and international organization.

The books in each of the streams are written by experts in the field, ranging from the most senior and respected authors to first-rate scholars at the beginning of their careers. In combination, the three components of the series—blue, red, and green—serve as key resources for faculty, students, and practitioners alike. The works in the blue and green streams have value as core and complementary readings in courses on, among other things, international organization, global governance, international law, international relations, and international political economy; the red volumes allow further reflection and investigation in these and related areas.

The books in the series also provide a segue-way to the foundation volume that offers the most comprehensive textbook treatment available dealing with all the major issues, approaches, institutions, and actors in contemporary global governance—our edited work International Organization and Global Governance (2014)—a volume to which many of the authors in the series have contributed essays.

Understanding global governance—past, present, and future—is far from a finished journey. The books in this series nonetheless represent significant steps toward a better way of conceiving contemporary problems and issues as well as, hopefully, doing something to improve world order. We value the feedback from our readers and their role in helping shape the on-going development of the series.

A complete list of titles can be viewed online here: https://www.routledge.com/Global-Institutions/book-series/GI

UNHCR as a Surrogate State (2018)
by Sarah Deardorff Miller

The British Media and the Rwandan Genocide (2018)
by John Nathaniel Clarke

The League of Nations (2018)
by M. Patrick Cottrell

Global Governance and China (2018)
edited by Scott Kennedy

Global Business Associations (2018)
by Karsten Ronit

A League of Democracies (2018)
Cosmopolitanism, Consolidation Arguments, and Global Public Goods
by John Davenport

Moral Obligations and Sovereignty in International Relations (2018)
A Genealogy of Humanitarianism
by Andrea Paras

Protecting the Internally Displaced (2018)
Rhetoric and Reality
by Phil Orchard

GLOBAL BUSINESS ASSOCIATIONS

Karsten Ronit

LONDON AND NEW YORK

First published 2018
by Routledge
2 Park Square, Milton Park, Abingdon, Oxon OX14 4RN

and by Routledge
52 Vanderbilt Avenue, New York, NY 10017

Routledge is an imprint of the Taylor & Francis Group, an informa business

© 2018 Karsten Ronit

The right of Karsten Ronit to be identified as author of this work has been asserted by him in accordance with sections 77 and 78 of the Copyright, Designs and Patents Act 1988.

All rights reserved. No part of this book may be reprinted or reproduced or utilised in any form or by any electronic, mechanical, or other means, now known or hereafter invented, including photocopying and recording, or in any information storage or retrieval system, without permission in writing from the publishers.

Trademark notice: Product or corporate names may be trademarks or registered trademarks, and are used only for identification and explanation without intent to infringe.

British Library Cataloguing in Publication Data
A catalogue record for this book is available from the British Library

Library of Congress Cataloging in Publication Data
Names: Ronit, Karsten, author.
Title: Global business associations / Karsten Ronit.
Description: Abingdon, Oxon ; New York, NY : Routledge, 2018. | Series: Routledge global institutions series | Includes bibliographical references and index.
Identifiers: LCCN 2018024940| ISBN 9781138960824 (hardback) | ISBN 9781138960848 (paperback) | ISBN 9781315660165 (ebook)
Subjects: LCSH: International business enterprises–Societies, etc.
Classification: LCC HD2755.5 .R675 2019 | DDC 338.8/806–dc23
LC record available at https://lccn.loc.gov/2018024940

ISBN: 978-1-1389-6082-4 (hbk)
ISBN: 978-1-1389-6084-8 (pbk)
ISBN: 978-1-3156-6016-5 (ebk)

Typeset in Bembo
by Taylor & Francis Books

CONTENTS

List of illustrations viii
Acknowledgements ix
Abbreviations xiii

   Introduction 1
1 Peak associations 21
2 Industry associations 55
3 Alliances of corporations and associations 90
4 Clubs and think tanks 115
5 Facilitators 140
6 Conclusion 165

Bibliography *179*
Index *183*

ILLUSTRATIONS

Figures

1.1 National business in global peak associations	30
1.2 The first headquarters of ICC	33
1.3 Annual Meeting of the BRICS Business Council	46
2.1 Associability in a bygone age: meeting of the International Federation of Master Cotton Spinners' and Manufacturers' Association in Cairo and Alexandria, 1927	69
2.2 Cyber Security Onboard Ships guidelines developed by industry associations	77
3.1 The multiple and variable roots of alliances	93
4.1 Hotel de Bilderberg—the first meeting place of the club	121
5.1 Tasks managed by facilitators in relation to associations (markets and politics)	144
5.2 The major consulting firms and their global market shares (2016)	153

Tables

3.1 Members, benefits and tasks in the FIDO Alliance	105
4.1 Location of think tank offices and entities	127

ACKNOWLEDGEMENTS

The idea to write this book has lingered on my mind for many years. I originally started out having a scholarly interest in the relations between business and politics as they play out in different national arenas, but soon realized that organized business was operating across jurisdictions. Hence, I began focusing on business and politics, first in a regional and then in a global context from the middle of the 1990s, leading to publications on different industries and various policy fields in which global business is active. Together with many other scholars I have provided smaller pieces of a much larger puzzle still uncompleted.

Over the years, I have led or been a part of many research projects that have focused on the role of business associations, and the book could not have been written without these inspirations and without the ensuing professional contacts and friendships. It is impossible to thank all those colleagues here, but some colleagues have provided specific comments on selected aspects of this concrete book project. I have more recently discussed the organization of food with Carsten Daugbjerg; mining and minerals and the role of BIAC with Aynsley Kellow; think tanks with Diane Stone; finance with Tony Porter; members of business associations with John Mikler; relations between associations and intergovernmental agencies with Bob Reinalda; and the role of facilitators in business with Lyne Latulippe. The same goes for the practitioners in the associations with whom I have had numerous contacts in the preparation of this book, but they generally prefer to remain anonymous, which I respect. However, it is important to stress that there is today an abundance of open sources on business associations, although they, as other actors, have their secrecy, and there is therefore a sound basis for studying their organization and political activities.

Although global business associations have been alive for decades and in certain cases centuries, it is still a virgin field. Many opportunities to advance the study of global business associations have been missed. Although their core interest is not really centered on business associations, some disciplines and sub-disciplines have relatively much to offer on the study of this group of organizations, for instance certain fields of comparative politics, political sociology and economic sociology to name a few; however, even they have largely failed to embrace the global activities of business associations, quite astonishing given the profound transboundary actions of business.

Yet, at the same time, studies dedicated to exploring international relations and international political economy, and corporate behavior and management, in principle all obvious candidates to investigate global business associations, have not provided a warm welcome to this group of actors into their various scholarly traditions. States, a focal point of political science, and markets, a key field for economics and business administration, are easily recognized in these disciplines, while intermediary actors such as associations performing key tasks in and between economy and politics are sidelined. This emphasis on and celebration of particularly dignified aspects in a discipline, and disregard of others, is known from many other areas of research and often prevents science from key insights and from moving ahead. As the renowned twentieth-century archeologist V. Gordon Childe wrote: "My Oxford training was in the Classical tradition to which bronzes, terracottas and pottery (at least if painted) were respectable while stone and bone tools were banausic."[1] His experiences can easily be translated to our field. The truly multi-disciplinary character of the study on global business associations is clearly a factor complicating research, but the rigidity of established paradigms, and simple lack of knowledge, are factors that effectively keep new or forgotten perspectives at bay. However, such new studies provide important insights and invigorate the field.

For many years, a book devoted to global business associations as a multidimensional species has been missing. Given the lack of concentrated effort in these multiple disciplines, it is hardly surprising that this volume comes relatively late in the series on global institutions. Having completed an earlier book in the series on *Global Consumer Organizations*, I discussed my ideas for a new book with the series editors and they encouraged me to write a proposal on a new volume on business associations. My proposal was immediately approved, and I began work on the manuscript in the summer of 2015.

The working title, also the final title of the book, was *Global Business Associations*, but right from the beginning I was aware that a study on these associations could not and should not be strictly limited to organizations that conceived themselves as associations in a formal sense and conceptually fulfilled these criteria in research. Indeed, there are a number of other actors that share a number of the same tasks as the associations in the business community but cannot be categorized as associations proper. If treating only those organizations that fulfill all the requirements of associations and leaving out those that belong to a wider population of business actors and in certain respects overlap with the associations, we would risk offering a somewhat incomplete image of the organization of the business community, and hence of the multiple challenges facing associations. For this reason, certain groups of other and quite heterogeneous actors are included, and the title of the book could be extended to the awkward title *Global Business Associations and Related Entities* to capture the wider ecology of actors. It is, however, important to stress that associations epitomize the political representation of collective business interests in the global realm and abound at all levels in the business community, hence giving the book its deserved title.

The work on the manuscript has been spread across a number of semesters, moving forward when time allowed. However, I had a good opportunity to make headway during a stay at the Department of Government at the University of Tasmania in the winter of 2015–16, and on various occasions I have presented bits and pieces of the work at conferences of the International Studies Association, at the International Political Science Association, and at the International Public Policy Association. I finally had the opportunity to complete the book during a research stay at the San Cataldo Institution, Costiera Amalfitana, in November 2016. Here it was possible to think through all the basic arguments behind the book one last time and how best to present them.

I am very pleased to have the book published in the Global Institutions series and that business associations are now presented alongside the many public and private organizations that make up the global political system. As series editors, Thomas G. Weiss and Rorden Wilkinson saw this right from the beginning and have secured a fast publication of the book, involving useful comments from anonymous reviewers. I also owe thanks to Nicola Parkin, later on Robert Sorsby, and their co-workers at Routledge, for reminding me of deadlines and seeing the manuscript through a speedy editorial and production process.

Karsten Ronit
St. Paul's Bay
April 2018

Note

1 V. Gordon Childe, "Retrospect," *Antiquity* 32 (1958): 69–74, at 69.

ABBREVIATIONS

ACAMS	Association of Certified Anti-Money Laundering Specialists
ACC	American Chemistry Council
ASC	Aquaculture Stewardship Council
B20	Business 20 Coalition
BBC	BRICS Business Council
BDI	Bundesverband der Deutschen Industrie/Federation of German Industries
BIAC	Business and Industry Advisory Committee to the OECD
BIMCO	Baltic and International Maritime Council
BIS	Bank for International Settlements
BRICS	Brazil, Russia, India, China, South Africa
BUSA	Business Unity South Africa
CAPE	Confederation of Asia-Pacific Employers
CCI Russia	Chamber of Commerce and Industry of the Russian Federation
CCOIC	China Chamber of International Commerce
CCPIT	China Council for the Promotion of International Trade
CEATAL	Business Technical Advisory Committee on Labor Matters
CEFIC	European Chemical Industry Council
CNI	National Confederation of Industry
CRT	Caux Round Table
EABC	European-American Business Council

ECOSOC	United Nations Economic and Social Council
EU	European Union
FAO	Food and Agriculture Organization of the United Nations
FBN-I	Family Business Network International
FICCI	Federation of Indian Chambers of Commerce and Industry
FIDO	Fast IDentity Online Alliance
FIO	Food Information Organization Network
FSB	Financial Stability Board
FSC	Forest Stewardship Council
GAA	Global Accounting Alliance
GAA	Global Agri-business Alliance
GAN	Global Apprenticeships Network
GATF	Global Alliance for Trade Facilitation
GATT	General Agreement on Tariffs and Trade
GBA	Global Business Alliance for 2030
GBC	Global Business Coalition
GBC-Education	Global Business Coalition for Education
GFMA	Global Financial Market Association
GIRN	Global Industrial Relations Network
GOSH	Global Occupational Safety & Health Network
IAA	International Advertising Association
IAB	Interactive Advertising Bureau
IACC	International AntiCounterfeiting Coalition
IAFN	International Agri-Food Network
IATA	International Air Transport Association
IBA	International Bar Association
IBCC	International Bureau of Chambers of Commerce
IBFed	International Banking Federation
IBLF Global	International Business Leaders Forum Global
ICA	International Court of Arbitration
ICAO	International Civil Aviation Organization
ICB	Industry Classification Benchmark
ICBA	International Council of Beverages Associations
ICC	International Chamber of Commerce
ICCA	International Council of Chemical Associations
ICCIMB	International Maritime Bureau
ICCTM	International Committee on Cotton Testing Methods
ICIS	Independent Chemical Information Service
ICMM	International Council of Mining and Minerals

Abbreviations xv

ICS	International Chamber of Shipping
ICTA	International Chemical Trade Association
IDC	International Diamond Council
IFBA	International Food and Beverage Alliance
IFPMA	International Federation of Pharmaceutical Manufacturers and Associations
IFRS	International Financial Reporting Standards
IGO	intergovernmental organization
IIBCC	International Information Bureau of Chambers of Commerce
IIF	Institute of International Finance
IISI	International Iron and Steel Institute
ILO	International Labour Organization
IMF	International Monetary Fund
IMO	International Maritime Organization
INGO	international non-governmental organization
INTERTANKO	International Association of Independent Tanker Owners
IO	international organization
IOE	International Organization of Employers
IPE	international political economy
ISDA	International Swaps and Derivatives Association
ISF	International Shipping Federation
ISIC	International Standard Industrial Classification of All Activities
ISO	International Organization for Standardization
ITMF	International Textile Manufacturers Federation
JCIA	Japan Chemical Industry Association
LCIA	London Court of International Arbitration
MEDEF	Mouvement des Entreprises de France
MNC	multinational corporation
MNE	multinational enterprise
MSC	Marine Stewardship Council
NGO	non-governmental organization
OECD	Organisation for Economic Co-operation and Development
PCI SCC	Payment Card Industry Security Standards Council
PMA	Produce Marketing Association
PWBLF	The Prince of Wales Business Leaders Forum
RT	Round Table of International Shipping Associations
SAC	Sustainable Apparel Coalition
SMEs	small and medium-sized enterprises

TABD	TransAtlantic Business Dialogue
TBC	Transatlantic Business Coalition
TNC	transnational corporation
UIA	International Association of Lawyers
UN	United Nations
UNEP	United Nations Environment Programme
UNESCO	United Nations Educational, Scientific and Cultural Organization
UNFCCC	United Nations Framework Convention on Climate Change
UNICEF	United Nations Children's Fund
UNITAR	United Nations Institute for Training and Research
UNWTO	United Nations World Tourism Organization
WBCSD	World Business Council for Sustainable Development
WCF	World Chambers Federation
WEF	World Economic Forum
WFA	World Federation of Advertisers
WHO	World Health Organization
WIPO	World Intellectual Property Organization
worldsteel	World Steel Association
WSC	World Shipping Council
WTO	World Trade Organization
WTTC	World Travel & Tourism Council

INTRODUCTION

- Global business associations and related private entities
- The profound historical background
- Meagre research traditions
- Toward an integrated approach: complementarities in the business community
- Outline of the book

While global civil society tends to be seen through a rich array of social movements, global business is generally perceived as a number of powerful multinational corporations (MNCs) capable of controlling markets, a series of disguised elite networks or an anonymous social class of capitalists that influence politics in domestic and international contexts. A relatively weak but organized civil society is seemingly opposed to a strong but comparatively fragmented business community often deprived of formal and identifiable coordination. The reality, however, is that business is highly organized at the global level. A plethora of associations and a variety of related private bodies bring together competing companies and conflicting national businesses in a rich variety of combinations. Indeed, global business associations have a long history,[1] and with accelerated globalization in recent decades, further opportunities have arisen for unified action in the business community.

Associations and other forms of collective action harness important resources to build strategies in different institutional contexts: first, many business norms and rules are defined by associations to guide the behavior of firms in the market; second, associations position certain interests in relation to other associations and forms of cooperation in business; third, coordinated responses are formulated to meet the challenges of labor unions, consumer organizations and various civil society groups; and fourth, business interests are represented before many different intergovernmental bodies to influence public regulation. Associations have different functions in relation to the market, civil society and the state, and may specialize in one of these roles, but often several roles are managed within the same association.

In scholarly work, only limited attention is given to global business associations and similar private entities. A systematic treatment is consequently needed to fill a major gap in the literature and confront prevailing assumptions and tacit understandings about the capacity of global business for collective action. This treatment needs to identify, classify and analyze very different formats of organized business, but we must also move beyond this exercise and offer some relevant theoretical lenses through which to study this phenomenon. Of course, this would be far easier if we already had a rich tradition of studies and vibrant discussion, but this is not the case. Hence, this volume has many demanding tasks.

It is important to recognize the complex character of global business associations: they have different constituencies, perform multiple economic, social and political functions, and engage in a variety of institutional contexts.[2] It is also important to analyze associations as based on sound historical traditions yet forming a dynamic category that includes established as well as many new entities to cope with changing demands and expectations in and beyond the global business community. Furthermore, it is necessary to recognize that concerns are not always managed by typical associations but are taken care of by other, related private organizations.

Global business associations and related private entities

Our approach to global business associations must be precise yet flexible enough to accommodate different groups under this general concept. We need a robust concept that can single out associations as particular manifestations of political action but, at the same time, is malleable and recognizes that associations perform multiple activities—for instance, downgrading political tasks and upgrading activities to help members in the market.[3] This view appreciates associational diversity and recognizes continuities in associational profiles.[4]

Time is important from this perspective. The tasks of global associations are not fixed but under continuous development, influenced by forces inside business and drivers in their institutional environment. In this evolution, associations become involved in areas and activities managed by other bodies in the business community, and, vice versa, these entities infringe upon the traditional activities of business associations.[5] Such trespasses show that although there are typical activities in which associations are involved, these are fluctuating and arbitrary and must be defined under the impact of broad institutional developments. A number of business-related think tanks, for instance, are important in global agenda-setting and prepare analyses and issue reports, a job held primarily by associations, and certain law firms offer various legal services, which are also provided by associations to their members and others on a commercial basis. By including these various private entities in our analysis, we will reach a better understanding of associations and other cognate entities in the global business community.[6]

When examining associational profiles, we need to take account of some key organizational properties. It is important to clarify which concerns they organize and represent (the membership domain), which purposes they have (the political domain), in which policy fields associations are active (the policy domain) and at which level they are present (the territorial domain).[7] We also have to acknowledge that there are various formal organizations that cannot be fully encompassed by the concept of associations, but, in many ways, these organizations are related to the core functions of associations. These related private entities compete with associations in some areas but mainly tangentially. They specialize in certain functions that already are or can potentially be covered by business associations, and they perform various auxiliary roles in the global business community.

First, global business associations organize and represent private enterprises of different kinds. They do this either directly, through the membership of corporations, or indirectly, through the membership of various types of associations that organize these corporations, and different membership models can be combined. There are many ways to recruit members, but it is essential that members come from the business world, represent interests from the private sector and are not compromised by other concerns. As a rule, publicly owned companies governed by other interests and accountable to actors beyond the market are not included or represented by these associations. Still, of course, instances of public involvement cannot be completely ruled out in private firms, and private owners and managers also come in many different forms; we may find instances of publicly owned companies joining private associations. There can also be cases of expert involvement that extend the member bases of business associations and help in coalition building.[8] As far as possible, however, we will concentrate on business associations as essential private organizations that are strong adherents of free-enterprise principles.

Second, global business associations have a distinct political orientation. Basically, they organize a wide spectrum of individual business concerns rooted in the economic, social and political conditions of producers and employers, and formulate collective business interests that can be represented in a variety of political contexts. Thus, associations provide examples of developing social capital and turning competitors into cooperators and colleagues within a specific organizational framework where mutual trust prevails. In economics, for instance, it is argued that cooperation is not a rarity among human beings,[9] and in our context, at a more aggregated organizational level, competition is replaced by principles of cooperation. This cooperation is not merely a social benefit for members; it is used for political purposes in exchanging with actors external to the associations. It is important to note that, since we are studying global business associations, which have to accommodate highly complex interests, they often build on already-aggregated interests in the form of, for instance, national associations, a factor facilitating collective action.

Third, global business associations cover a variety of policy fields. They depart from some fundamental interests in the business community, and the most common distinction in organized business is between employer associations and producer associations.[10] Accordingly, associations can develop into rather specialized entities that divide labor and concentrate on either employer issues or producer issues, including how they are addressed by global regulations. They also have the opportunity, however, to embrace multiple concerns and become hybrid organizations that unite both tasks and consequently engage in a much broader field. A realistic assessment indicates that there can be many mixed forms where not all but at least some activities are administered by the same organization without attempting to embrace producers' as well as employers' issues *in toto*. Although the distinction between basic forms of organizations is very useful and, in many cases, adequately captures the situation in associations, one must observe the emergence of new global policy fields as well as the changing interpretations of their mandates, factors that compel associations to adapt and question existing boundaries.

Fourth, global business associations aim to organize and represent global concerns. Business is organized at different territorial levels (subnational,

national, regional and global), but at the global level, associations organize business from many countries, and, in principle, their ambition is to have members from all continents.[11] Although we do find many countries, or rather their businesses, represented through global associations, this does not suggest that all parts of the world are equally well covered. Many countries are, indeed, catching up, but often there is a bias toward developed countries, whose business communities are stronger and more varied. Following this pattern, global associations do not harbor the same global aspirations in their recruitment strategies. While focusing on global associations and other private entities, it is important to acknowledge that the issue of territorial coverage, to some extent, lends itself to a certain degree of interpretation. It is therefore relevant, in some cases, to include actors that are not global in every sense but still have a global position in specific contexts by addressing global polices and by exchanging with and participating in global policy-making structures.

The profound historical background

The emergence of global business associations is not just a feature of contemporary global politics but rests on a solid historical foundation. The emergence of global business associations is closely related to the globalization of markets, but several caveats must be made here. Globalization is not accomplished in a sweeping stroke but is often preceded by various steps of internationalization. Globalization of the economy does not automatically produce collective action but shapes only some conditions for the organization of business, and the global organization of business does not always take on an associational format.

Essential in our context, however, is that early in history businessmen learned to cooperate beyond their local and national domains, and established institutions to define joint interests and set important standards to regulate markets. Various forms of cooperation were established at less aggregated levels, such as cities and districts, and the basic lessons of these institutions were transferred to the international realm, where, however, a clearly defined public authority was often missing. The classic example of the strong international organization of business is the merchant guild, which came in different forms in medieval Europe.[12] However, an interesting and never fully resolved question is whether the international institutions that emerged to represent and regulate business resulted from the organization of private business interests by expanding states or from the organization of state interests by an expanding business community. The Italian city states, the Hanseatic League and the chartered companies in many European countries, each in their way, showed that local powers and states were keenly interested in promoting business and vice versa, and public and private institutions shared many ambitions.[13] These developments facilitated transboundary business action, but in cases when the interests of states and empires initiated or governed these institutions, there were still important barriers to international cooperation in business. Indeed, these examples demonstrate that collective action was not always held in a genuinely private framework, and often, cooperation was international rather than global.

The emergence of independent business associations, institutionally differentiated from states,[14] came later and ushered in an era of institutional change. In the latter part of the nineteenth century and in the early twentieth, many intergovernmental agencies and associations were founded and reflected a general spirit of optimism for international cooperation.[15] This cooperation was temporarily halted in light of the world wars, but the process gained momentum after the Second World War, and has accelerated in recent decades with the inclusion of China and Russia in the world economy and the coverage of many third world countries.

With time, the material basis of business has also changed, with the emergence of many new industries that soon engaged in transboundary activities, and business has come to address ever new concerns and policy fields through an increasingly complex associational system. At the same time, the regulation of business became international and intergovernmental bodies were established in an increasing number of policy fields both to control business and to facilitate the global operations of firms. Reflecting strong economies, global associations in business often have a regional origin, and many were founded in Europe and North America and then globalized.[16] This associational system includes bodies at all levels, from industry associations, such as the International Chamber of Shipping (ICS), to peak associations representing international business as a whole, such as the International Chamber of Commerce (ICC).

In sum, the emergence of associations in the global arena is related to economic, social and political drivers. The relative importance of each of the drivers as well as their combined impact vary considerably and influence which sectors of business become organized, which countries are drawn into this cooperation, and which policy areas such associations embrace. As we shall see, globalization is highly uneven.

Meagre research traditions

Certain parts of these historical and current developments have been captured in research. Indeed, there is a rich tradition in economic history, study of institutions, and here, some of the precursors to modern associations have been investigated, but their part in forming a long tradition leading up to our time has rarely been studied. On the other hand, studies in political science and sociology on current business associability seldom draw on historical works to display how institutions are brought into a new era and how elements of continuity exist in the organization of business. In this way, otherwise productive connections and mutual inspirations are not sufficiently exploited.

In the literature, different business actors have different potential roles in global politics and, accordingly, we may roughly distinguish between individual and collective actors. Cognate disciplines, such as economics, business administration and management, all adopt a firm-centered approach and are dominant in the study of business, while political science, sociology and their various sub-disciplines give greater weight to the role of collective actors.[17] The former approaches are extremely influential and have clear spill-over into studies in political science and international relations, where the role of firms is echoed in various research traditions.

First, on one end of the scale, there is a long and multi-disciplinary tradition of studying MNCs, less frequently referred to as multinational enterprises (MNEs) or transnational corporations (TNCs); another strong focus in the study of business history is the role of firms.[18] This research tradition has investigated concrete practices in the market, but the distinct political dimension in the work of corporations is generally rather opaque. However, many MNC studies have provided important insights: the economic might of corporations produces structural political power,[19] and the instrumental influence of large corporations in particular issue areas and situations documents the transboundary effect of corporations. In this tradition, however, the firm remains the key unit of analysis, and research has difficulty in moving beyond this micro-level and encompassing aggregated forms of business action, such as associations. As such, MNC studies tend to provide an under-institutionalized approach to global business.

Second, on the other end of the scale, there is a tradition of studying capitalists and corporations as forming a specific social class. This approach asks broader questions about political power in society and addresses how the capitalist class is increasingly coordinating interests across borders.[20]

Some studies move from the more abstract concept of social class to elite networks as representing broader class interests to empirically document behavior.[21] Social classes, as such, do not operate directly in the market but are concentrated in the political sphere, and both structural power and instrumental power are discussed as relevant tools to manifest economic interests. In this tradition, however, the key unit of analysis are actors very distant from the market, and research is primarily centered on the macro-level of class with little attention paid to less-aggregated but highly coordinated forms of business behavior.

The approach taken in this book directs attention to business associations and kindred forms of collective behavior, and seeks a middle ground between the individualistic and over-fragmented picture offered in studies of corporations and the collectivistic and over-coordinated image of business presented in research on social class. Global business also gives high priority to these kinds of organized behavior. Indeed, we find a rich and highly diversified population of organizations that are arranged for political action and that seek to organize and represent larger or smaller groups in the business community but do not aspire to represent social classes in their entirety. The community of associations is characterized by a high degree of stability and by significant dynamics leading to the emergence of new associations and forms of cooperation. The focus on this group of actors acknowledges that global business is now characterized by many and varied forms of institutionalization that the micro- and macro-approaches discussed above cannot capture.

The inspiration to study global business associations comes from many avenues of research as studies on organized business are scattered around many fields, but there are lots of disappointments as associational action is often neglected. Contributions from these various traditions, some more dominant than others, are found in the huge and somewhat diffuse research field of "state and market," which overlaps with the international political economy (IPE) tradition. IPE research, however, has a clear advantage, seen in the context of this volume at least, in that it is particularly concerned with economic and political behavior at the international level. IPE studies, for instance, teach us that the economy and politics are intimately connected and affect power relations in society. The economy is not an autonomous force but is affected by the choices of actors, and organized business that coordinates business interests may be an interesting factor. IPE studies also provide insights into how business is regulated, and this provides some clues as to how regulation may encourage coordinated action.[22]

Although the IPE tradition has a strong potential to embrace institutions beyond market and state, such as associations, we largely search in vain for research contributions on global business associations that explicitly position themselves within this tradition. Also, in broader works about the IPE field, the study of associations is largely missing. The more we delve into different strands of research on transnational relations and global governance,[23] with which the IPE field is interwoven, the stronger the interest for various intermediate actors, but systematic attempts to cover organized business are rare and weak.

Moving on to international relations research, which has strong roots in political science and some element of international law, we still find limited recognition of business associations as interesting and politically important actors. Global business associations belong to the broad category of international organization (IO) studies, but IO research tends to be occupied with intergovernmental organizations (IGOs), and theories to capture global business associations are not readily available. What is even more astonishing is that research on international non-governmental organizations (INGO) and non-state actors that are committed to capturing private organizations generally ignore organized business. However, the finding from general IO research that international organizations, whether public or private, must attend to a huge diversity of regional and national interests, is helpful in comprehending the complicated decision-making structures in associations and understanding the variety of interests that need to be accommodated.

However, studies of IPE and IGOs have shown that business interests can, for instance, be channeled through powerful states and empires.[24] Indeed, states can be seen as proxies for business in the global arena when business manages to capture states and when there is a prevailing state ideology and practice to forward the interests of business. We here come close to seeing states as actors capable of representing social classes. From a wider perspective, business can also be seen as dominating the agendas of IGOs, especially organizations such as the World Bank, the International Monetary Fund (IMF), the World Trade Organization (WTO) and the Organisation for Economic Co-operation and Development (OECD), which are based on strong pro-market principles, but elements of active private diplomacy from corporations can also be included to study their directed influence.[25] However, the unit of analysis tends to be shifted from business to states and intergovernmental bodies, and independent scrutiny of organized business is pushed into the background. The mechanisms briefly described here are important, but there is a risk that capitalism is being studied without highlighting the agency of capitalists and their organizations.

Greater help in analyzing global business associations and related actors is obviously offered in research that has an explicit ambition to analyze collective action, but such research is scattered between economics, political science and sociology, and sub-disciplines such as economic sociology and political sociology. Some areas of comparative politics, including related comparative political economy,[26] also embrace interest groups and organized business and offer good sources of inspiration, although in the main they focus on diversity across nations and sectors rather than on global business. Studies in this domain of research see business as capable of fostering collective action and organizing competitors in the representation of interests. In other words, members may bring many disparate and contradictory preferences into the associations (logic of membership), but the management of associations plays an active and strategic role in finding realistic compromises and reaching a unified position in order to optimize negotiations with key institutions in their environment (logic of influence).[27]

These mechanisms are found across organized business, in small and specialized associations as well as in encompassing peak associations, and the ability to balance conflicting concerns is important in achieving recognition in business and in politics. Interestingly, associations may, under specific circumstances, become so capable in harnessing the resources of a particular group in business that they assume responsibility for certain elements of public policy through arrangements of self-regulation.[28] These perspectives on coordination are primarily developed with variation across countries in mind, but they are potentially applicable on the global level, although collective action must here build on a much higher degree of heterogeneity, and interests are not represented before the same kind of centralized public authority. Research into global business associations and the various private actors surrounding them in the broader business community shows that collective action unfolds in many areas, as will be discussed in the following chapters, but the recognition of business associability at this level is lacking somewhat in studies of countries.

We find further interesting contributions to organized business at the global level in the form of, for example, clubs, networks and social classes.[29] This literature reiterates that business can coordinate beyond states. In their way, each of these actors is a manifestation of business action, but they are not representative and recognized organizations like associations, which cannot rely on informal types of coordination and have to exhibit some kind of accountability in the public realm. While including entities beyond associations, we offer a broader view of collective business action and contextualize the role of associations in the organization of business. However, the brief note on global business associations offered in this chapter cannot do full justice to the literature, and in each of this book's chapters, existing research will be drawn further into the discussion.

Toward an integrated approach: complementarities in the business community

Taking a middle-ground approach that highlights associational action does not imply that single-firm action is inappropriate in business or that social classes are irrelevant, for business interests are expressed in a huge number of formats, but the adopted approach confers centrality to associations as common vehicles for the engagement of business in global politics.

Although some associations, especially peak organizations and some clubs, have very general tasks, they still cannot speak for such a large group as the capitalist class. Neither can they effectively address the concerns of individual corporations, although associations, and especially industry associations, can become involved in many issues that often have a direct bearing on corporations. Obviously, this approach implies that business needs its own independent organizations to define and voice interests and cannot simply rely on governments or IGOs, even if these are considered business-friendly.[30]

In general, we may refer to associations and related entities as a population of actors in the global business community.[31] In fact, however, we find several subpopulations in this community. While the associations are genuine interest groups and must overcome the challenges of coordinating their interests, most of the related entities referred to in this book are not organized as interest groups *per se*, do not challenge their status as representative associations, and form a qualitatively different, yet heterogeneous set of actors. This has various consequences for our understanding of their relationships.

Several entities must be scrutinized simply because associations are, indeed, located at very different levels in the global business community, and perform different economic, social and political functions in this ecology. As associations have different horizontal and vertical orientations, they consequently meet different demands and expectations from their constituencies as well as their environments. Fostering collective action at the global level is highly demanding, and the adaptation of actors and emergence of new organizations are rooted in existing patterns of cooperation. These historical foundations inform the strategies of the actors, indicate opportunities and show constraints, but they also open up space for change. Accordingly, we can observe that such adaptations usually lead to gradual changes rather than sudden shifts.

Given these conditions, it is less likely that associations will come into head-to-head competition with other associations that are designed to organize the very same members and focus on exactly the same tasks. Associations may experience some overlap and compete in certain dimensions but rarely in their core functions. Indeed, major efforts will be made to avoid competition and establish a division of labor wherever possible, and associations will find and actively carve out their own niches and roles.[32] Hence, complementarities will be a key feature of the global business community.

Competition between associations and related entities is of a quite different nature. Essentially, these entities are not geared toward the representation of business and do not host ambitions to replace the associations. However, they have capacities to solve a range of problems more effectively than the associations, and we expect that they will challenge the associations—and compete among themselves, for that matter—in particular areas. In this regard, there is an important element of adaptation because associations will tend to surrender or avoid certain activities, for instance the production of various services, where they have less competence. Therefore, they will be inclined to outsource certain activities, but there is always a risk that, in some respects, this may deprive them of knowledge and resources. Finding the right balance between managing these different functions is a perennial challenge.

Outline of the book

Chapter 1 deals with peak associations in global business. There is a rather small group of peak associations that organizes large sections of business, including many industries, groups of firms and national businesses, and, accordingly, the associations formulate rather broad interests. This is a challenge for collective action. Although these associations are general in scope, they tend to specialize in different ways: they do not organize the same members, they do not engage in similar issues and they do not have key relations with the same public authorities in the global realm. We find various elements of competition between them, but there are also opportunities for cooperation, and each of the peak associations needs to adapt to find its own role.

Chapter 2 studies important vertical structures in the associational system. Many industries are organized through global associations: we find business associations in the extractive industries, in the manufacturing industries, and in the wholesale, retail and service industries. Some date back many decades, even centuries, and some are quite recent, reflecting the emergence of new industries, products and technologies. The chapter provides a general overview and analyzes a variety of industries in greater depth. Many industries face specific regulation, and a major task is to leverage intergovernmental agencies with which they often have close relations. However, the degree to which industries can coordinate through associations varies, and the industry associations must balance a diversity of interests.

Chapter 3 scrutinizes alliances of corporations and associations. In a number of cases, existing peak associations and industry associations prove insufficient, and ad hoc or permanent alliances become relevant. The traditional associations cannot always cope with new challenges because they lack relevant knowledge and support in their constituencies. Therefore, it is easier to establish new entities than to reform the old associations because it is demanding to develop the necessary expertise, expand tasks and formulate strategies in new areas. Usually, alliances organize and represent a small and particularly committed group of corporations and associations. Consequently, the alliances are highly focused and do not have to wait for support from all firms in a given industry, where some remain undecided or have other preferences.

In Chapter 4, attention is given to clubs and think tanks. Some organizations take the form of clubs, which combine different tasks, involve selected and committed groups of businessmen and -women and firms, and constitute complex organizational hybrids. Clubs have important social functions in building and maintaining networks, but they also deliberate policies, and they have different ways of disseminating their work. In some cases, a club may even act as a kind of think tank, and in the second part of the chapter, the work of key business-based and -oriented think tanks will be examined. Like associations, think tanks are involved in producing knowledge on specific issues and setting important agendas of relevance to business. It is important to discuss both clubs and think tanks to complement the analysis of business associations and their many and related entities.

Facilitators play an essential role in global business and are studied in Chapter 5. These organizations facilitate the operations of firms in the market, dispose of special knowledge, and offer a number of services to firms to help them market their products and enhance their reputation by following prescribed norms and rules, and they also assist associations in various ways to profile businesses. These specialized bodies also aid in resolving various conflicts and, in some cases, develop regulatory functions as an alternative or complement to public regulation. Some of the functions are performed by associations, discussed in the preceding chapters, and by handling a number of the same tasks, the facilitators may both challenge and assist business associations.

Chapter 6 synthesizes the major findings of the book. It states that collective action in global business is advanced and that a rich variety of associations are active in different areas and institutional contexts. Indeed, a fine-tuned but in no way planned global community of associations has evolved to organize and represent business. There is a strong continuity in the patterns of associations, but there are also demands to adjust to changes in business itself and in its environment. The recognition of business as an organized actor has consequences for our understanding of international affairs more generally. Indeed, by highlighting the role of associations, we also confront existing assumptions in various research traditions that have either ignored or underestimated the role of these actors in global politics.

In sum, business contributes in different ways to global governance, sometimes as the result of a determined effort of organized business. Broadly speaking, associations influence governance in three domains: state, market, and civil society. Such opportunities have existed since the emergence of associations in the corporate world and the evolution of globalization, but in a more contemporary context these influences were recognized at a programmatic level by the Commission on Global Governance in the early 1990s.[33]

A core argument in the debate on global governance is that global politics is shaped not only by states and IGOs, but increasingly by a plethora of public and private actors that alone or together may provide the basis for governing the world.[34] In this context, reference is sometimes made to a pluralist perspective.[35] As far as global business is concerned, we meet long-held views that business is manifested through the dispersed actions of strong MNCs, a perspective somewhat related to the pluralist approach, or assumptions that power lies in the hands of highly coordinated and perhaps even secret corporate groups, a position echoing elite theories. However,

Introduction 15

the role of business in global governance is not adequately captured in these approaches as there are strong historical traditions and a rich variety of current practices for collective action. The adoption of such a research focus does not suggest that we will have to adopt a more optimistic or a more pessimistic view as far as the role of business in global governance is concerned, but instead a different approach.

Research reflects the condition that governance is and cannot be produced entirely by states and their organizations but is also provided by various private organizations. However, the recognition of "business" as a potent contributor to global governance fails to recognize that business is a highly complex category that needs to be unpacked. On closer inspection, we find global associations at many different levels in the business community: first, associations have a key role in relation to the governance of markets. Markets are not institution-free but governed by a rich array of rules and norms deliberated and adopted by associations, and for business it is often an advantage to move first and define these in a private framework. Second, global associations represent members in many contexts and influence public policy in a range of fields as they deliver important input into intergovernmental agencies. Sometimes associations encourage regulation, and sometimes they do their utmost to forestall political initiatives in cases when the overall principles of free enterprise or the concrete interests of business are challenged. Third, associations engage with civil society actors. Civil society uses many ways to challenge business authority and business needs a "social license" to operate and, hence, a more responsive strategy is required by business associations. Various mechanisms of consultation with countervailing powers in civil society are therefore created. These different roles of business in global governance are discussed in research, but "business" is a very broad category and further attention should be directed toward specific organizations, such as associations. The gaps in understanding the many and varied roles of business associations will be addressed in this book.

Notes

1 Broader overviews of the modern situation as well as its historical roots are missing. Some glimpses of historical associational action are provided in Craig N. Murphy, *International Organization and Industrial Change: Global Governance since 1850* (Cambridge: Polity Press, 1994); Kees van der Pijl, *Transnational Classes and International Relations* (London: Routledge, 1998); John Braithwaite and Peter Drahos, *Global Business Regulation* (Cambridge: Cambridge University Press,

2000). Some organizational biographies, of course, give detailed insights into specific associations.
2 The role of business associations in markets, politics and society are theorized in Ernst-Bernd Blümle and Peter Schwartz, eds, *Wirtschaftsverbände und ihre Funktion* (Wissenschaftliche Buchgesellschaft: Darmstadt, 1985); J. Rogers Hollingsworth and Robert Boyer, "Coordination of Economic Actors and Social Systems of Production," in J. Rogers Hollingsworth and Robert Boyer, eds, *Contemporary Capitalism: The Embeddedness of Institutions* (Cambridge: Cambridge University Press, 1997), 1–49. For a management approach to the multiple task of groups, see e.g. Asli M. Colpan, Takashi Hikino and James R. Lincoln, "Introduction," in Asli M. Colpan, Takashi Hikino and James R. Lincoln, eds, *The Oxford Handbook of Business Groups* (Oxford: Oxford University Press, 2010).
3 Traditional leverage is important, but in an abundant literature on governance also the self-regulatory functions of global associations are recognized. For some examples: Christian Tietje and Alan Brouder, eds, *Handbook of Transnational Economic Governance Regimes* (Leiden: Brill, 2009); Thomas Hale and David Held, eds, *The Handbook of Transnational Governance* (London: Polity, 2011); Fabrizio Cafaggi, ed., *Enforcement of Transnational Regulation: Ensuring Compliance in a Global World* (Cheltenham: Edward Elgar, 2012).
4 This aspect could be given more attention in the population-ecology approach to associations but is treated as "variational evolution" in biology. A major job is to establish clear taxonomies of species but also to identify the many continuities between subspecies; see Ernst Mayr, "Speciational Evolution or Punctuated Equilibria," *Journal of Social and Biological Structures* 12 (1988): 137–158.
5 It is hard to pin down each of these facilitators. For a treatment of different institutions in the market, and also associations, see Avner Greif, "Commitment, Coercion, and Markets: The Nature and Dynamics of Institutions Supporting Exchange," in Claude Ménard and Mary M. Shirley, eds, *Handbook of New Institutional Economics* (Springer: Heidelberg, 2005), 727–788. A framework for the financial industries is offered in Heather McKeen-Edwards and Tony Porter, *Transnational Financial Associations and the Governance of Global Finance: Assembling Wealth and Power* (Routledge: London, 2013).
6 These private entities are treated in separate literatures, and under different concepts, but the specific bearing of these activities on associations is not addressed.
7 Different concepts are available to characterize the active space of associations, such as domain, field or sector. Also "niche," see Virginia Gray and David Lowery, "A Theory of Interest Representation," *The Journal of Politics* 58, no. 1 (1996): 91–111, is relevant but may bring connotations of something marginal. In our context, the definition of associational niches is closely related to the corporate activity of the members of associations. The niche concept was first applied in biology, or more specifically in ornithology, by Joseph Grinnell, "The Niche-Relationships of the California Thrasher," *The Auk* 34 (1917): 427–433. Great care is needed when transferring this concept to the social sciences.
8 A case is, for instance, the Sustainable Apparel Coalition (SAC), see https://apparelcoalition.org/ (accessed 12 November 2017).
9 Herbert Gintis, Samuel Bowles, Ernst Fehr and Robert Boyd, eds, *Moral Sentiments and Material Interests: The Foundations of Cooperation in Economic Life* (Cambridge: MIT Press, 2005).

Introduction 17

10 John P. Windmuller and Alan Gladstone, eds, *Employers Associations and Industrial Relations* (Oxford: Clarendon Press, 1984); Luca Lanzalaco, "Business Interest Associations," in Geoffrey G. Jones and Jonathan Zeitlin, eds, *The Oxford Handbook of Business History* (Oxford: Oxford University Press, 2008), 293–315; ILO, *Report on the ILO Symposium on Employers' Organizations. The Business of Representing Business* 5–6 September 2011 (Geneva, Switzerland, 2011); Karsten Ronit, "Global Employer and Business Associations: Their Relations With Members in the Development of Mutual Capacities," *European Review of International Studies* 3, no. 1 (2016): 53–77.
11 There is an old debate on the difference between internationalization and globalization. International associations are numerous in regional contexts, especially in Europe, but these have received considerable attention already and are not analyzed in this book. As a basic criterion for characterizing associations as global, and not just international, associations should draw members from at least three continents and aspire to include all.
12 Barry R. Weingast, Avner Greif and Paul Milgrom, "Coordination, Commitment, and Enforcement: The Case of the Merchant Guild," *Journal of Political Economy* 102, no. 4 (1994): 745–776; Regina Grafe and Oscar Gelderblom, "The Rise and Fall of the Merchant Guilds: Re-thinking the Comparative Study of Commercial Institutions in Premodern Europe," *Journal of Interdisciplinary History* 40, no. 4 (2010): 477–511. Of an even older day were the craft guilds in various trades and professions.
13 Philippe Dollinger, *Die Hanse* (Stuttgart: Alfred Kröner Verlag, 1964); Edwin S. Hunt and James M. Murray, *A History of Business in Medieval Europe, 1200–1550* (Cambridge: Cambridge University Press, 1999); Philip Jones, *The Italian City-State: From Commune to Signoria*, 1st Edition (Oxford: Clarendon Press, 1997).
14 In the mercantilist era, trade companies, such as the British East India Company, were in one way or another organized by states. Nick Robins, *The Corporation That Changed the World: How the East India Company Shaped the Modern Multinational*, 2nd Edition (London: Pluto Press, 2006).
15 L.C. White, *The Structure of Private International Organizations* (Philadelphia: Ferguson, 1933); F.S.L. Lyons, *Internationalization in Europe 1815–1914* (Leiden: A.W. Sythoff, 1963).
16 Both the World Economic Forum and the World Business Council for Sustainable Development began with offices in Europe, then extended to North America and then to other parts of the globe through members, partners, networks and offices. e.g. WEF, "About," see: www.weforum.org/about/contract; and WBCSD, Global Network, see: www.wbcsd.org/Overview/Global-Net work (accessed 19 November 2017).
17 The sub-discipline of economic sociology, recognizing the market-based relation of business associations is a promising candidate to embrace global business associations, especially if fused with elements of political sociology, emphasizing behavior in political contexts, and political economy. For some treatises, see: Neil Fligstein, *The Architecture of Markets: An Economic Sociology of Twenty-First-Century Capitalist Societies* (Princeton: Princeton University Press, 2001); Jens Beckert, "How Do Fields Change? The Interrelations of Institutions, Networks, and Cognition in the Dynamics of Markets," *Organization Studies* 31, no. 5 (2010): 605–627; Mark Granovetter and Richard Swedberg, eds, *The Sociology of*

Economic Life (Boulder, CO: Westview, 2011); Patrik Aspers and Nigel Dodd, eds, *Re-imagining Economic Sociology* (Oxford: Oxford University Press, 2015).

18 In numerous publications and at endless international conferences reference is commonly to "MNCs and NGOs" as if only civil society, and not business, were capable of coordinating interests, a view contradicted by the real-life activity of global business associations. Studies on MNCs can be valuable and provide important insights into corporate action; see John Dunning, *Alliance Capitalism and Global Business* (London: Routledge, 1997); Susan Strange, John M. Stopford and John S. Henley, *Rival States, Rival Firms: Competition for World Market Shares* (Cambridge: Cambridge University Press, 1991); and for a recent overview, John Mikler, ed., *Global Companies* (Chichester: Wiley, 2013). This body of literature, however, does not address how individual action is combined with associational action. Usually, the role of associations is completely sidestepped, e.g. in an otherwise inclusive volume by Alan M. Rugman and Thomas L. Brewer, eds, *The Oxford Handbook of International Business* (Oxford: Oxford University Press, 2017). In some cases, is it argued that large corporations today prefer to act on their own, Cornelia Woll, "Politics in the Interest of Capital: A Not-So-Organized Combat," *Politics and Society* 44, no. 3 (2016): 373–391, a position that is not defensible in global politics, however.

19 Doris Fuchs, "Theorizing the power of global companies," in John Mikler, ed., *The Handbook of Global Companies* (Chichester: Wiley, 2013), 77–95; John Ruggie, "Multinationals as Global Institution: Power, Authority and Relative Autonomy: Multinationals as Global Institution," *Regulation & Governance* 2017 (early view): http://onlinelibrary.wiley.com/doi/10.1111/rego.12154/full; Pepper D. Culpepper, ed., "Special Issue: Structural Power and the Study of Business," *Business & Politics* 17, no. 3 (2015).

20 Leslie Sklair, "The Transnational Capitalist Class and the Discourse of Globalization," *Cambridge Review of International Affairs* 14, no. 1 (2000): 67–85; Clifford L. Staples, "Board Interlocks and the Study of the Transnational Capitalist Class," *Journal of World-Systems Research* xii (December 2006): 309–319; William K. Carroll, *The Making of a Transnational Capitalist Class: Corporate Power in the 21st Century* (London and New York: Zed Books, 2010); Peter Phillips and Brady Osborne, "Exposing the Financial Core of the Transnational Capitalist Class," *Global Research* (13 September 2013), www.globalresearch.ca/exposing-the-financial-core-of-th e-transnational-capitalist-class/5349617 (accessed 24 November 2017).

21 William K. Carroll and Colin Carson, "The Network of Global Corporations and Elite Policy Groups: A Structure for Transnational Capitalist Class Formation?," *Global Networks* 3, no. 1 (2003): 29–57; Michael Nollert, "Transnational Corporate Ties: A Synopsis of Theories and Empirical Findings," *Journal of World Systems Research* XI, no. 2 (2005): 289–314; Georgina Murray and John Scott, eds, *Financial Elites and Transnational Business: Who Rules the World?* (Cheltenham: Edward Elgar, 2012).

22 Peter Drahos and John Braithwaite, *Global Business Regulation* (Cambridge: Cambridge University Press, 2000); Walter Mattli and Ngaire Woods, eds, *The Politics of Global Business Regulation* (Princeton: Princeton University Press, 2009); Tony Porter and Karsten Ronit, eds, *The Challenges of Global Business Authority: Democratic Renewal, Stalemate or Decay?* (Albany: State University of New York Press, 2010).

23 While international relations focused on states, the transnational approach included private actors and made a promising start through Joseph S. Nye, Jr. and Robert O. Keohane, "Transnational Relations and World Politics: An Introduction," *International Organization* 25, no. 3 (1971): 329–349. Essentially, this tradition mainly came to recognize civil society non-governmental organizations (NGOs) while little attention to organized business is found.

24 The literature is considerable and cannot be adequately reviewed here. Robert Gilpin, *Global Political Economy—Understanding the International Economic Order* (Princeton: Princeton University Press, 2001), offers a realist account with a key role attributed to states. Jeffry A. Frieden, *Global Capitalism: Its Fall and Rise in the Twentieth Century* (New York: W.W. Norton, 2006) presents a liberal view with more actors involved but still attributes an important role to states, especially the United States and the United Kingdom. For studies on global economy and politics, see e.g. André Broome, *Issues & Actors in the Global Political Economy* (Houndmills: Palgrave, 2014). Also the small but informative book by Benjamin J. Cohen, *Advanced Introduction to International Political Economy* (Edward Elgar: Cheltenham, 2014) provides interesting insights into the (US-UK) debate.

25 This is discussed in contributions on intergovernmental agencies. There is also a specific literature on private, economic or commercial diplomacy. Huub J.M. Ruel and Robin Visser, "Commercial Diplomats as Corporate Entrepreneurs: Explaining Role Behavior From an Institutional Perspective," *International Journal of Diplomacy and Economy* 1, no. 1 (2012): 42–79.

26 A valuable link-up with internationalization and globalization is the recognition that national business is to different degrees exposed to globalization. Jürgen R. Grote, Achim Lang and Volker Schneider, eds, *Organized Business Interests in Changing Environments* (Houndmills: Palgrave, 2008).

27 This approach was developed and applied to the study of business associations in Philippe C. Schmitter and Wolfgang Streeck, *The Organization of Business Interests. Studying the Associative Action of Business in Advanced Industrial Societies* (MPIFG: Cologne, 1999 [1981]).

28 Karsten Ronit and Volker Schneider, "Global governance through private organizations," *Governance* 12, no. 3 (1999): 243–266; David Vogel, "Private global business regulation," *Annual Review of Political Science* 11 (2008): 261–282; Tony Porter and Karsten Ronit, "Implementation in International Business Self-Regulation: The Importance of Sequences and Their Linkages," *Journal of Law and Society* 42, no. 3 (2015): 413–433.

29 Jean-Christophe Graz, "How Powerful are Transnational Elite Clubs? The Social Myth of the World Economic Forum," *New Political Economy* 8, no. 3 (2010): 321–340; Jason Struna, "Global Capitalism and Transnational Class Formation," *Globalizations* 10, no. 5 (2013): 651–763.

30 This does not suggest that public sector organizations are irrelevant to business. On the contrary, governments as well as international agencies can be tremendously important, but an active and continuous effort is required to keep them "friendly" to business interests.

31 Guidance can be found in classical studies on population and organization ecology. Michael T. Hannan and John H. Freeman, "The Population Ecology of Organizations," *American Journal of Sociology* 82, no. 5 (1977): 929–964. These

approaches must be carefully adapted to the global and associational level and avoid biases that researchers may carry over from studies on national ecologies. Furthermore, studies on international organizations may be helpful: Rafael Biermann and Joachim A. Koops, eds, *Palgrave Handbook of Inter-Organizational Relations in World Politics* (Houndmills: Palgrave, 2016). However, we must take care when transferring understandings of intergovernmental agencies to private organizations. Finally, studies on interest groups provide a relevant starting point: Karsten Ronit and Volker Schneider, "Organisierte Interessen in nationalen und supranationalen Politökologien: Ein Verglecih der G7 Länder mit der Europäischen Union," in Ulrich von Alemann and Bernhard Wessels, eds, *Verbände in vergleichender Perspektive* (Berlin: Sigma, 1997), 29–62. Darren Halpin, David Lowery and Virginia Gray, eds, *The Organization Ecology of Interest Communities. Assessment and Agenda* (Houndmills: Palgrave, 2015).
32 This ecological view on the complementarity of actors has some affinity with the one found in Peter A. Hall and David Soskice, *Varieties of Capitalism: The Institutional Foundations of Comparative Advantage* (Oxford: Oxford University Press, 2001).
33 The Commission on Global Governance, *Our Global Neighbourhood* (Oxford: Oxford University Press, 1995).
34 A useful summary of the debate and an attempt to move forward is found in Thomas G. Weiss and Rorden Wilkinson, "Rethinking Global Governance? Complexity, Authority, Power, Change," *International Studies Quarterly* 58, no. 1 (2013): 207–215.
35 Philip G. Cerny, *Rethinking World Politics: A Theory of Transnational Neopluralism* (Oxford: Oxford University Press, 2010).

1
PEAK ASSOCIATIONS

- Overview: major features and challenges of peak associations
- Relations between peak associations: members and markets
- Activities: policy fields and service provision
- Multiple exchanges: relations with IGOs and other actors
- Profiles of peak associations: similarity and variation
- International Chamber of Commerce
- International Organization of Employers
- World Chambers Federation
- Business and Industry Advisory Committee to the OECD
- World Economic Forum
- World Business Council for Sustainable Development
- Global Business Coalition
- BRICS Business Council
- Conclusion

A small group of very large associations known as peak associations aspire to organize vast sections of global business, and these horizontal structures occupy a central place in the associational system. While the trans-industry character of peak associations gives them a unique commitment to addressing concerns shared by the global business community, there is a considerable distance between these organizations and the conditions of individual firms in markets around the globe, and it can be difficult to trace the impact of associations on their economic situations. As a rule, however, peak associations are linked to corporate interests in two ways: they build on national peak associations and, in a few cases, on individual firm membership,[1] and they are designed to represent the general interests of these diverse constituencies.

Their mutual status as peak associations does not suggest that they are all similar. As we shall see, they manage their roles as "peaks" and their roles as "associations" somewhat differently.[2] As horizontal organizations with potential overlaps with other associations in the small cluster of peak associations, they have to observe how adjacent associations administer their roles. They find many ways to adapt, mindful of broader trends in and beyond the global system of business associations. This interesting differentiation among peak associations is attributable to multiple factors. They do not organize exactly the same members, they do not specialize in exactly the same fields, and they do not face quite the same environment. This important variation is also related to their different historical backgrounds. The chapter opens with an overview to introduce these factors.

In this overview, we discuss issues that are of concern to all associations but of particular interest to peak associations, which meet different challenges than do the industry associations and alliances studied in the following chapters. Theoretically, it is a strategic issue how associations define their various tasks, domains and relations, as this will ultimately impact on their competition with kindred associations and crucially affect their chances of survival. Hence, in a comparative perspective, we analyze the patterns of relations that exist between the associations, identify and discuss their concentration on different policies as well as some aspects of their service provision and, finally, examine their relations with relevant international agencies and civil society organizations. These bodies have traditionally played a key role in the environment of peak associations.

In a further step, the chapter analyzes and offers a profile of the following actors: the International Chamber of Commerce (ICC), International Organization of Employers (IOE), World Chambers Federation (WCF), Business and Industry Advisory Committee to the OECD (BIAC), World Economic Forum (WEF), World Business Council for Sustainable Development (WBCSD), Global Business Coalition (GBC), and the most recently formed, BRICS Business Council (BBC). We first draw a general profile of each of the associations and highlight aspects of their history, their membership bases, leadership structures, norm- and rule-building activities, and external relations. These associations were founded during different time periods, and we will analyze them in chronological order gradually adding to the ecology of organizations. Although their emergence is not a neat chain of related events, it is important to understand the shifting organizational contexts in which new associations have materialized. Finally, we conclude the chapter by discussing the apparent similarities and differences among this small group of organizations and by placing the associations into the context of the general system of business associations and related entities.

Overview: major features and challenges of peak associations

Global peak associations have, in principle, more or less identical tasks as they all seek to organize business on a global scale, but nevertheless there is huge variation as to how this task is defined. It is clear that they try to recruit some of the same members and cover some of the same parts of the world, but the definition of these domains is not always very precise. The same applies to the fields of activity, and not least the policy issues they are engaged in, where they both specialize and tend to concentrate on some of the same issues. This activity is also related to their relations with the environment, where peak associations establish relations with important intergovernmental agencies. Before we study specific peak associations, it is useful to highlight these general theoretical challenges and see how they are addressed in a comparative perspective.

Relations between peak associations: members and markets

In an attempt to differentiate themselves and define their own roles, peak associations rarely refer to other peak bodies. However, there has always been a profound awareness of the broader context in which the peak associations find themselves and especially a great and constant attention paid to their closest "neighbors," with whom opportunities for competition or collaboration are particularly strong, an issue that is of key theoretical and practical importance. Accordingly, they have found various ways of adaptation and specialization. We can distinguish between different organizations at the peak level in terms of territorial scopes, member properties, and market orientations, all factors that are crucial to their profile.

First, the associations vary in their territorial scopes. All of them seek to organize global interests, but not all of them cover the entire globe, either because their constitutions and ambitions do not point to such goals or because they are not able to achieve a global presence. This palpable variation in globalization and the different profiles have consequences for their legitimacy as global actors. ICC, WCF and IOE all have a substantial global basis and cover all continents soundly. BIAC also has many members and has managed to expand its membership domain over time, moving from an inter-regional organization covering mainly North America and Western Europe to a global organization with members on several continents. GBC has a global presence, albeit stunted in recent years, but it only attends to large economies and big business communities, and here we find some deficiencies. BBC has a global basis but also accommodates very large countries and few members. WEF and WBCSD organize firms from many countries, but those from developing countries are quite few. There is clearly a bias toward developed countries, especially the United States and Europe, and there are important limitations to the representation of global business.

Second, the associations vary in relation to the basic member properties. We can distinguish between associations with first-order membership (direct), which organize single firms, and second-order membership (indirect), which organize associations.[3] This has various implications for how collective action is organized. ICC, WCF, IOE, BIAC, GBC, and BBC are federations, and they all have associations as members—in most cases, national associations. There are also some consultations with large companies in, for instance IOE, but core membership is restricted to national associations that present a unified national business position, somewhat akin to the role of states in IGOs. However, it is important to note that the different peak associations do not link up with the same national associations, as the national associations tend to cater to different groups in the national business community, but some of the peak associations also have some of the very same members. WEF and WBCSD form another group of associations. They apply the direct-membership model, and especially large firms have direct access to the decision-making structures of the two organizations and, hence, do not represent national business interests in general. These patterns give rise to different opportunities for governing the associations, and in some cases, single corporations are important in influencing leadership structures.

Third, the associations vary according to their market orientations. Typically, they define their formal status as employer related, producer related or a mix, and this shows that there are many drivers for associability related to different markets.[4] With a few minor exceptions, IOE organizes national employer associations (some of which are mixed) and also classifies itself as an all-out employer association, whereas BIAC defines itself as a mixed association and has both employer and producer associations among its members. There are also some overlaps between IOE and BIAC in terms of members and orientations, especially when it comes to questions relevant for developed countries, but formal coordination mechanisms exist between the two bodies to discuss issues of common concern. Occasionally, GBC may address employer-related issues, though its engagement in this field is weak. The rest of the peak associations, ICC, WCF and BBC, concentrate on issues not related to unions and to the labor market, and an agreement adopted in the 1970s stipulates the division of labor between ICC and IOE.[5] As mentioned, WEF and WBCSD organize firms only, and firms, of course, are an embodiment of both producer and employer functions, but WEF has paid little attention to employer issues, and WBCSD has not displayed an active interest in labor issues.

Activities: policy fields and service provision

The profile of the associations, and the way they define membership, is closely related to their policy engagement, and the involvement in policy fields is, of course, also an area in which the associations may come into competition. Indeed, in a theoretical perspective there are also many dimensions of competition. We observe that policy portfolios differ between the peak associations, and we witness not only different styles of engagement but also different priorities for the development of policy in relation to other tasks, such as service provision. Indeed, there is space for specialization and a refined division of labor, but cases of intersection also occur.

First, as peak associations, the eight organizations reviewed in this chapter are committed to addressing a relatively broad array of issues, yet there are remarkable variations in their approaches. ICC definitely has the broadest coverage—this also has some benefits for WCF, an organization which thinly covers its policy fields—and ICC has a much broader engagement than GBC, also spanning strong capacities in areas of self-regulation. BBC seems to host an ambition to systematically cover areas embraced by BRICS. WEF engages in a huge number of areas and is able to bring many fresh ideas forward through reports and events but, like WBCSD, without an explicit obligation to represent a negotiated compromise supported by members. In comparison with ICC, both IOE and BIAC have defined a smaller but slowly growing number of policy fields, BIAC because of its dual commitment to employer and producer issues. Because of the focus on employer concerns, the two associations are active in areas where the other organizations are largely absent.

From a wider perspective, however, the stricter division of labor between peak associations that existed in the past is giving way to flexible approaches in more or less all associations, and employer and producer issues have become harder to separate. Add to this the circumstance that all associations today try to grapple with a range of new issues, for instance in the broad area of corporate social responsibility, where complex issues of economic, social and human rights force associations into often-unknown terrain where they meet experienced experts from intergovernmental agencies and civil society organizations.

Second, the associations have different styles in their communication of policies. Some try to reach beyond the business community and traditional interlocutors, such as the most important intergovernmental bodies, and address the general public. This is clearly the dominant strategy of WEF, which has been very successful in setting agendas and staging different kinds of events and is seen by some, perhaps, as the quintessential voice of business. As an association only based on firms, WBCSD is also an active player but is confined to a relatively small field and for more special audiences. The attention received by WEF is often envied by other peak associations, which may seem less innovative and energetic, but it is important to note that these other associations face strikingly different conditions because they are representative organizations with a commitment to members and are not broad forums for deliberation.[6] They have to go through the often-tedious process of negotiation before joint positions are reached and communicated. Also, ICC is an active communicator and uses many channels, but while GBC has maintained its level of communication, especially in relation to the G20 summits, BBC has still to develop its own style. These organizations are somewhat underprivileged, and they are not supported by strong secretariats and committee systems. WCF mainly relies on ICC, and IOE and BIAC are very active in the context of their primary institutional environments but less so in a general public context.

Third, the peak associations also have strategies regarding their internal and external activities and how to balance the development of policy with the development of services. Members will appreciate active organizations that set important agendas, but they will also expect various services to be provided. In general, all the associations seem to have become increasingly aware of the value of services and, accordingly, they have tended to upgrade this activity. However, ICC has substantial experience and by far the most significant capacity to provide a range of services to its diverse constituency, and it further assists WCF in these activities.[7] The IOE offers a considerably smaller number of services and does so primarily to its members in developing countries, whereas BIAC is modestly involved in service activity and has members with strong capacities. This lack of profile is even more characteristic of GBC, whose activities do not cover this dimension at all, and of BBC, whose service provision is limited but may increase. Also, both WEF and WBCSD, the latter in its relatively narrow field, include service production, but WEF seems to couple this activity to the social benefits of members in the joint development of ideas and initiatives, and the large members have other ways of obtaining traditional services offered, for instance, by ICC. As we have seen, the associations have different profiles and give different degrees of attention to services and politics, but as demonstrated by ICC, strong profiles in both areas are achievable.

Multiple exchanges: relations with IGOs and other actors

In addition to relations built up with other associations and actors in the business community, peak associations interact with different intergovernmental agencies that regulate the activities of business, and with civil society actors that challenge the power of business and mobilize for alternative agendas. The prominence and pattern of these relations vary significantly between the peak associations and can be analyzed by taking a closer look at the policies developed by the associations, their participation in intergovernmental bodies and their contacts with civil society groups. Theoretically, we move into problems on organizations and their environment.

First, the policy portfolio of the associations tends to match squarely or have a strong similarity with that of primary institutions in their environment.[8] The strong focus of intergovernmental agencies on core issue areas, some of them even promoted by business, urges the associations to follow these closely. As many agencies are also experiencing a rapid expansion of policy fields, this may drive associations to develop their activities accordingly.[9] These portfolios, and the dynamics they underlie, are important aspects in solidifying the role of the associations and giving them a special place among other peak associations.

IOE is involved in a variety of economic and social issues with relation to the labor market, and these are the core fields of the International Labour Organization (ILO); BIAC has a broader focus and embraces both employer and producer issues; OECD also has an exceedingly broad scope and is responsible for areas not always covered by BIAC; GBC is committed to following G20 summits carefully and formulating strategies in many of the same fields, although meetings between heads of state have broader agendas.[10] The same very much applies to BBC, which is closely related to the overall BRICS institutionalization. However, such patterns of parallel public and private activity do not exist everywhere. ICC, including WCF, has no single IGO that is of primary relevance, and it covers a variety of areas and policies managed by several agencies. The same can be said about WEF, which has an enormously broad portfolio. Compared with the other peak associations, WBCSD has a somewhat thinner policy portfolio with a key emphasis on environment and sustainability, but such issues are managed by multiple agencies, and hence, the centrality of a single body cannot be claimed.

Second, all peak associations are essentially independent, and they rely on the economic and political support they receive from their members. This support is decisive in the formation of the associations and in their later life. However, indirect and direct support is also provided by IGOs, which often have intimate relationships with the peak associations, which are admitted into various decision-making structures. Indeed, IGOs help define the membership of some of the associations, essentially because the associations recruit members from the same countries that are represented in the intergovernmental bodies.

Correspondingly, some associations are designed to represent business in relation to particular agencies. This applies precisely to BIAC, GBC and BBC, and, in fact, they have these obligations written into their names. BIAC, especially, enjoys a long tradition of recognition from OECD, and "BIAC's expert counsel remains an indispensable part of our OECD 'family'," as emphasized by Ángel Gurría, secretary-general of the OECD.[11] This is also very much the situation for IOE. The IOE is strongly influenced by the ILO as the latter was founded on the principle of tripartism involving governments, labor and employers, and at the operational level, ILO assists in establishing employer associations in third world countries.[12]

ICC, WCF, WEF and WBCSD face quite different conditions because their work is not distinctly related to specific agencies. However, ICC and, to a lesser extent, WBCSD, enjoy the same degree of recognition as BIAC, GBC, BBC and IOE, and they are invited to participate in relevant committees set up by IGOs to prepare different aspects of public policy. Adding to the support received by their members and acquired in a historical process, these different forms of backing from important IGOs are key factors in establishing and tuning the various profiles of the global peak associations.[13]

Third, the roles of the peak associations are further defined in their relation to organized interests beyond the business community, with which various kinds of conflict and cooperation are likely. In principle, several types of interests may have relevance. ICC, including WCF, engages in a rich variety of issues, but it does not have any firm relations with, for instance, unions, consumer groups or environmental movements and, in the main, its activities do not seem to address these groups *per se*. The same applies to GBC and BBC, although it is important to note that, in G20, there exists a forum for unions, L20, and for civil society, C20—but much of this work and possible connections are still in an early stage.[14]

The situation is quite different for BIAC and IOE. As both organizations are mixed associations, the role of unions is central to their work, and they meet with global unions in different institutional contexts and address many of the same issues. The emergence of WBCSD was and is also related to strong activities from the environmental movement since the Earth Summit in 1992, but it should be borne in mind that the work of WBCSD is also geared by independent processes in business and the ambition to profile firms more effectively in areas with new business opportunities. WEF has reacted in quite a special way to challenges from other interests in society by creating forums for civil society and knowledge holders inside the organization, in line with its ambition to find innovative solutions, but this does not cripple the ability of WEF to speak for business. Therefore, the impact of other organized interests on global peak associations is highly variable.

Profiles of peak associations: similarity and variation

Global peak associations are few in number. It is open for debate which associations to include and which criteria to apply. In this chapter, associations that draw members (associations and firms) from three or more continents are considered global; for instance, transatlantic forms of cooperation involving only Europe and North America are too restricted to qualify as global cooperation. This study's criteria also include only associations that represent business in general and do not cater to particular industries, a task fulfilled by industry associations and other specialized actors; the study only includes associations that embrace a relatively broad portfolio of issues pertaining to a wide array of businesses, although some specialization is common; and it only includes associations that give priority to the private sector and avoids or at least limits the role of publicly owned companies. Interestingly, these criteria are important in terms of scientific inquiry,[15] but they are also of great concern to associations, which must define their domains to maintain and adjust their profiles. Indeed, the specification of profiles has huge consequences for the relations between the peak bodies and how they compete, cooperate, and complement each other.

Figure 1.1 offers a first impression of the membership structure of the current peak associations.[16] We must remember that national business is organized in many different ways and is often represented, at the global level, through, for instance, employer organizations, producer associations or chambers of commerce, giving countries different "input" opportunities. Accordingly, some peak bodies cover many countries while others have rather few members, and this alone gives us an idea about the different ways in which they are globalized.

The peak associations have emerged in different historical contexts and reflect processes in business as well as in their institutional environments, and together, this small population of actors constitutes a horizontal layer in the associational system of global business. We do not find global peak associations that serve exactly the same sections of the business community, nor do we see global peak associations that exclusively cater to each of their

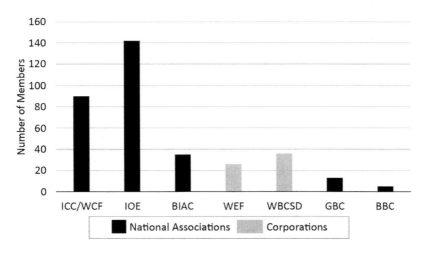

FIGURE 1.1 National business in global peak associations

segments. Profiles can in some cases and various elements of competition are identifiable.

Many policy fields are of interest to global business, and there are rich opportunities to formulate a general business voice. The pattern of activity basically departs from the formal requirements and identities written into their constitutions as well as from their historical legacies. However, it is always a question where to concentrate their effort. The specialization on either classical employer or producer concerns gives a good indication of priorities. A further question is whether to engage in the production of various services and make these available to members. Obviously, services must be provided on a rather general basis and cannot be tailored to meet the demands of particular industries (as will be dealt with in the next chapter). Still, there are a variety of strategies for the development of services to keep and attract members.

As encompassing organizations, peak associations are entitled to exchange with many other actors to represent the interests of global business. Indeed, recognition by, for instance, intergovernmental agencies will help solidify the role of peak associations as legitimate organizations of global business, and formal participation in their work is generally an important goal of the associations. Some associations will also give attention to relations with other parties, such as civil society, to foster a dialogue and shield business from critical civil society groups. Although peak associations have broad commitments and are likely to be drawn into a range of general issues, again based on their obligations and historical traditions, there is variation in their commitments. It is always a key matter how much they can expand into new areas because the changing of profiles requires additional resources and entails a number of risks.

International Chamber of Commerce

ICC is the oldest of the peak associations treated in this chapter, and this gives it a special status among the group of encompassing organizations.[17] Founded in 1919, just after the end of the First World War, it came to represent the general interests of international business. ICC was a follow-up of previous organizations in business, and after the Treaty of Versailles it could build on private cooperation in a time when national political interests could be a serious obstacle to business.[18] The idea was also to contribute to the revival of international trade that had seen a remarkable upswing in the decades before the war. Thus in a wider context, ICC was part of a peace-building project where business was to have its place in the civilized cooperation between nations. Placed in Paris, where it still resides, ICC could reach out to all the national chambers of commerce in the world and to relevant intergovernmental bodies, such as the League of Nations, but also to specialized agencies in different regulatory fields. It has always given priority to exchanges with intergovernmental bodies, as will be discussed in depth later, and it has strong relations with several agencies and does not give top priority to a single body.[19]

In those days, ICC could not be a truly global association simply because large parts of the globe did not have independent associations to join this international initiative. Still, however, it was considered the international business voice *par excellence* and, for its time, the number of members enrolled was significant. Later, more countries joined ICC, and it has been a strategy of the organization to encourage the formation of local chapters, called "national committees," helping them institutionalize at the domestic level and connect with ICC.[20] In this way, domestic business is attended to on the ground, and ICC, as a global body, has become ever more representative of business. These efforts are less important in countries that already have a thriving business community and a strong tradition of associability, but in both a historical and contemporary context, this function of ICC has been quite important in developing countries.

Today, the membership consists of national committees from a large number of countries, and they have already established a unified national position that they bring into ICC. In its development of a global strategy, ICC can then build on the many and different positions aggregated and negotiated at national levels. As a membership category, national committees are not the same everywhere, however. Different meanings are attached to the chamber institution across the world, although ICC, to some extent, tries to homogenize things and refers to the national committees as branches of ICC. This reflects the fact that national chambers have been created not only at different times in history but have emerged in different business cultures and exercise different roles.

With so many countries represented, it is a key task to design representative management bodies to meet the demands and expectations of the constituency. National chambers represent economies of quite different size and complexity, and it is important that the organization is not unilaterally governed by the richest countries and their strong associations. This gives rise to the management of various dilemmas: although it is important to give leading economies and experienced national chambers a central role, it

FIGURE 1.2 The first headquarters of ICC
Source: Charles Hodges, *The Background of International Relations: Our World Horizons: National and International* (London: Wiley, 1931).

is also necessary to include members from different continents and groups of countries in the relevant management bodies.

A further point is to allocate resources and find appropriate structures that can respond effectively to member concerns and position ICC in a diversity of policy fields and institutional contexts. ICC controls significant resources and runs a strong and highly diversified secretariat that is able to build up expert knowledge in a range of areas, but, in general, it refrains from addressing employer issues.

In addition to these political efforts, ICC provides members with an equally significant variety of services. Interestingly, ICC is involved in various forms of self-regulation and administers a number of codes, for instance in advertising and marketing.[21] A specific capacity is found in the area of arbitration where ICC, or more precisely, a body closely attached to the organization, namely the International Court of Arbitration (ICA), formed in 1923,[22] provides a unique judicial framework for conflict resolution in the global business community. This body has an important role in solving transboundary conflicts in global business. It is one of the factors that contributes to the strong reputation of ICC as a global business voice and, together with other activities, as an organization with a prominent service profile. Moreover, these activities are important for financial reasons as services provide significant revenues for ICC itself. This kind of business activity means that the organization has several sources of income and does not rely on member fees alone; from the members' perspective, it means that the burden of running the organization is shared by large parts of the global business community and not shouldered by members alone.

International Organization of Employers

The IOE was formed in 1920, in the same immediate post-war era as ICC. While ICC could further cooperation and peaceful relations in business, the IOE, with its distinct profile as an employer organization, could contribute to civilizing relations in the labor market and, thus, contribute to social peace between employers and workers.[23] Although the formation of the two associations, specializing in different markets and areas of business activity, were not, as such, part of a grand scheme to organize global business coherently, their almost-simultaneous foundation is interesting and gives an indication of the general vision that pervaded business.

That vision, to civilize and institutionalize relations between capital and labor, was not just the result of parallel national projects. In addition, this was a declared international ambition, and the regulation of conflicts in the labor market by means of peaceful cooperation was inscribed in the statutes of the ILO,[24] which was founded as a new intergovernmental agency related to the League of Nations. This model still exists and, therefore, the relations between IOE and ILO are of a special nature, but today, IOE has relations with a large number of international agencies and has moved into many policy fields beyond narrow employer issues.[25]

Whereas many countries had experience with the organization of business, fewer had experience with the specific organization of employers. In Europe, especially, there existed many national employer associations. Although IOE enjoyed support from many countries, it particularly gained strength from its European members, and only slowly did it globalize its activities, concomitant with the slower globalization of labor markets relative to many commodity markets. However, membership has expanded considerably, and in recent decades, many national associations have joined IOE. In the overwhelming majority of cases, only one national member association is admitted, and thus, different national members bring into IOE positions that have already been settled among employers, a feature facilitating coordination in IOE.

Somewhat breaking with the traditions of the federated model, IOE introduced a kind of direct-membership model in 2013 through the IOE Partner Company Initiative.[26] This scheme gave employers with membership in national associations an opportunity to take part in the work of IOE and enjoy the many opportunities of networking in general and through the Global Industrial Relations Network (GIRN), Global Apprenticeships Network (GAN), and Global Occupational Safety & Health Network (GOSH). Although national member associations are still the basic units, balancing the participation of associations and firms has become ever more crucial.

Because it draws members from across the world, where employers have discrete experiences with organizing interests and where national labor-market institutions are markedly different, collective action is demanding. It is, however, an official task to facilitate national member associations, especially in developing countries, professionalize their activities and build strong domestic employer associations.[27] The eventual success of this endeavor is important for IOE, which has become increasingly representative of global employers.

It is crucial to balance different concerns and the positions of employer associations in the leading bodies of the organization. As a basic guideline, the management board of IOE consists of the "top seven contributing members."[28] This gives these associations a special power, of course, but it is also a huge commitment and requires support from their relevant national secretariats. Indeed, participation is both an opportunity and a burden. However, the task is not to represent the main contributors, which, to some extent, come from strong economies, but also to include member associations from different continents and specific member groups whose participation is desirable. Regional representatives are entitled to membership on the board, and the board can co-opt members. In this way, different countries are integrated into the leadership structures. This also reflects the fact that regional associations of employers provide a forum for the discussion of various international issues, and they serve as vehicles of interest intermediation without enjoying membership in IOE.[29] In some cases, national employer associations may find it more relevant to address and solve issues at regional levels, and thus, some energy is taken out of activities at the global level.

The daily tasks are not carried out by the elected bodies alone. Much work is delegated from the General Council and the Management Board to other bodies and the secretariat. These entities are supported by a relatively small number of special policy working groups, which are supposed to gather experience and deliberate policies and filter this into the decision-making structure. These groups have only been created recently, however, and this shows that, in spite of the broad membership base, collective action has not always been so advanced. A strong organizational infrastructure has been lacking. An upgrading of the secretariat, based in Geneva, Switzerland, took place over a number of years, enabling IOE to focus on servicing member associations and companies, and assisting in the development of policy and management of relations in a complex environment. Keeping sufficient staff is a significant challenge but is necessary to cope with the many different demands and expectations and to secure funding for activities.[30]

World Chambers Federation

The WCF, as it is now called, has a unique history. It is basically an offspring of ICC which, in the 1940s and 1950s, saw an increasing need for a special forum for the many national and local chambers of commerce that found their way into the organization in a time when ICC was expanding. ICC itself was not in a position to accommodate the different needs of the chambers through its existing structures, however. Instead of overburdening these, it decided to create an entirely new organization that had strong links with the mother organization. The WCF goes back to 1951, and various models were applied over the following decades to find an appropriate structure.[31] Today, WCF is formally an independent organization, but in many respects, it is under the umbrella of ICC forming a special department. For many years the two organizations were housed in the same stately building in Paris, but they have relocated, though are still under the same roof.

While ICC has national and encompassing chambers as members, WCF specializes in organizing and, to some extent, in representing the many local chambers. Today, around 12,000 local chambers from all continents,[32] a significant outreach, are affiliated, and they typically have other concerns than the big national chambers, which bring coordinated national interests into the organization.

The smaller entities tend to bring issues from locally based SMEs into the discussion. These interests, however, are not only dealt with in the context of WCF, which alone cannot provide a sufficient backing in global politics. They are also filtered through ICC, which tries to integrate and respond to their concerns in the development of political strategies and in their relations with intergovernmental agencies. In this way, WCF can be seen as an institution that both gives its huge number of local members a specific voice and provides them with an additional entry point, but the strong political arm is provided by ICC, showing the considerable variation in political involvement among peak associations.

The leading bodies draw on members from local chambers from many parts of the world, and multiple criteria, such as private- and public-law bodies and geographic distribution, are used in the composition of the leading bodies to enhance the representativeness of the organization. Interestingly enough, many members of the General Council, the leading body of WCF, do not have a background in local chambers but come from national chambers in the same way that members are represented in the key bodies of ICC, so attention to the local dimension is not consequentially applied. In the context of WCF, however, we find that local chambers from a number of other countries are represented and, taken together, the two organizations provide access to a large group of chambers in the leadership. It is also important that WCF and ICC have different commitments and are supposed to work with different issues and take different approaches to chamber interests.

In reality, the WCF secretariat is just a small section of the large ICC secretariat and has a small staff, but the organizations are not very informative about this. Obviously, it cannot meet all the demands for service from the chambers, nor can it assist properly in the development of policies in all those areas where local chambers are affected by regulation. It needs to draw on logistical support and relies to a considerable degree on ICC in many service areas, and in this way, it attempts to avoid duplication.

Business and Industry Advisory Committee to the OECD

BIAC was created in 1962,[33] in a very different time than were ICC and the IOE but not without similarities on the broader scene. While the two older associations related to historical projects after the First World War, BIAC was related to important Western schemes of advancing prosperity and building modern market economies under the OECD umbrella. This uniting of Western countries was further linked to the Cold War and political conflicts with the socialist bloc, and in this context, organized business had its role to play in economy and society.

BIAC is not, as the name might suggest, a body under the auspices of OECD but an autonomous association designed to represent the interests of business in a specific institutional context. BIAC did not face the same burden of organizing members as ICC and IOE. The members were, so to speak, already available when the association was founded: in the same way that countries were admitted to the OECD, associations from the very same group of countries were welcomed by BIAC. With subsequent expansions of the OECD, BIAC's membership base was also enlarged, but it is not possible for BIAC to go beyond the domain of the OECD and recruit members on a broader basis, further globalizing the organization. Only associations from countries with an observer status are somewhat integrated into BIAC. This suggests that the organization has a global reach, counting members from North and South America, Europe, Asia, Australia, but not from Africa. Therefore, there are certain limitations to its global character. There is also some coordination with a group of associations called "associate experts" that include various European and global industry associations, but they are not listed as members.[34]

The countries that joined the OECD all had sound economies and solid institutions, such as developed employer and business associations. Therefore, BIAC did not have to assist in the professionalization of these organizations or in their creation. Instead, national associations, some of them with significant resources and experience, bring important input into the deliberations of the organization. As members, the association has always included employers as well as business associations with a focus on producer interests, and this gives BIAC the status of a mixed organization that pays equal attention to its two roles. This has profound consequences for its commitments and policy portfolio, where different perspectives must be aligned and many issues covered. As will be dealt with later, BIAC has a broad policy coverage and is also active in policy fields where the OECD is present.

The inclusion of employer and producer interests implies that in countries where business is not represented by a single encompassing association, two members are represented instead of just one. BIAC, therefore, has a good deal more members than there are countries in the organization, but this does not give the countries with double representation any advantages in decision making. No attempts are made by BIAC to encourage the formation of single organizations in these countries and, accordingly, different national models and memberships are recognized. However, it is expected that members coordinate their strategies when representing national interests in the organization and that potential conflicts are ironed out.

Today, many member associations have the capacity to contribute to the leadership. The major countries and economies will always be represented on the executive board while some of the smaller countries will typically be represented on a rotating basis according to specific keys and practices among members. This pattern of representation brings them into leadership functions at intervals and, in principle, helps to balance different interests. This concern is essential in an organization that draws members from many countries and must formulate its strategies while mindful of this diversity.

It is important to understand that the many policy groups established by the assembly and the board have major responsibilities in the development of policy, and they bring the many associations and their members together at a more operational level where concrete initiatives are formulated. This role is not and cannot be taken by the small secretariat, today numbering just below ten staff,[35] whose job is primarily to coordinate activities in the political field rather than provide services, a task carried out by the member associations themselves.

Interestingly, OECD is able to fund some BIAC activities,[36] and the financing of the organization is, therefore, not solely dependent on the collective action of members and their willingness to support BIAC. But it is important to note that many activities hosted by BIAC depend on strong participation from its member organizations, which spend time, resources and expert knowledge on running the association.

World Economic Forum

Again, we must take a major leap forward in history, to the early 1970s. WEF was founded in 1971 as the European Management Forum and slowly grew into the organization we know today.[37] In the beginning, the initiative was predominantly European and focused on relatively narrow management issues in the business community, and only gradually did it engage in global issues and begin to address the general public. But reforms of the organization's structure and of its outlook catapulted it into a position as an important global player. As such, the organization has received considerable attention, most strikingly in relation to its hosting the annual event in Davos that draws business people and statesmen and -women, plus an array of celebrities, from around the world, and provides a unique place for top-level networking. Indeed, some of its activities could be hosted by the UN, but WEF is, after all, a more informal setting,[38] and depending on the activity, it looks alternately like an intergovernmental agency, an event bureau, a business association or a think tank.[39]

WEF has a strikingly different membership structure than the associations studied above and it does not build on national or local associations.[40] Only single firms are admitted as business members, and even stand-alone corporations, such as Facebook and Google, unaffiliated with industry associations have joined WEF. Direct firm membership implies that members cannot bring already-negotiated interests, such as national business voices, into WEF, and WEF is the first real level of collective action. In other words, it is mainly possible for WEF to represent these companies and not broader parts of the business community. This leaves WEF with the huge task of finding a common denominator between the many firms, which today include around 300 large companies,[41] but its goal is not to represent members in a strict sense, and hence the integration of members in decision making is relaxed. This is both a strength and a weakness: a strength because WEF can address issues without waiting for the scrutiny and consent of all members and the tedious process of negotiation, and a weakness because it is less representative and cannot rely on the support of members. The arrangement gives the organization more flexibility than other peak associations, indicating the variation in policy style within the community of these large associations.

A further complicating factor is that WEF admits members from outside the business world. Other categories of members include experts and civil society actors, and this shows that WEF is not a typical business association. Despite this hybrid character, certain parts of the organization can, indeed, be considered a business association, and a novel entity experimenting with different models in both the organization and the representation of interests.[42]

The member firms generally come from the most affluent parts of the world, such as the United States, the United Kingdom, Germany, Switzerland, the Netherlands, Japan, and China, all of which are well represented in the organization.[43] They have strong resources, and they assert their interests directly without liaising with other firms in national peak or industry associations. Members from developing countries are rare, but a few examples exist, and WEF clearly has an ambition to have as members large firms from these parts of the world and so demonstrate global coverage.

Because of its complex leadership—different entities may qualify as governing bodies for different sorts of activities and different groups of communities—it can be difficult to pin down the way the organization is led by business. However, the Board of Trustees and the Managing Board are the primary entities, and here we find leading MNCs. The Executive Committee runs the many activities of the organization. Furthermore, large parts of the work are delegated to, and carried out by, a range of relatively autonomous committees and working groups that draw on both members and external experts. They provide analyses of many topical issues in global business and society, but we should be careful not to see these many initiatives as negotiated in and necessarily backed up by the membership, although they are issued in the name of WEF. However, the organization has been exceedingly active in setting agendas in global politics and in establishing relations with a number of IGOs, indicating that there are many ways for peak associations to become recognized on the global stage.

A resourceful secretariat in Zürich, employing, together with offices abroad, in the vicinity of 60 staff,[44] contributes to the strong infrastructure of WEF. It is able to support different clusters of industries, a wealth of working groups and a series of events. Interestingly, WEF has also "regionalized" its secretariat by setting up offices in the United States, China, and Japan to attract firms, provide meeting places for them and more generally globalize its activities.

World Business Council for Sustainable Development

Although the WBCSD can be ranked as a peak association and is engaged in multiple trans-industry issues, it does not have the same broad profile as the other associations discussed in this chapter. Again, this shows the significant variability among the small population of peak associations in global business,[45] and the organization, therefore, has some similarities with alliances and facilitators, actors which will be analyzed in later chapters.

It was not possible to accommodate sustainability issues effectively in traditional business associations; hence, the WBCSD was created as a new association in 1992.[46] From the outset, it had a special purpose: to organize and represent companies with a clear environmental agenda irrespective of their country or industry of origin and, in principle, embrace all sectors of the global business community. Indeed, the foundation of this new initiative reflects a time when business began to hold commercial interests in environmentally friendly technologies and did not oppose the environmental movement *en bloc*.

In previous decades, environmental issues were often bluntly perceived as anti-industry and not something to be readily embraced by profit-seeking firms, but economic and technological changes, as well as changes in the perception of environmental challenges, led business circles to reorient their activities. These new positions were often hard or impossible to attend to within the framework of existing associations with more conventional approaches. In specific industry associations, firms with a sharper environmental profile were often a minority, and it became feasible for a larger organization to embrace different areas of business with the emergence of a critical mass of firms.

Like WEF, WBCSD organizes single firms only. With its distinct sustainability agenda, its potential membership base is much smaller than WEF's, but it appeals to different companies and does not have the same strong focus on very large companies, although it does have several of them among its members. Today, the membership base typically originates in advanced industrial countries, where sustainability technologies are most developed and where there is generally a more profound pressure on business to be environmentally friendly. Therefore, some regions have a strong presence in the association while others have none.[47]

Consequently, firms from countries such as the United States, Switzerland, Japan, Germany, France and the United Kingdom, and increasingly also China and India, make up the bulk of members, whereas Latin America, Africa and the Middle East are weakly represented, but it is difficult to improve coverage because the material basis of firms with potential to become enrolled in WBCSD is missing. Almost unavoidably, this bias is echoed in the Executive Committee, which primarily consists of leading multinationals.

With corporations as direct members, collective action is not premediated at other levels, as, for instance, in different national or industry contexts, and then brought into the organization. WBCSD must, therefore, provide all the necessary structures to deliberate policies and define joint strategies between firms from different industries but with "sustainability" as their common hallmark. This can be a complex exercise.

Different bodies, consisting of both the Council, which functions as the general assembly, and the Executive Committee, help formulate a coherent strategy, but the various committees and clusters also relate to different industries. However, WBCSD is not a traditional business association with a primary emphasis on formulating relevant policies, and it is active in a range of sustainability projects.[48] Because there are other success criteria in its work, it is less dependent on producing compromises and finding support for its political work in the membership.

Related to this project activity is also the provision of services to its members, who need the organization as a forum for exchanging experiences and for improving competitiveness in the market, services not readily available in other peak associations. At the same time, resources are invested in the development of policies and in maintaining a presence in a variety of institutional contexts. It is important to bear in mind that all the work devoted to examining and finding solutions to concrete sustainability problems also has a political dimension and enables the association to formulate strategies and exchange with intergovernmental agencies and other interests beyond business.

These priorities are mirrored in the organizational structure of the association. The headquarters, located in Geneva, Switzerland, together with offices in the United States and India, has around 60 staff and includes various divisions and functions.[49] Interestingly, the secretariat has globalized in recent years, with new offices established in the United States and India, not only to embrace firms in these countries but also to work vis-à-vis governments and, thus, help the organization build a stronger global platform. Much of its work is oriented toward the sharing of information, and professional networking in and across industries plays a crucial role. Although the association promotes some key values and norms regarding business and sustainability through its various charters,[50] limited attention is given to creating and administering strong systems of self-regulation.

Global Business Coalition

GBC is the youngest of the peak business associations but only if judged by the recency of its name. In the past, it was known as the B20 Coalition, sometimes further abbreviated to B20. It was tasked with representing business on a global scale in connection with the business summits under the G20,[51] but it was rebranded GBC in November 2016.[52] Like many of the other peak associations, B20 Coalition started life in a smaller and more modest form. Attempts by the major powers to establish policy-making structures beyond the UN system led to a series of summits between heads of state, initiated by the G5, and this framework has expanded in different directions to include more countries, one of the events now known as G20.[53] As many issues in the world economy were of great relevance to business, there was a need for a consolidated business opinion. An appropriate way of representing global business interests in this special context was considered and found through the B20 Coalition, an initiative that, in many ways, is still under development. However, a number of traditions have evolved, policy priorities have been set and members have agreed on many recommendations over the short span of years in which the organization has been active.

Only national business associations are members of this relatively new group, and they bring already-coordinated interests into the coalition, but in the past, a few exceptions (e.g., Mexico and India) indicate that more than one organization per G20 country has been participating.[54] National business interests were already organized by several bodies, a condition B20 did not interfere with.

Organized as a federation, collaboration is, in principle, based on member associations from the same countries as represented in G20, plus Business Europe as a joint representative of associations in the European Union. In the past, some have been missing, however, and today, not all countries are taking part in the work of the coalition. Currently, China's presence is missing, as is that of Russia. Highly active a few years ago in preparing the B20 before the 2013 G20 meeting in St Petersburg, Russia is not listed as a member of B20, suggesting that the organization is vulnerable to conflicts in world politics. These are very delicate issues, of course. In general, however, the organization does not have to go out and recruit new members on a broad basis: it is obvious who may constitute the membership base, and it is a kind of closed forum with global reach.

Although GBC is still a very small organization that is supposed to form a coherent voice for global business, collective action is not always an easy task. Many different interests are present in this small and heterogeneous body, where both old and new economic powers are present. However, collective action is not needed everywhere. The organization has a broad agenda, but given the types of interest represented through the national associations, producer interests and not employer concerns are discussed first and foremost.[55]

Although the coalition has a presidency, there is no real permanent leadership in the form of a board with selected members, and it has a rather flat structure, acknowledging that the participating national associations all represent significant business interests. In 2014, it held its first plenary meeting.[56] Leadership functions are also alternating and delegated to the business associations of the country hosting G20, and they form an executive committee to prepare GBC meetings as well as to formulate recommendations to the G20 summit. This gives the host association opportunities to coordinate with its own government, but there is a risk that the host country will not sufficiently accumulate and evaluate its experience by the time the role is passed on, after the meeting, to another member of the coalition.

Decision making is, in some ways, simple within such a relatively small organization, but cooperation is under-resourced. In fact, the association does not have any traditional secretariat with a capacity to prepare meetings effectively. Most functions are taken care of by the business association in the host country, together with the French member of GBC, Mouvement des Entreprises de France (MEDEF), which runs a small secretariat for GBC. In addition, various working groups and task forces are involved in the preparation of reports, policy papers and recommendations, and they involve representatives from the member associations. The association can, to some extent, also rely on input from other global peak associations.

BRICS Business Council

The most recent organization to take on the character of a global business association at the peak level is BBC, which was inaugurated in 2013 following the BRICS summit in Durban, though cooperation started a few years earlier.[57] As the name indicates, this association is limited to relatively few countries and their businesses, and includes Brazil, Russia, India, China and South Africa, but spans several continents. It is not open to all countries and is, therefore, global only in a limited sense, but this condition also applies to peak associations such as BIAC and GBC, which only welcome associations from the OECD and G20 countries, respectively. It is still difficult to predict how BRICS will develop as an institution, but there have been rumors about new countries joining. By focusing on BRICS countries and their specific challenges in the global economy, BBC has taken up a unique mission, and the organization is part of a general division of labor in the organization of global business interests. Certainly, some of its members

FIGURE 1.3 Annual Meeting of the BRICS Business Council

are, for instance, also closely related to GBC, but the institutional focus of BBC, the BRICS summits, is, of course, a very different scene.[58]

The emergence of BRICS and its gradual institutionalization were major incentives for businesses to organize interests and present these in a coherent form, but a major driver for BBC was also the member states' ambition to encourage a new platform and involve business in the BRICS process. These dual motives are essential in explaining the emergence of BBC. Today, the organization is already integrated into the policy-making structure of BRICS, where it is attributed a key role at the BRICS Business Forum, an activity that is organized as part of the annual summits. This event also gives the organization an opportunity to meet political leaders and vice versa. As noted by Indian Prime Minister Narendra Modi, "the BRICS Business Council also has matching priorities of ease of doing business, dismantling trade barriers, promoting skills development, establishing manufacturing supply chains and infrastructure development. The Council's work holds much promise for expansion of trade and business among BRICS countries."[59]

It is interesting to note that each of the member countries is represented in the Council through one association only, or rather, each member association sends representatives from five different corporations with an interest in BRICS issues. Each country forms a chapter of the global body—for instance, the China BRICS Business Council—and thus, new entities are created at domestic levels with the concrete purpose of delivering input into the global body. To varying degrees, however, these chapters are related to and, in some cases, identical with the leading business association in the country.[60] Although new entities in the form of chapters have been added to existing national associations, it is doubtful whether the global association has stimulated the reorganization of business associations at domestic levels, but it gives the various chapters specific roles in coordinating with their respective governments in developing and implementing policies adopted by BRICS.

The work of BBC is centered on the annual BRICS meetings, but activity also unfolds between these events where the chapters meet. A number of working groups have been established to develop strategies in selected policy areas where there seem to be particularly good prospects for cooperation. Efforts are made to further trade and host activities that enhance cooperation between business in the member countries. The organization provides some services but still at a miniscule level, reflecting its infancy.

There is currently a small secretariat in New Delhi hosted by one of the Indian peak business associations, the Federation of Indian Chambers of Commerce and Industry (FICCI), but coordination also rests with the alternating presidency of the organization, the relevant national chapter and even the company of the chairman.[61] In the future, a stronger administrative foundation will be required. Greater stability is important to secure the further development of BBC, and steps have been taken to form various working groups assisting the secretariat to underpin strategy development. Very likely, cooperation on the business side will be strengthened alongside parallel development of cooperation between the member states of BRICS.

Conclusion

Among global business associations, there is a particular horizontal layer occupied with trans-industry issues. This layer consists of a limited population of peak associations that organizes and represents broad categories of members in the form of national associations and individual firms. Yet, there are considerable variations in the global associations in terms of, for instance, their territorial coverage, leadership structures, and policy portfolio. In other words, the category of peak associations is not always easily defined.

Global peak associations have largely gone unobserved in research and are undertheorized, but the existence of highly active peak associations demonstrates that encompassing collective action is possible in global business and with activities in many areas. Neither social classes nor individual corporations can speak for encompassing business interests, and there are many issues faced by global business that warrant different organizations to interpret these varied challenges and take action. Indeed, there is a tradition for organizing global business at this top level that goes back to the early twentieth century, processes that have unfolded alongside the development of intergovernmental and international civil society cooperation.

This stability, however, does not exclude organizational dynamics. At long intervals, new entities have been added. It is no easy task to set up such organizations, but new demands and incentives have occasionally led to the emergence of new associations, showing the evolutionary trends in global peak associations. This relative stability is, in part, attributable to peak associations having a much greater distance to changes in particular economic, industrial and technological developments than is the case in industry associations that are more sensitive to these processes, a point we will return to later.

The peak associations largely cater to different members or, at least, to different perspectives of the same members, such as producer and employer concerns. They also adapt, specialize and engage in different policy fields to represent the diverse interests of their members, but there are certain limitations to finding appropriate and defendable niches. Indeed, the horizontal terrain can be interesting for all peak associations, and in some cases, they come into competition with each other. For peak associations, the finding of niches is quite different from industry associations that are exceedingly specialized, an issue that will be discussed in the next chapter.

An important factor in the division of labor between peak associations is their institutional specialization. In addition to representing different members in the form of single firms and national associations, they are oriented toward different institutions in their environment. In some cases, the peak associations exchange with one particular intergovernmental agency and develop their policies according to the agendas typical for this institutional framework and, hence, clear examples of co-evolution can be documented. This is one of the important rationales for the historical formation of peak associations as well as their current activities. Today these profiles of peak associations and the different capacities of business to coordinate interests at a large scale have also wider implications. When there is no single association that speaks for global business in its entirety, contributions to global governance are rather through different organizations specializing in different policy fields. However, only have a certain potential. Interests are a determining factor in influencing how much can actually be achieved in different forums.

Complementarity is a significant feature in the relations between associations, but it is also clear that there are different forms of rivalry between them. This rivalry can occur both when they engage in similar issues and when they stick to their own domains. Because they endeavor to represent general business interests, and thus have major tasks in common, there is a somewhat diffuse competition as to who is most effectively representing business. Such a problem seems unavoidable. What should be avoided however, is the formulation of contradictory strategies, the duplication of efforts and fragmentation in resource allocation, and efforts are made to hinder this through various forms of coordination between some of the associations. To date, these mechanisms are not sufficiently developed and cause some frustration. There are voices in the associations that see the current situation as untenable and advocate for a new form of organization or, at least, a new coordinating body on top on the existing ones. This has not been accomplished so far, and it also has several downsides as many and heterogeneous interests would need to be aligned. Indeed, the associations represent different interests and perspectives in global business and face different institutional challenges, both key factors that invariably set barriers to concerted action.

Notes

1 In this sense, peak associations, constituted as federations, benefit from collective action in a number of small groups. This perspective is also applicable to global interest groups. See Mancur C. Olson, *The Logic of Collective Action: Public Goods and the Theory of Groups* (Cambridge: Harvard University Press, 1965).
2 It is always difficult to define when organizations turn into peak associations. The WBCSD is no doubt the most specialized of the peak associations in terms of policy fields addressed. In another context, I have labelled it a "multi-sector association": Karsten Ronit, "Global Business Associations, Self-Regulation and Consumer Policy," in Achim Lang and Hannah Murphy, eds, *Business and Sustainability: Between Government Pressure and Self-Regulation* (Heidelberg and New York: Springer, 2014), 61–79.
3 This has implications for the debate on globalization. However, the different forms of membership in global business association have not been systematically addressed in research.
4 Franz Traxler, "Employer Organizations," in Paul Blyton, Edmund Heery, Nick A. Bacon and Jack Fiorito, eds, *The SAGE Handbook of Industrial Relations* (London: Sage, 2008), 225–240.

50 Peak associations

5 ICC and IOE, *Protocol of Agreement Between the International Chamber of Commerce and the International Organization of Employers* (Paris and Geneva: ICC and IOE, 1976).
6 Personal communication with staff from other peak associations.
7 The roles of ICC and WCF are difficult to entangle, and "WCF's extensive chamber membership plays a pivotal role in connecting ICC to SMEs [small and medium-sized enterprises] worldwide," indicating the particular function of WCF as an arm of ICC. ICC, Chamber Services, see: https://iccwbo.org/cham ber-services/world-chambers-federation/ (accessed 1 December 2017).
8 Kenneth W. Abbott, Philipp Genschel, Duncan Snidal and Bernhard Zangl, "Orchestration: Global Governance Through Intermediaries," in Kenneth W. Abbott, Philipp Genschel, Duncan Snidal and Bernhard Zangl, eds, *International Organizations as Orchestrators* (Cambridge: Cambridge University Press, 2015), 3–36; Bob Reinalda, "The Co-Evolution of Non-Governmental and Intergovernmental Organizations in Historical Perspective," in William E. DeMars and Dennis Dijkzeul, eds, *The NGO Challenge for International Relations Theory* (London: Routledge, 2015), 107–129.
9 "Mandate creep" or "mission creep" are analyzed from different perspectives: e.g. Jessica Einhorn, "The World Bank's Mission Creep," *Foreign Affairs* 80, no. 5 (2001): 22–35; Jacqueline Best, "Ambiguity and Uncertainty in International Organizations: A History of Debating IMF Conditionality," *International Studies Quarterly* 56, no. 4 (2012): 674–688.
10 Also the OECD plays an important role in the G20 process, however, and this even brings BIAC into the role as an active player in business coordination, see: OECD, "Stakeholders," www.oecd.org/g20/stakeholders.htm (accessed 30 March 2018).
11 BIAC, Ángel Gurría, secretary-general of the OECD, in *BIAC Annual Report 2015* (BIAC: Paris, 2015), 5.
12 Sandrine Kott and Joëlle Droux, eds, *Globalizing Social Rights: The International Labour Organization and Beyond* (Houndmills: Palgrave, 2013).
13 Current relations seem relatively stable, but institutional innovations may lead to new bodies. In December 2017 the First Business Forum was held under the auspices of the WTO involving ICC and WEF but also GBC. See, Ministerio de Producción/Precidencia de la Nación and ICC, MC 11 Business Forum, businessforummc11.com/en/ (accessed 23 April 2018).
14 In the G20 process, different "engagement groups" that meet with sherpas and ministers are created: B20 for business, C20 for civil society, L20 for labor, T20 for think tanks, W20 for women, Y20 for youth, see for instance: www.g20a ustralia.org/news/deepening_g20_engagement_business_civil_society_labour_yo uth_and_thought_leaders and www.c20turkey.org/page/dynamic/38 (accessed 29 December 2016).
15 A discussion of relevant criteria to define global peak associations is found in Karsten Ronit, "Global Employer and Business Associations: Their Relations with Members in the Development of Mutual Capacities," *European Review of International Studies* 3, no. 1 (2016): 53–77.
16 Most peak associations build on national associations and in the figure the number of countries covered by national member associations is recorded (ICC: "national committees"; IOE: "business or employers' organizations"; BIAC:

"member organizations"; GBC: "members"; BBC: "members"). However, there are some deviations from this pattern. WCF is based on "chambers of commerce and industry" but only data on ICC are provided in the figure, as the many chambers are not always represented through coordinating national committees. WEF and WBCSD only organize individual corporations among their business members, and the origin of countries is recorded, hence the different shades of the bars. In a very few cases, we find more than one member association per country but in such cases only one membership is recorded in the figure. In some cases, also observer status is granted to members but in the figure only full members are counted. For further elaboration see note 20.

17 For a historical study on the ICC, see George L. Ridgeway, *Merchants of Peace. The History of the International Chamber of Commerce* (Boston: Little, Brown and Company, 1959 [1938]). The 1938 edition appeared under a slightly different title. For a more recent contribution: Dominic Kelly, "The International Chamber of Commerce," *New Political Economy* 10, no. 2 (2005): 259–271. Often certain activities of ICC are researched rather than the organization as such, as for instance its engagement in arbitration through the International Court of Arbitration (ICA). Alex Stone Sweet and Florian Grisel, *The Evolution of International Arbitration: Judicialization, Governance, Legitimacy* (Oxford: Oxford University Press, 2017).

18 Kees Van der Pijl, *Transnational Classes and International Relations* (Routledge: London and New York, 1998), 118–120.

19 To some degree, it can be considered a *primus inter pares*, and in 2016 it was granted observer status by the United Nations (UN) General Assembly, as the first and until now only global business association. ICC, "ICC granted UN observer status," see: www.iccwbo.org/News/Articles/2016/UN-General-Assembly-grants-Observer-Status-to-International-Chamber-of-Commerce-in-historic-decision/ and www.un.org/en/ga/search/view_doc.asp?symbol=A/C.6/71/L.7 (accessed 26 December 2016). For many years, ICC, and a number of other business associations, have enjoyed consultative status with another central UN body, the United Nations Economic and Social Council (ECOSOC).

20 ICC, *ICC Constitution*, Article 2 and 3 (ICC: Paris, June 2017). The membership of ICC consists of "national committees" as well as "direct members" where the former category refers to bodies with a broad coverage of economic sectors, and the latter class refers to chambers where encompassing committees are missing, making them less representative of national business but still testifying to the outreach of ICC. Thus, different approaches can be made when describing and analyzing ICC membership; see for the inclusion of countries: Karsten Ronit, "Global Employer and Business Associations: Their Relations with Members in the Development of Mutual Capacities," *European Review of International Studies* 3, no. 1 (2016): 53–77. In this book, however, a more restrictive approach is adopted, emphasizing full national member organizations. In addition to the full members of ICC, 93 in spring 2018, "direct members" are drawn from 48 countries: ICC, *2017–2018 Programme of Action* (ICC: Paris, 2017). The figure has gone up in recent years, but there can be a huge variation in their capacity to represent broader business interests.

21 ICC, *Advertising and Marketing Communication Practice. Consolidated ICC Code* (ICC: Paris, 2011). Document No. 240-46/660 (2011).

22 ICA, *Arbitration Rules*. *Mediation Rules* (ICC: Paris). https://cdn.iccwbo.org/con tent/uploads/sites/3/2017/01/ICC-2017-Arbitration-and-2014-Mediation-Rule s-english-version.pdf.pdf (accessed 4 April 2017).
23 Jean-Jacques Oechslin, *The International Organization of Employers. Three Quarters of a Century in the Service of the Enterprise (1920–1998)* (Geneva: IOE, 2001).
24 George N. Barnes, *History of the International Labour Office* (London: Williams and Norgate Limited, 1926).
25 IOEs policy fields, see IOE, "Policy Areas," www.ioe-emp.org/policy-areas/ (accessed 10 May 2017).
26 IOE, "Become a partner of the International Organization of Employers," www.ioe-emp.org/networks/gan/.
27 Karsten Ronit, "Global Employer and Business Associations. Their Relations with Members in the Development of Mutual Capacities," *European Review of International Studies* 3, no. 1 (2016): 53–77.
28 IOE, *Statutes (As amended and adopted by the General Council on 4 June 2017)*, Article 6,e (IOE: Geneva, 2017).
29 This involves BusinessEurope (Europe), Business Technical Advisory Committee on Labor Matters (CEATAL) (the Americas), Confederation of Asia-Pacific Employers (CAPE) (Asia and the Pacific), and Business Africa (Africa). They all have close collaboration with regional intergovernmental bodies.
30 The secretariat has experienced changes and currently has around 25 staff. IOE, *Annual Report 2015–2016* (Geneva: IOE, 2016).
31 Its former names were International Information Bureau of Chambers of Commerce (IIBCC) (1951–66), and International Bureau of Chambers of Commerce (IBCC) (1966–2001). ICC, *World Chambers Federation*, see https://iccwbo.org/ chamber-services/world-chambers-federation/ (accessed 5 November 2017).
32 ICC, *World Chambers Federation*, https://iccwbo.org/chamber-services/world-c hambers-federation/ (accessed 1 December 2017).
33 Nathalie Aubry, "Business and Industry Advisory Committee to the OECD," in Christian Tietje and Alan Brouder, eds, *Handbook of Transnational Economic Governance Regimes* (Leiden: Nijhoff, 2009), 51–60.
34 BIAC, *Member Organizations*, http://biac.org/our-members/ (accessed 1 December 2017).
35 BIAC, "Our Team," http://biac.org/biac-team/ (accessed 2 December 2017).
36 Richard Eccleston and Aynsley Kellow, *International Business Peak Associations: The International Chamber of Commerce, BIAC and Tax Reform*, IPSA Congress, Madrid, 8–12 July 2012.
37 WEF, *The World Economic Forum: A Partner in Shaping History. The First 40 Years 1971–2010* (Geneva: WEF, 2009).
38 Jean-Christophe Graz, "World Economic Forum," in Kenneth A. Reinert, Ramkishen S. Rajan, Amy Joycelyn Glass and Lewis S. Davis, eds, *Princeton Encyclopedia of the World Economy* (Princeton: Princeton University Press, 2009), 1179–1182.
39 WEF represents an excellent case of mimicry. Mimicry is treated in an often cited contribution in organization theory, see: Paul J. DiMaggio and Walter W. Powell, "The Iron Cage Revisited: Institutional Isomorphism and Collective Rationality in Organizational Fields," *American Sociological Review* 48, no. 2 (1983): 147–160. A much more sophisticated treatment of mimicry is offered in

biology, see: Georges Pasteur, "A Classificatory Review of Mimicry System," *Annual Review of Ecology and Systematics* 13 (1982): 169–199; Gabriel A. Jamie, "Signals, Cues and the Nature of Mimicry," *Proceedings of the Royal Society B: Biological Sciences*, 22 February 2017; 284 (1849): 20162080.
40 Geoffrey Allen Pigman, *World Economic Forum: A Multi-Stakeholder Approach to Global Governance* (London: Routledge, 2006).
41 A particular group of members, the "strategic partners," enjoys special privileges in the organization. WEF, Strategic Partners, www.weforum.org/about/strategi c-partners (accessed 16 April 2018).
42 Today, WEF is led by a board of trustees to which a managing board is responsible. According to WEF, "it is now on the next phase of its journey as the global platform for public-private cooperation," but still "the World Economic Forum provides a platform for the world's 1,000 leading companies to shape a better future." WEF, "Members and Partners," see: www.weforum. org/about/our-members-and-partners (accessed 1 December 2017).
43 WEF, "Industry Affiliation," www.weforum.org/about/industry-affiliations (accessed 17 September 2017). Around 300 figure under the category "industry affiliation," while 100 enjoy the supreme status of "strategic partners."
44 WEF, "Leadership and Governance," www.weforum.org/about/leadership -and-governance (accessed 17 October 2017).
45 There is not one form of peak associations in global business association but several forms. Accommodating several forms under one main type of organization shares some features with subspecies in biology. See the authoritative work of Ernst Mayr, *The Growth of Biological Thought: Diversity, Evolution and Inheritance* (Cambridge: Harvard University Press, 1982), 286–297.
46 Originally, the Business Council for Sustainable Development was established in 1992 and in 1995 amalgamated with the World Industry Council, initiated by the ICC, into the World Business Council for Sustainable Development. Although the WBCSD is today a leading force in sustainability issues, the ICC has not left the scene and is an important player, see Amandine Orsini, "Thinking Transnationally, Acting Individually. Business Lobby Coalitions in International Environmental Negotiations," *Global Society* 25, no. 3 (2011): 311–329.
47 WBCSD, "Our Members," www.wbcsd.org/Overview/Our-members (accessed 2 December 2017).
48 WBCSD, "Our Partners," www.wbcsd.org/Overview/Our-partners (accessed 2 December 2017).
49 WBCSD, "Our Team," www.wbcsd.org/Overview/About-us/Our-team; WB-CSD, "About US India," www.wbcsd.org/Overview/About-us/India; WBCSD, "About US North America," www.wbcsd.org/Overview/About-us/ North-America (accessed 16 April 2018). However, full information on staff can only be recovered by visiting additional project-related websites of the organization.
50 WBCSD, "Governance," www.wbcsd.org/about/organization/governance.aspx (accessed 4 April 2017).
51 Karsten Ronit, "Global Employer and Business Associations: Their Relations with Members in the Development of Mutual Capacities," *European Review of International Studies* 3, no. 1 (2016): 53–77.

54 Peak associations

52 GBC, "Press Release: The Global Business Coalition Calls for International Cooperation" (30 November 2016).
53 Andrew Cooper and Ramesh Thakur, *The Group of Twenty (G20)* (London: Routledge, 2013). With the formation of the B20 Coalition, and later the GBC, we hear less from business coordination in relation to other summits, but sometimes action is taken, for instance, before the G7 through B7 consisting of peak member associations from Germany, Canada, Italy, Japan, France, the United States and the United Kingdom. Bundesverband der Deutschen Industrie/The Federation of German Industries (BDI), "Industrial Innovation for a Sustainable World. Recommendations from the B7 to the G7," see: www.busi nesseurope.eu/sites/buseur/files/media/imported/2015-00391-E.pdf.
54 www.globalbusinesscoalition.org/wp-content/uploads/2017/03/GLOBAL-BU SINESS-COALITION-B7-2015-Germany-Summit-Statement.pdf (accessed 30 March 2018). B20 Coalition, "Business Organizations," see: www.b20busi nesssummit.com/guests/business-organizations (accessed 25 May 2013).
55 Employer associations are not affiliated with GBC, but IOE and some national employer associations maintain contacts with the organization.
56 B20 Coalition, "Events," www.b20coalition.org/coalition-activities/events/ first-plenary-meeting-of-b20-coalition (accessed 29 December 2015).
57 BBC, *Joint Statement of the BRICS Business Council Meeting Held on 19 August.* Sandton Convention Centre, Johannesburg, South Africa. Business Meeting, 26 March 2013. For earlier developments, Ministry of External Relations (Brazil), "Main Areas and Topics of Dialogue Between the BRICS," see: http://brics.itamaraty.gov.br/about-brics/main-areas-and-topics-of-dialogue-betw een-the-brics (accessed 1 January 2016).
58 So far, BBC has not been examined in scholarly research and only briefly referred to. Oliver Stuenkel, *The BRICS and the Future of Global Order* (Lanham: Lexington Books, 2015); Andrew F. Cooper, *The BRICS: A Very Short Introduction* (Oxford: Oxford University Press, 2016).
59 Ministry of External Affairs, "Intervention by Prime Minister at BRICS Business Council Meeting," 16 October 2016, http://mea.gov.in/Speeches-Statements. htm?dtl/27489/Intervention_by_Prime_Minister_at_BRICS_Business_Council_ Meeting (accessed 12 September 2017).
60 This applies to the following organizations: China Council for the Promotion of International Trade (CCPIT), but also the recent APEC-China Business Council, and the China Chamber of International Commerce (CCOIC) are relevant in these processes, see: http://en.ccpit.org/info/info_4028811758d70820015d63 d7901c0171.html, http://en.ccpit.org/info/info_4028811758d70820015d54c2714 70164.html; Chamber of Commerce and Industry of the Russian Federation (CCI Russia), https://tpprf.ru/en/news/the-brics-business-council-held-its-annual-meet ing-2017-in-shanghai-i204237/; FICCI; www.bricsbusinesscouncil.in/bbc-india. php; Brazilian National Confederation of Industry (CNI); www.vale.com/EN/a boutvale/news/Pages/vale-participa-da-primeira-reuniao-do-conselho-empresarial -brics.aspx; and Business Unity South Africa (BUSA) (all websites accessed 19 October 2017).
61 COSCO, "Group News: Capt. Xu Lirong Attended the BRICS Xiamen Summit," http://en.coscoshipping.com/art/2017/9/5/art_6923_63737.html (accessed 10 September 2017).

2
INDUSTRY ASSOCIATIONS

- Overview: major features and challenges of industry associations
- Population: many and specialized entities
- Principles: competition and cooperation
- Governance: members and management
- Activities: policies and services
- Engagements: participation and regulation
- Profiles of industry associations: strong specialization
- Conclusion

Almost all industries are, in one way or another, organized through global associations, and consequently, their populations are significant. Indeed, associations abound in all parts of the production and value chain: we find business associations in the extractive industries, in the manufacturing industries, and in the wholesale, retail and service industries. Some date back many decades or even centuries, and some are quite recent, reflecting both the solidity of business sectors and the continuous emergence of new industries, products and technologies.

The principle of associability as a means to represent collective interests is universally applied, but the degree to which industries coordinate through associations varies depending on such factors as inter-firm conflicts, tensions between national industries and the character of external challenges.

Industry associations must balance the interests of large influential corporations that tend to dominate many industries as a result of economic concentration and globalization, and they must further seek out compromises between powerful national industry interests. Strong attention to key institutions in their environment is equally required.

Many industries face specific regulation, and a major task is to leverage intergovernmental agencies to adopt rules beneficial to business and to forestall initiatives that go in the opposite direction. Unlike peak associations, industry associations tend to have close relations with agencies that have more specialized mandates. These agencies, and sometimes only certain departments and offices, receive valuable knowledge from the industries but also gain support from industry associations in cases when strategies are adopted and rules are implemented—initiatives the ultimate success of which depends on the backing of the industry in question.

Typically, these interactions are formalized through the participation of industry associations in a range of bodies and further nourished by contacts at different political and bureaucratic levels, but relations can also have a more conflictual character. Regulation, however, is not only a domain of important agencies. In many cases, industry associations develop their own systems of self-regulation to govern markets, and these initiatives sometimes emerge quite independently in business without being observed or contested by public authority. They are often taken on with the deliberate intention to avoid traditional public regulation.

For obvious reasons, this chapter does not cover all global industry associations or their rich variety of activities. First, it provides a general overview of the basic theoretical challenges facing industry associations, the principles on which they are based, how they are governed and the diversity of functions they perform. This part will include experiences from a variety of industries. Second, it analyzes industry associations in selected areas to reach a better understanding of variations in their work while stressing that associations can thrive in extremely varied settings. Without capturing the full diversity of this particular population of organizations, the analyses provide important insights into their complex life and include associations in minerals, foods, textiles, steel, chemicals, shipping, airlines, finance and advertising. In examining the major features of the associations, we show that there is variation as well as similarity across the industries. In the concluding section, we stress the key features of the challenges they face and place them in the context of other organizations in global business.

Overview: major features and challenges of industry associations

Global industry associations are found in more or less all sectors of the economy, and we begin the analysis with an overview of the population of the world's industry associations. They all grapple with a number of challenges characteristic of interest organizations, yet they also confront specific problems that set them apart from other associations within and beyond the business community. They must find ways to balance cooperation and competition between members who are often active in the same markets; they have to integrate members into leadership structures and establish a professional management; they must offer various kinds of services to attract and keep members; and, as private actors, they become involved in regulation with or without public authority. Before we study concrete industries, it is important to understand these properties: how they are organized and how they work.

Population: many and specialized entities

Whereas the community of peak associations is quite small, the population of industry associations is overwhelming. Indeed, they are not a phenomenon restricted to national industries, where members find cooperation in comparatively smaller groups feasible and where challenges from actors in their environment are easier to identify. Instead, cooperation is found in organizations involving members from across the world, where they face a number of different challenges from regulators and civil society. Furthermore, this form of cooperation is not a rare occurrence found only in some industries where specific drivers are in place to facilitate collective action; instead, associations are found across industries and are a customary way of organizing business on the global scene. And, finally, this multitude of associations shows that cooperation does not only, or primarily, occur through the peak associations discussed in the last chapter, where rather broad interests are defined and represented; instead, cooperation is related to highly specific issues, and industry associations perform tasks that have not been mastered at the peak level.[1]

There is no agreed-upon classification of "industry" or of what an industry association is supposed to cover. Finding a suitable definition of an industry, the material and constitutive element of industry associations, is complicated, and a range of approaches and standards are available.[2] Usually, the associations have quite precise definitions and understandings of their industries and, hence, of their membership domains. However, there is also an element of historical tradition and pragmatism in carving out domains, and these can be more or less inclusive and vary between what comes close to narrow product groups or what includes several connected clusters of industries, indicating that the profiles of industry associations can vary along a vast spectrum from homogeneity to heterogeneity. Furthermore, many dynamics in the development of business continuously wipe out and create new sectors in the economy, changing demands for collective action.

Accordingly, there are different strategies to form and manage industry associations. Sometimes they have quite plain membership structures, as, for instance, the International Air Transport Association (IATA), which only represents airline companies, and sometimes they are internally differentiated units embracing several member categories under an encompassing industry body like, for instance, the Institute of International Finance (IIF).[3] These patterns, which will be further elaborated below, have important implications for the population of industry associations.

Industry associations occupy and seek to shape niches for themselves so as to avoid competition for members and for representation.[4] In many ways, this tends to be an easier exercise than for peak associations, which all focus on general interests, although different territorial, functional and legal criteria are employed to differentiate between them. Among the industry associations, we often find elaborated divisions of labor, where specific products, services and technologies are defined to institute and sustain relevant domains. Escaping overlap is a perennial task, but in general, domains are not seriously challenged, and they are either respected by associations close to the domain or simply ignored by other and more distant associations.[5]

Certain domains, may however, intersect in the population: some associations compete for the same members, or specified segments in the membership in the form of national associations or, at least, certain of their interests, or for some firms, or a fraction of their interests. For instance, conglomerates, such as Siemens, are members of many and related associations, and there are opportunities to disperse or concentrate membership on relevant industry associations.[6] However, it is important to note that initiatives are not necessarily taken to outcompete other associations but rather to make smaller adjustments. In fact, some forms of associational competition can become problematic and will be adamantly opposed by many members, corporations and national associations alike, which prefer peaceful settlements of possible domain disputes or the creation of new associations or mergers instead of waging costly and devastating battles.

Principles: competition and cooperation

As a basic principle, global industry associations are constituted of cooperation between members in the form of firms, national associations and, in some cases, other entities. On an individual level, members cannot respond in a timely and effective manner to all challenges, and they come together to address matters of joint concern, exchange experiences and formulate appropriate strategies to advance their interests in a variety of informal and formal global contexts. The associations provide an essential platform for deliberation and action, but there are also clear barriers that need to be observed and that hinder or affect cooperation.[7]

Cooperation in industry associations is based on the premise that members are competitors. The same factor that propels strong cooperation, the relative homogeneity in member profiles, is also a factor that threatens it. Member firms either are or may become immediate competitors or near-competitors in the market, offering identical or substitutable goods and services to other business actors or to end consumers. There is a risk of collusion, and associations may turn into cartels. Given this proximity to the market and the possible confrontations between members around negotiations that have direct or indirect consequences for market competition, global industry associations are in a different situation than the peak associations, with their greater heterogeneity. The broad strategies and policies of peak associations will not in the same way risk affecting competition in markets.

In industry associations, this problem may be somewhat relaxed in cases where they consist of national associations, as illustrated for instance by the International Council of Beverages Associations (ICBA) and the International Council of Chemical Associations (ICCA), because such associations are not market actors that come into direct competition, but there is competition at a more general level between national industries that seek to represent different national economies and, as such, they may press for different initiatives in the associations.

Given this situation among global industry associations, it is important that they respect the autonomy of firms and not only avoid interfering in their decisions to hire, fire, produce and invest, but also avoid interfering with competition in ways that privilege certain firms and associations over others. Therefore, there are issues that cannot be addressed at all and issues where utmost care and attention are needed.

However, industry associations of all kinds cannot escape the fact that members are of disproportionate size, and when associations have corporations of exceedingly different sizes and national industry associations of very different volumes, significant asymmetries are represented. Of course, members will have different incentives and opportunities to influence associational decision making in ways that are particularly beneficial for them and work against initiatives that harm them.[8] Although cooperation is a key principle for the associations, it is difficult to ignore the importance of the economic conditions that surround them and are filtered into them. But it is important to moderate those factors in order to avoid alienating members and jeopardizing cooperation. Many practices of cooperation have evolved and have been built into associations, giving members expectations of how cooperation and competition should be balanced.

Governance: members and management

Global industry associations have basically two categories of members: national industry associations, representing approximately the same type of producers and service providers, and single and often internationally operating firms, where national associations are not available to organize interests and represent business. This distinction is applicable in a great many cases of global business.

However, there are a number of exceptions to this general pattern, and there are cases where associations conflate the two principles but in different ways and for different reasons. Material factors in business are important.[9] In some domestic contexts, there is simply no association to represent a given industry. There is, for instance, no relevant industrial activity, or a few but dominant firms have reduced the demand for associations and stand alone; even at the global level, there may be few corporations in an industry. In other cases, global associations have created additional membership categories for large firms to improve funding and offer these firms better access to the decision-making structures of the organizations. In the pharmaceutical industry, for instance, the International Federation of Pharmaceutical Manufacturers and Associations (IFPMA) has included large firms as a specific membership category, adding to the traditional members category of national associations.[10]

There is significant variation in the capacities of members: obviously, national associations represent industries of different levels of economic importance, and the same applies to individual corporations. This produces different kinds of asymmetries and, in turn, gives rise to the adoption of statutes and practices that both reflect and correct these imbalances. In other words, cooperation is not only between partly competing associations and firms, as we discussed above, but also between unequal members and illustrates different power relations. However, this is a basic condition of cooperation and something that global industry associations are highly experienced in managing.

These membership properties have a bearing on the governance of associations. The existence of such asymmetries has a clear impact on the integration of members into the governing bodies and committees of the associations. Large members pay higher fees, are endowed with differentiated voting rights, draw on a substantial pool of experiences and tend to be better represented in these organizational structures.

Such patterns are highly important for analyzing both the relations between members, and between members and management of global industry associations. Because the members of these associations are all organizations—and not individuals as in many other kinds of global associations—many of them have resources that easily match those of the industry associations and, hence, they have special opportunities to control management. In other words, there are various measures to limit the autonomy of these associations and their bureaucracies.[11]

We saw that there is much variation in the secretariats of peak associations and also that industry associations display significant differences in the size and complexity of secretarial resources. Some have modest staff while others have strong secretariats, and this pattern will affect their various functions, which we will discuss later. To fully appreciate the strengths and weaknesses of industry associations, we need to recognize that there are different models for organizing secretariats, displaying different steps in collective action and organizational development. The more modest secretariats are hosted by members, perhaps on a rotating basis where the secretariat goes from one firm to another, usually large corporations, or from one association to another, usually leading associations.[12]

The more full-fledged secretariats have permanent locations and their own independent staff, but of course, this type also varies according to the resources allocated to the associations and the trust that members have in delegating tasks to professional experts. Usually, however, these secretariats have greater capacities and can embrace far more issues, and they tend to dispose of greater autonomy vis-à-vis members. In addition to these basic types, we find many intermediate forms, for instance, when a secretariat builds on permanent sections specialized in different areas and attached to national and regional associations. This is the case in the chemical industry, where the secretariat of the ICCA is virtual and shared between associations in North America, Europe and Japan,[13] reflecting a logistical but also a political compromise.

Activities: policies and services

Essentially, industry associations are non-market actors: they are active in the political realm and work to have interests represented in a variety of global forums to influence the regulation of business in a specific area. These efforts are largely collective good-oriented (i.e., in the sense that they seek to influence agendas and decisions by public authority that are beneficial for their members). However, free riders also tend to benefit from public policy in the same way as members when global regulation cannot distinguish between members and non-members. Non-members cannot, of course, exert any influence on political initiatives taken by the associations, so there are still important incentives to be a part of such a community and influence strategies.

Industry associations have a comparatively narrow point of departure and are not compelled to go into broader issues, usually the domain of the peak associations. Still, the portfolios of these associations can be quite extensive. Many issues need attention, and often, associations dispose of highly specialized knowledge not held by any other private or public actors. Today, many industry associations experience an expansion of their policy domains, and they also move into areas that are partly covered by the peak associations, such as the application of human and labor rights.[14] In particular industries, such as textiles and sporting goods, these are big issues.

Yet, there are relevant activities other than the formulation and representation of policies. A common feature of many associations is the development and provision of particular services to members, i.e. a range of selective goods. Indeed, some industry associations have specialized and put stronger emphasis on service activities than on political activities, and it is, therefore, problematic to see industry associations as invariably putting the political dimension first. For example, an association such as the Baltic and International Maritime Council (BIMCO) is particularly strong in servicing the maritime sector.[15] Further and careful scrutiny of the profiles of industry associations is required.

In general, services are offered free to all members or supplied on favorable conditions. They are closely related to the profile of the industry, enabling associations to draw on and further develop the knowledge already accumulated in secretariats and to use and extend their networks. Therefore, the provision of services cannot be seen as an apolitical, isolated mechanism of no or little value to the political arm of associations but, rather, an effort that, to varying degrees, interacts with and benefits their political work.

These services are, in some cases, an important source of income, making associations less dependent on fees. Indeed, associations have become increasingly aware of services as a means to improve their finances, but they run into competition with other actors in the business community who are offering similar kinds of services. This problem will be addressed in a later chapter on facilitators.

Engagements: participation and regulation

As global organizations, industry associations exchange with a host of other global bodies. IGOs tend to be of utmost importance because they are central in the formulation, adoption and implementation of rules and norms that regulate a given industry. For many associations, participatory practices with these bodies are well established. In some cases, interest intensity is high and one or a few rather specialized agencies, committees or offices belong to the principal interlocutors of a given industry association.

There can be a high degree of interdependence in the exchange of resources and support when public and private entities cover the same policy field. Examples of such close relations are, for instance, between associations representing airlines, including IATA and the International Civil Aviation Organization (ICAO); pharmaceuticals, including IFPMA and the World Health Organization (WHO); ship owners, including the International Chamber of Shipping (ICS) and the International Maritime Organization (IMO); and tourism, a more fragmented industry, including the World Travel & Tourism Council (WTTC) and the United Nations World Tourism Organization (UNWTO).[16]

Hence, formal relations are often established between industry and IGOs, and the industry associations are granted some kind of consultative status testifying to their representativeness. In many areas, industry associations have become the sole and unchallenged business voice, and thus, official recognition cements these positions. Although agencies generally recognize several associations in and beyond business, they usually accept only one association per interest category; representation from several would be dysfunctional in that it would enhance competition between associations and send differing messages about the interests of the same industry.

Global regulation, however, does not only occur through public agencies.[17] Today, much regulation is adopted by private bodies in the business community, including industry associations. These activities can be summarized under the generic concept of self-regulation, a model frequently referred to by the industries themselves. Indeed, industry associations are very relevant vehicles of self-regulation, which is found across many industries and some of which will be analyzed in depth below. In many cases, business prefers to have its own rules and uses self-regulation as a means to forestall traditional public regulation. However, such initiatives do not exclude deliberations with governments and IGOs and, from a wider perspective, consultations with relevant civil society organizations.

Associations also provide an established institutional framework for regulation: they have a stock of committed members that have built up a high degree of mutual trust, they have established a sound basis of specific industry knowledge and they have an organizational basis with which to monitor and evaluate implementation. Usually, industry associations organize leading corporations and major national associations, and they can, if not guarantee the ultimate effectiveness of self-regulation, then at least present it as a credible alternative to public regulation and perhaps even ensure that a large part of the industry will actually comply with the rules of self-regulation. Experiences with industry self-regulation also show that associations in many industries are involved in such arrangements. However, industry engagement does not cease with schemes initiated and managed by industry associations but encompasses a rich variety of institutions, involving groups in civil society as well as various third parties holding expert knowledge.[18]

Profiles of industry associations: strong specialization

With the help of these general *problematiques*—summarized under the headings of principles, governance, activities and engagements—that, to different extents, confront and produce differing results in all industries, we can draw a profile of the organizations.[19] However, there are also important associational properties that cannot be accommodated under these broad themes and, therefore, some other aspects of their activities are given attention in the following sections. We show that the organization of these industries displays a number of commonalities that characterize industries and are different from other levels of organized business, but the industries range from highly established to new and innovative businesses, and they are located at different points in the production and value chain—the organizing principle in the analysis below.

Obviously, the industries examined are examples from a much larger pool of industries, but they cover major parts of the world economy, and the selection is broad enough to place industry associations into the overall picture of organized business. Further analysis will no doubt confirm a number of important findings while also leading to new discoveries and bringing even more nuance into the study of global industry associations.

Mining and minerals

Mining covers broad fields and methods of extracting minerals from the earth. It is found in many countries and accomplished under substantially different economic, technical, social and political conditions. With the help of new technologies, new ores are discovered and better access is achieved, including remote parts in the world, thereby connecting markets. In a similar vein, new applications of minerals make mining profitable, and mining is, therefore, related to many upstream industries in the global production chain. The relative geographical fixation of the mining business means that the industry is embedded in local and national environments, and many problems are first and foremost addressed in these contexts. However, global concerns are becoming increasingly salient.

Today, the International Council of Mining and Minerals (ICMM) is the lead organization in the mining business,[20] although there are other organizations that specialize in certain minerals, for instance, the International Diamond Council (IDC), and there are corporations that stand outside the organization. For a global business association, ICMM was founded astonishingly late, in 2001, and many years of active mining preceded the formation of a global outlet. It was also founded much later than many associations in, for instance, the energy business, and, until recently, the industry faced a handicap in coordinating interests and matching other organizations.

This suggests that the existence of an industry is, in itself, not a sufficient condition to facilitate collective action through an industry association. Additional factors are needed to foster cooperation of this kind. Important pressures came especially from the environmental movement, and mining companies were requested to develop a coherent strategy and, thus, avoid being singled out and targeted by campaigns aimed at individual firms. With the formation of ICMM, new policies were formulated to address sustainability, an area where mining had performed poorly in the past. ICMM has formulated ten principles with which members must comply,[21] but they are not so precise than they cannot be interpreted loosely and circumvented, and the industry still has serious image problems. However, the principles show an ambition to engage in some kind of self-regulation.

The member base is quite complex, embracing national mining associations as well as leading mining corporations, giving a variety of corporate interests a voice. Thus, the association combines two classical principles in the organization of business interests and integrates interests that mirror the diverse membership. First, ICMM draws members from a number of mining countries, embracing countries that have been less represented in global industry associations (e.g., South Africa and Chile). Second, different branches have been created, encompassing almost every type of extracted mineral, from iron to gold. Third, both smaller and larger players are included, reflecting the variable economic importance of mining companies and national mining associations.[22] As a consequence, various interests must be accommodated and balanced to avoid the dominance of specific groups in the industry, and this is a major task of the management, the board and the many committees that operate within the association.[23]

The mining industry has no obvious intergovernmental agency to exchange with. In fact, there is an apparent lack of organizations to formulate and implement policies with regard to mining, and little global regulation is in place. Given this institutional background, the industry is not forced to coordinate and present a unified view to match strong regulators in the same way as many other global associations. Additional factors, however, may compel collective action in the industry. Countervailing powers in the form of the environmental movement and human rights groups are monitoring the industry and its behavior in sensitive areas, and other business interests in and beyond mining challenge the association and formulate strategies in some of the same policy fields, such as environmental policy and energy policy.

Foods

The global food industry is extremely complex and consists of many separate industries that grow, manufacture and market a large number of products. The industry further comprises a mix of small firms that specialize in particular commodities and work in local contexts and large MNCs, such as Nestlé, Unilever and Coca-Cola, that span several product groups and are present in all corners of the world. Indeed, the prevalence of large corporations may, to some extent, hinder collective action through associations, especially in cases when the corporations feel strong enough to take independent political action and in cases when they are exposed to different campaigns targeting individual companies. Add to this that much regulation is national or regional and encourages actions from corresponding national and regional associations but does not require global industry coordination around the same issues and does not demand leverage of the same regulators.

Under these circumstances, it has not been imperative to unite the heterogeneous interests in the food industry and create an encompassing body. Instead, foods tend to be represented through a diversity of smaller associations that are more or less global, specialize in specific products or, as we shall see in the next chapter, liaise through alliances. Coordination is also achieved through collaboration between American and European associations that represent significant parts of the food industry, but these collaborations are trans-continental rather than global.

One of the associations that has become truly global by building on members from different continents but not from all countries is ICBA, which was established in 1995 and represents a specific part of the overall food industry.[24] National associations from the United States and the European Union (EU), as well as from Canada, Mexico, Australia, Brazil, China, Hong Kong, India, Taiwan, and South Africa, have joined ICBA. Interestingly, a few corporations have also joined on a direct firm-membership basis, and thus, we find an association with a mixed membership, a trait found in many other global industry associations. It is a clear indicator of the considerable role played by the major companies in beverages, and this feature spills over into the governance of the organization.

Another association in food is the specific product-oriented association SNAC International, which goes back to 1937. Its activities are still centered on the US market and politics, but in recent years, it has internationalized and globalized, extending its constituency to include foreign companies and address issues for American companies operating abroad. It is an interesting case of how national associations, if emerging from key markets and representing multinationals, may gradually transform into global associations. A somewhat similar case is the Produce Marketing Association

(PMA), an American association founded in 1949, which began expanding to include members from other continents in the mid-1990s.[25]

Different intergovernmental bodies are of relevance to the food industry, but the UN Food and Agriculture Organization (FAO) is the principal agency, and the standard-setting Codex Alimentarius Commission, a key body in global food regulation and labelling, is especially important. Because there is no single industry association in food, interactions occur between smaller and more specialized associations, and it seems that there has not been sufficient encouragement from FAO to form a joint body for the food industry as a whole. However, we should not forget that FAO is a highly knowledge-based organization and tends to call for expert participation rather than interest-based input alone and it is specifically geared toward safety matters. Indeed, there are also several global and private initiatives that mix commercial, technological and informational tasks, including, for instance, the Food Information Organization (FIO) Network.[26]

In addition to leveraging certain IGOs, food industry associations manage different forms of self-regulation. Strong guidance is delivered by the ICC, which has adopted its own general rules in advertising and market communication, and even adopted the ICC Framework for Responsible Food and Beverage Market Communication,[27] thus entering the domain of the food industry. However, the food industry and the beverages association do not see these efforts as competing with the industry's schemes and have welcomed this initiative as complementary. Against the backdrop of these general rules in global business, ICBA has issued its own International Council of Beverages Associations Guidelines on Marketing to Children,[28] an example of how peak associations and industry associations may combine their efforts.

Textiles

Textiles are a truly basic commodity with production and consumption all over the world. It is also a highly diversified industry, using different processes and types of fibers, and supplying other industries in the production and value chain, such as the apparel industry. The textiles industry globalized early. It has a long tradition of national and international associability that relates to production and marketing of textiles but also embraces a number of educational and professional aspects. These factors have given rise to the emergence of different associations.

The principal association in the textiles industry is the International Textile Manufacturers Federation (ITMF), founded in 1904 during the initial globalization of the industry as the International Federation of Master Cotton Spinners' and Manufacturers' Association,[29] based in Manchester, England, then an important hub of the world's textile industry. Many decades later, it moved to Zürich to weaken ties with British interests and better connect with other centers, not least those in developing countries.

ITMF is organized today in a triple membership format, including national associations as full or associate members and a large number of single corporations, especially from countries such as China, India, Bangladesh, Indonesia and Pakistan, indicating the historical relocation of the textile industry to developing countries. These changing ramifications also have a bearing on the governance structure of the association. The role of Europe and North America in the board has declined, and the impact of developing countries has increased. Compared with most other industry associations, this composition is unusual, however. Various mechanisms

FIGURE 2.1 Associability in a bygone age: meeting of the International Federation of Master Cotton Spinners' and Manufacturers' Association in Cairo and Alexandria, 1927

exist to balance the diversity of interests. In the committee of management, for instance, only national associations have voting rights and, according to ITMF itself, it strives to take unanimous decisions when meeting annually.[30] It is a perennial problem for industry associations to find an appropriate balance between adequately representing the raw forces of the market and including different member segments in the membership.

The association is engaged in many kinds of activities, and various services are provided to members to update them on the general development in the industry; these services include economic analyses and statistics and certain educational activities. However, other organizations in the global textiles community are available to bear the burden of at least some of these tasks. Members are serviced to improve market performance and benefit from technological advances, such as the perfection of testing methods. In fact, much collaboration in the different committees of the organization is geared toward challenges in the market. Some initiatives take the form of self-regulation to establish standardized testing, such as the Guideline for Standardized Instrument Testing of Cotton, used to guarantee functionality in the supply of identical textile qualities to other parts of the industry.[31]

The organization is a place for the exchange and dissemination of information and for the formulation of strategies in dealing with other private and public organizations. Indeed, there are many organizations making up the textile community and with which contacts have been established. Relations with some of the governments that represent key producer or consumer countries can be important, but no IGO is of paramount importance to the world textile industry. Nevertheless, the drive toward cooperation in the industry has been strong enough to sustain a coherent association through many decades and many structural reforms.

The industry takes an interest in a variety of agencies but primarily those focusing on economic, competition, trade and standardization issues that, in one way or another, are important to the global textile industry. Agencies such as WTO, in earlier times the General Agreement on Tariffs and Trade (GATT), and the International Organization for Standardization (ISO), are, therefore, some of the bodies that are of major relevance to the industry, but ILO also addresses textiles, clothes, leather and footwear and has adopted a special program to improve working conditions.[32] However, it should be remembered that production, rather than employer-related issues, are central to ITMF. Interestingly, the increased concern with topical issues, such as fair trade and development, labor rights and sweatshops, has not led to a strong and increased focus in ITMF on extending its policy portfolio.

Seemingly, other actors in the wide-ranging textile industry have embraced such issues; in apparel, for instance, there are closer contacts with end consumers and, hence, the industry is more affected by these new agendas and demands.[33]

Steel

Steel is not a pure mineral itself but an alloy of different elements, such as iron and carbon. It is produced through complex processes of, for instance, smelting and casting, leading to a variety of highly standardized grades of steel that are supplied to other industries in the production and value chain, such as the car, construction and shipbuilding industries. The link-up with other industries is crucial to understanding the role of steel, but steel is also an industry unto itself with its own specific actors and issues. Therefore, the global steel industry has its own business association, the World Steel Association (worldsteel).

While other bodies are called to represent other metals, the position of worldsteel as the sole representative of the steel industry is unchallenged. Established as the International Iron and Steel Institute (IISI) in 1967 under a somewhat different format to focus on specific industry issues, it became the World Steel Association in 2008,[34] and activities have gradually expanded.

The entrance barrier to this industry is high, requiring significant capital to engage in steel production. Relatively few countries can today boast of an important and diversified steel industry. These material ramifications spill over into associational politics: members are drawn from a limited number of countries hosting major steel producers, showing that global associations do not necessarily represent all countries but primarily the most relevant countries in a particular industry, a condition to which associations must always adapt when organizing a given industrial activity. Unlike global industry associations, which are based on national associations only, many individual firms are affiliated with worldsteel, together with some national and regional associations and steel research institutes focusing on technical issues of production. Still, however, the companies play a leading role in the organization as direct members, labelled "regular members."[35] Given the high economic concentration in the industry, we only find large companies, and only companies with a certain steel output are admitted.

These market conditions have further repercussions on the governance structure of the association, where large companies from a few countries play a dominant role. To adapt to these conditions, the Board and

Executive Committee include major producers, and they are structured to integrate a diversity of interests in the constituency. Furthermore, the governing bodies of worldsteel consist of a quite elaborate infrastructure that includes several committees and working groups assigned special policy tasks. These entities retain relevant expertise and draw this into policy formulation, and thus, they assist the Brussels- and Beijing-based secretariats, numbering together around 40 staff,[36] in keeping track of relevant developments and taking necessary initiatives. This provides special opportunities for the secretariat to make a variety of services available to members, including analyses, statistics, forecasts and training courses and to inform other relevant institutions about important trends in the industry.

In some ways, worldsteel may look like a cartel, simply because the cooperation between corporations with relatively similar profiles potentially facilitates coordination in the market. However, such collusive practices would jeopardize the position of the association and conflict with international and national competition policy, so outright coordination of economic behavior is, for principal reasons, avoided. Nonetheless, various activities are launched to enhance the competitiveness of steel producers, and thus, worldsteel is involved in various self-regulatory initiatives in the general promotion of the industry and in communications with various institutions outside the industry. worldsteel is alert to allegations of conspiracy and "with a membership of the leading steel companies in the world, must be particularly antitrust sensitive."[37] Accordingly, it has adopted a set of "Antitrust Compliance Guidelines" to which members must adhere.[38]

Basically, cooperation also aims to profile the associations in political matters of mutual concern. Interestingly, however, the organization is not linked to any particular intergovernmental agency. The work of WTO and G20 are important, but no special agency has oversight of the industry or caters to "steel policy" in particular. This is a different situation than, for instance, in shipping and airlines, where such bodies encourage a unified industry voice. Instead, worldsteel has relations with a number of intergovernmental bodies, reflecting its expanding policy engagement, and important environmental and sustainability problems have been added to traditional economic concerns.

Chemicals

The chemical industry is highly complex and is, in reality, made up of a range of industries. In the production and value chain, the industry supplies and interacts with other businesses as well as end consumers. This gives rise to a complex system of specific associations in the industry, some of them attending to unique problems that are hard to address by general chemistry associations and which are not always understood and classified as part of the chemical industry. The pharmaceutical industry, for instance, is a field characterized by its own agendas and relations in health policy, so it runs its own global industry association, IFPMA, which speaks independently for this part of the wide-ranging chemical industry.

However, general industry interests also need to be organized. Indeed, there are many traditional issues that are common for different branches, and the chemical industry undergoes changes and must respond to these. With innovation, new substances emerge and add to existing compounds and products, new pressures come from critical voices in civil society and new demands come from regulators. There is a strong tradition of organizing the chemical industry in some countries and regions.[39] Again, as with many other industries, collective action in the chemical industry dates back in time, and cooperation on an international scale also has strong roots, but for many years, the founding of a global association was not considered imperative. In fact, the formation of a global association is a relatively recent phenomenon. ICCA was established in 1989, reflecting the demand for unified action in a time of increasing challenges in an already globalized industry.[40]

Leading firms in the industry as well as strong associations work to have a joint platform to become more representative. As the name of the association suggests, national associations are members, not single companies, but a number of MNCs are affiliated via several of these national member associations. In this respect, ICCA is different from other global associations based on the principle of mixed membership, which has been introduced in recent decades. It is noteworthy, however, that other special organizations in the global chemical industry are not affiliated with ICCA, which uses a different model than in Europe, where a plethora of specialized associations are members of the encompassing chemistry association, the European Chemical Industry Council (CEFIC). Hence, ICCA is characterized by a different principle of member integration.

The strong focus on member associations is reflected in the structure of the secretariat. There is no permanent global secretariat but, somewhat unusually, a rotating secretariat hosted by shifting associations in the United States (American Chemistry Council—ACC), Europe (CEFIC), and Japan (Japan Chemical Industry Association—JCIA). These changing secretariats receive input from national associations and companies that have considerable resources, and they assist committees in the coordination of interests and in the adoption of policy. In fact, much work is still done within a regional framework, and member associations, especially those from major chemical industry countries, such as the United States, Germany and Japan, are important in the governance structure of ICCA, while countries like China, India and Russia are listed as observer members.[41]

In the chemical industry, the introduction of Responsible Care Programs, a kind of self-regulatory tool, has been a major driver of cooperation between ICCA members. Various "guidelines" and "principles" adopted by ICCA belong to its regulatory toolbox.[42] The UN Rio Conference in 1992 was also very important in bringing together the chemical industry and creating a stronger environmental profile. As is the case with many other industries, there is no single intergovernmental agency that regulates the affairs of the chemical industry, and different agencies are of relevance (e.g., the UN Environment Programme—UNEP, the UN Institute for Training and Research—UNITAR, the OECD, the UN Framework Convention on Climate Change—UNFCCC, and WTO), indicating a primary focus on environmental, trade and general economic issues. As part of the ICCA strategy, it is not only oriented toward impacting traditional public regulation but is also an advocate of developing projects and partnerships with other parties to solve problems in the industry. Stronger and coordinated efforts on behalf of global regulators might, however, create incentives in the chemical industry to find unified responses, and, in turn, upgrade the work of ICCA, but recent history shows the globalization of organizing interests is generally accomplished through a series of smaller steps.

Shipping

Shipping is a major global form of transport and draws on a long economic, social and political history, and it is still important in connecting markets. However, the industry must compete with other forms of transportation, such as air transport and long-haul transport. Over time, this competition has led to more innovative and efficient ways of carrying goods, while passenger transport has suffered an irrevocable decline.

The organization of ship owners, ICS, is today the central and undisputed representative of the world's ship owners, but it would be fair to see ICS as one among many associations in maritime policy broadly defined. The association has no immediate rivals, but adjacent associations engage to some extent in similar issues. For instance, the World Shipping Council (WSC) was established in 2000 to represent the liner shipping industry and, interestingly, gives access to individual liner companies and not to national associations,[43] which is the model in ICS, of which it is associate member. Initially, WSC was geared toward maintaining strong relations with the US government and the European Commission, but its global activity and aspirations are today also expressed through its relations with various intergovernmental agencies, including the IMO. There are also specialized associations for specific types of shipping, such as chemical, gas and oil tankers, and they attend to these interests through the International Association of Independent Tanker Owners (INTERTANKO), founded back in 1970.

ICS was founded in 1921 and has shown the ability to engage in global collective action in modern times as well.[44] It has been able to keep its key position as a representative of the industry without engaging in mergers or turbulent organizational changes, instead gradually adapting to the development of the industry and its regulatory environment. We also find the International Shipping Federation (ISF), founded in 1909, a close partner of ICS that is somewhat under its umbrella. As an independent association, it specializes in industrial relations and represents ship owners in their capacity as employers in different global forums.[45] This is a unique organization because global employer interests are only exceptionally organized at the industry level, testifying to the need to match the organizations of transport workers.

ICS is a staunch advocate of the principle of the "free seas" (i.e., that ships can operate in all international waters without restrictions, allowing for a maximum of free competition in shipping), a strong tradition.[46] Traditionally, it has been against so-called excessive regulation, but in fact, shipping is subject to much global regulation, and consequently, the association must be active in many policy fields. Safety and environment, trade, and insurance issues all have high priority. Policy is deliberated and adopted through a number of panels focusing on specific sectors and carriers of shipping but also through a number of committees with cross-sectoral commitments, such as maritime policy, labor policy, environmental affairs, and insurance. It is the special obligation of the board, which includes virtually all full members, to coordinate these many different areas and priorities.

While all dimensions of maritime policy are central to ICS as the lead organization for shipping, the organization also supplies various kinds of services to its members, especially publications on key maritime issues, and it has a comparatively strong secretariat to engage in these tasks. However, other associations are much keener on maintaining a service profile; first and foremost, BIMCO has a strong tradition in services.

The principal intergovernmental agency in the environment of ICS is, indiscriminately, the IMO, the UN special body designed to manage all aspects of maritime policy, both traditional and in new dimensions of the field.[47] The relationship between ICS and IMO is very close, assuming almost a symbiotic character. The two organizations cover nearly the same areas, and logistically, since both are based in London, communication between staffs is easily facilitated around issues of mutual concern.

Although a number of other maritime associations also enjoy consultancy status with IMO, the recognition of ICS seems particularly solid, and ICS has maritime expertise in areas that can assist IMO in governing public policy. The focus on traditional sides of public policy does not in any way exclude self-regulation, however. In recent years, ICS has, for instance, adopted Guidelines for Cyber Security Onboard Ships (see Figure 2.2) together with other maritime organizations in the Round Table of International Shipping Associations (RT)[48] and defined Best Management Practices in relation to handling piracy. Interestingly, the activity of ICS, as an industry association, here meets the activity of ICC, as a peak association, which assists shipping in the recording and investigation of crimes through a specialized ICC International Maritime Bureau (ICCIMB).

Airlines

The organization of airlines is an element in the global organization of air transport and travel more broadly. Airline companies have their own distinct association, IATA, established in 1945 and building on earlier forms of cooperation through the International Air Traffic Association, dating back to 1919.[49] Members are individual companies, not national associations, but given the historical legacy of the companies many operated out of a domestic base, because they were run as government-owned companies and to some degree could be seen as quasi-governmental actors. Cementing its business character, ownership in the industry has become increasingly privatized, however, and today a major goal of the association is also the liberalization of air transport, but there are also conflicts here.[50] On various occasions, the organization has undergone reforms, especially in an attempt not to be associated with a cartel, but a number of members still engage in tariff coordination.

Industry associations 77

FIGURE 2.2 Cyber Security Onboard Ships guidelines developed by industry associations

Source: www.ics-shipping.org/docs/default-source/resources/safety-security-and-operations/cyber-security-onboard-ships-awareness-poster.pdf?sfvrsn=11.

Although the association's name refers to "air transport," the association is exclusively for cargo and passenger airlines. A host of other organizations cover related activities, such as airports, handling firms, travel agencies, and more. Therefore, IATA has no rivals in the organization and representation of airlines. However, the organization may come into competition with some of the above-mentioned actors when it comes to defining broader dimensions of air transport policy, where they also have major interests to represent.

Its members are all active in the market. In many cases, members are obviously in hard and direct competition when they have the same destinations and offer the same connections to passengers, either alone or through the various alliances that are typical of the industry. Yet, they must find ways to cooperate within IATA that do not privilege particular members but assist in the regulation of the industry.[51] The leading bodies of IATA, headed by its Board of Governors, integrate smaller airlines but are primarily run by airlines from developed countries, and these major airline companies represent not only stronger economies but bring into IATA more expertise and consolidated knowledge. IATA has a complex organizational structure and runs many types of committees involving members and staff, and, in addition, it has a number of regional offices and country offices round the world, an exceptional feature for a global business association.

IATA has, as an elaborate relationship with the UN organization in the field, ICAO, which is likewise based in Montreal and engaged in the regulation of all sorts of issues pertaining to air transport. It is important that the airlines and their organization can match this body effectively, influence regulation and offer technical expertise at the same high level. As a recognized industry body enjoying consultative status, IATA participates in much of ICAO's work. In many ways, the two organizations work in tandem and are mutually dependent, as expressed by former IATA Director General Tony Tyler: "As you know, aviation is a global industry. We connect the planet. And global standards are the foundation on which it is built. IATA and the ICAO are the custodian of those standards. IATA and ICAO are located across the street from each other in Montreal. And we share a long history of cooperation that continues to this day."[52]

However, the efforts of IATA in public policy do not stop its cooperation with ICAO. The organization is involved in various forms of self-regulation that are either a follow-up of public regulation or an independent effort to regulate the industry.[53] Members must comply with these various standards, including safety measures, to maintain membership, become members, and keep a license to operate.

Building on its profound expertise in a range of aviation matters, the association is also heavily engaged in the provision of services relating, for instance, to advertising, security, finance, training and environment as well as more advanced forms of consulting. This shows that the association is now not only engaged in all kinds of political issues but has a strong profile as a business entity. It even offers services to firms other than airlines; for instance, it is strongly involved in the accreditation of travel agents. Following this strategy, IATA meets competition from firms in the large aviation community that offer similar services but do not have an associational link-up, and in this game, the organization has certain competitive advantages.[54] With this complex profile, the organization is involved in struggles with different service providers outside the associational system and, thus, differs from many other global industry associations. This testifies to the great variation in industry associations.

Finance

Finance occupies a special place in global business. It is an industry unto itself or, rather, a highly diverse cluster of related industries, and at the same time, it is a horizontal layer in business that interacts with all other industries. In that sense, the financial industries have certain facilitating functions and share interesting features with the facilitators, which will be discussed in a later chapter. These classical roles have undergone important changes. Recent decades have been characterized by globalization and innovation of financial products,[55] enabling actors to embrace multiple sectors of finance and making boundaries increasingly porous but still serving general facilitating functions in the economy.

Although large individual players exist in the market, and in some cases can speak for themselves, we also find a number of industry associations that bring differing interests together and represent these on a global scale.[56] Finance is highly complex in terms of organizing interests, and today, a multiplicity of associations exist to further cooperation, from the broad Global Financial Market Association (GFMA) to the narrow International Swaps and Derivatives Association (ISDA). One of the core pillars in finance is banking, but boundaries between the associations in banking and beyond are not always sharply demarcated.

IIF, founded in 1983 and headquartered in Washington, DC, is a key representative of the financial industry, but it does not have a purely private character. Membership is also open to central banks, government development banks and even the World Bank Group, factors that all blur its distinct business profile. IIF includes a diversity of firms in the financial industry, primarily commercial banks but also insurance companies, investment management firms, hedge funds and many more. This helps build capacity in many areas and involves consultations with many intergovernmental bodies, but it also gives the association a very heterogeneous character. This character is further exacerbated by admitting non-banks, such as consulting firms, law firms and rating agencies, all actors to be studied as facilitators in a later chapter.

Banks have their own global association, the International Banking Federation (IBFed), headquartered in London and established as late as 2004, although many forms of international cooperation in banking go further back in time, when banking was organized mainly at national and regional levels. Members are banking associations and not individual banks,[57] and thus, different national interests and traditions in the world of banking are brought into IBFed via member associations that cover the major financial centers as well as banking in some smaller countries.[58] Unlike other associations, where there are different membership categories to balance interests at the leadership level, we here find a simple and highly traditional model where national business interests meet. Experts from individual banks may take part in the work of various working groups but on behalf of their respective national associations.

Strong traditions of domestic collective action in banking were important in fostering the new banking association, but the movement toward greater global coordination was further triggered by the combination of economic globalization in the industry as well as greater pressure on banking by intergovernmental agencies. IBFed sees itself as "the key international forum for considering legislative, regulatory and other issues of interest to the global banking industry"[59] and is unchallenged as a purely private organization for banks.[60]

There is no single body responsible for the global regulation of banking; several agencies are pertinent. In addition to the IMF, the World Bank, the Financial Stability Board (FSB) and the Bank for International Settlements (BIS), organizations such as the OECD and G20 have become more and more engaged in banking issues. It has become increasingly necessary to formulate a unified position in the associations, and endeavors to leverage governments at home are not satisfactory for banks as a whole. Consequently, IBFed is now very active in consulting with the OECD secretariat and with the G20 when banking issues are on their agendas.[61] Indeed, the financial industry as a whole has, in recent years, come under severe attack and must do its utmost to demonstrate responsible behavior. A particularly volatile case is tax evasion.[62] In this case, the efforts of IBFed are mainly directed toward leveraging regulators, and there is no elaborated policy to offer self-regulation as an alternative tool to traditional public regulation, although other actors in the financial community are considering self-regulatory practices in this field.

Advertising

For corporations and industries to promote their products and engage in broader public-relations activities, they rely on a specific group of firms, the advertising industry, which has special competencies to devise strategies and market products and brands in relation to their customers, using different media. Indeed, advertising companies provide various services and share a number of features with the facilitators analyzed in a later chapter, but advertising is also an industry in its own right. With the marketing of ever-new products and services and with the simultaneous development of new media, advertising is a fast-changing business, a challenge for the organization of the industry.

Like in other industries, many key interests are organized through global associations.[63] An organization emphasizing professional and educational elements is the International Advertising Association (IAA), established in the United States in 1938. Members include national chapters of IAA and a number of corporations, especially from the United States, as well as national advertising associations from a number of major countries.[64] We here even find other international associations, including the World Federation of Advertisers (WFA). These different members support the general ideas of professionalization in the advertising business and its ambition to heighten standards, adopt best practices, and create self-regulation schemes.

A related but quite different organization, WFA was founded in 1953 by European organizations and gradually globalized to cover other continents. As part of this process, it became increasingly relevant to organize not only national advertiser associations in the federation but to include corporations on a direct membership basis as well, and in 1984, membership was extended to single corporations. While national advertising associations tend to put greater emphasis on the professional dimension of marketing communication, the focus of firms has a stronger commercial angle. Typically, these are not firms specializing in assisting in the marketing of other firms but, rather, are firms who market their own products and services, and a large and familiar group of multinational companies are today members of WFA.[65] In other words, these companies use the organization as a vehicle for their specific marketing interests and work through other associations, for instance in foods or pharmaceuticals, for the representation of their industry's interests. In this way, the activities of WFA resemble those of alliances whose members meet to organize issue-specific interests across different industries, and which will be analyzed in the next chapter. However, WFA is an established association, can draw on a long history and is far from an ephemeral entity.

Given the specific constituency of WFA, the governance of the organization is influenced by a combination of national associations and multinationals. Thus, its board consists of representatives from corporations and from national associations, and the statutes regulate the composition: "an equilibrium shall be respected within the Board of Directors so that the two groups of members are represented in a balanced way."[66] How this affects specific policies of the organization must be examined concretely, but here it suffices to say that these different concerns are highlighted and explicitly filtered into decision making, and as such, they are a challenge to be addressed in many other industry associations with similar membership structures.

The association is involved in a number of issue areas relating to marketing, with offices in London, Brussels and Singapore. It is the key representative of this business, but interestingly, it does not have a specific intergovernmental body with which to exchange as we have seen in some other industries. General issues pertaining to marketers in different industries are embraced, but WFA also formulates policies in relation to specific industries, such as the food industry, or in relation to specific customer segments, such as children (who are a particularly vulnerable group of consumers). Its policy domain is, however, relatively narrow as members tend to have many other interests represented via other associations, but WFA is fairly unchallenged in its core domain. Interestingly, it engages with certain issues that are also addressed by peak associations, such as ICC, but instead of seeing this in competitive terms, it mentions explicitly that it follows and implements ICC codes on advertising in addition to its own self-regulation.[67] In fact, the association has quite a large program to define and administer joint rules, the implementation of which is, in part, delegated to various facilitating organizations on a commercial basis, altogether indicative of the strong role of private actors in global marketing and the corresponding weakness of public authority.

Conclusion

A large number of global industry associations serve specific sections of the business community and are distinguishable from the peak associations treated in the last chapter. Interestingly enough, members who, in one way or another, are likely to meet each other as competitors in the market simultaneously develop organizations as forums for cooperation. The industry associations organize comparatively narrow segments of business, engage in comparatively few policy fields, and exchange with selected intergovernmental agencies. Therefore, the relatively small and homogenous groups have important drivers for cooperation in politics that override market competition, a phenomenon in business associability that needs further theorizing.

The global population of industry associations reflects both old and new industries. There is clearly a high degree of continuity because many old and established entities manage to survive, adapting to new demands and expectations, and at the same time, the emergence of ever-new products and technologies gives rise to the formation of novel associations. The total population of industry associations is clearly increasing in this process, reflecting the globalization of business and gradual replacement of actors. Some associations are able to redefine their domains—for instance, in the chemical industry, where new substances and products are continuously added, or in tourism, where new forms of travel are invented by tour operators. However, new business activities, for instance in communications and media (e.g., Google and Facebook), cannot always be accommodated under an existing organizational framework.

Many associations are sensitive in embracing new concerns in their membership and in their political environment, factors that are enormously important to their adaptability and survival, and under these conditions, new bodies are not needed. This yields great stability to the industry associations as key elements in global business. In some cases, however, associations are not sufficiently alert and flexible enough to follow impulses in their membership and in their environment, and new entities are required.

There is no fixed model for all industries, however, and we find substantial variation in the organization of industries. Industry associations along the production and value chain display great variation along theoretical issues outlined in the initial overview of this chapter, and the small number of industries and their associations that we have examined in this chapter demonstrate some aspects of this variation: some have national associations as members while others build on firms, often large multinationals; some have large secretariats and dispose of considerable resources while others have quite rudimentary structures; some have a clear focus on political issues while others are more orientated toward the provision of services; some are clearly run by powerful firms or national associations from strong economies while others seek to integrate broader groups in the governance of the associations; some direct all their energy toward political institutions while others create various forms of self-regulation as ordering alternatives to traditional public regulation; and some associations have firm and almost symbiotic relations with a single agency while others have fragmented contacts with a variety of IGOs.

The population of industry associations shows that their proliferation is characterized by strong specialization in which each industry seeks to avoid competition with other associations in the organization and representation of its domain. This kind of specialization is, in many cases, successful, but we also find cases where industry associations have certain overlapping domains. It is a perennial task to avoid or at least minimize such conflicts in a world where a combination of economic, industrial and political dynamics influences the boundaries of the associations. It is, however, much easier for industry associations than for peak associations to investigate and verify whether they occupy some of the same niches and, hence, to find means to avoid or moderate conflicts, for instance, by negotiating boundaries and dividing labor, by merging existing bodies, by founding new associations, or by creating new and flexible platforms for cooperation in selected areas.

Notes

1 Without attempting to define peak and industry associations *per se*, Rutgers University hosted in June 2016 a conference on industry associations, mainly from a legal perspective, and with ideas about international associations. Rutgers University, *Conference Report: Industry Associations and Transnational Regulation*, see: https://cclg.rutgers.edu/wp-content/uploads/Industry-Associations-and-Transnational-Regulation-Conference-Report-1.pdf (accessed 12 September 2016).
2 Different international taxonomies exist to classify industries, the most authoritative perhaps the International Standard Industrial Classification of All Activities (ISIC) managed by the UN Statistics Division. Also the Industry Classification Benchmark (ICB) is useful and is followed in stock markets and by exchanges.

However, the associability of business does not mechanically reflect the material properties or the investment profiles industries, as industry associations are shaped by several economic, social and political factors.

3 John Braithwaite and Peter Drahos, *Global Business Regulation* (Cambridge: Cambridge University Press, 2000), 454–471; Heather McKeen-Edwards and Tony Porter, *Transnational Financial Associations and the Governance of Global Finance: Assembling Wealth and Power* (London: Routledge, 2013), 38–41.

4 In the biological understanding, niches are not something just available to species, and niches need to be identified and actively prepared. Ernst Mayr, *This is Biology: The Science of the Living World* (Cambridge: The Belknap Press of Harvard University Press, 1997), 207–226. This theory is also applicable to our case.

5 In this case, we do not have to do with large n-studies as often assumed in classical studies on population ecology, see: Michael T. Hannan and John H. Freeman, "The Population Ecology of Organizations," *American Journal of Sociology* 82, no. 5 (1977): 929–964. However, there is still much to learn from this perspective in organization theory.

6 E-mail communication with Lars Rohwer, Corporate Communications and Government Affairs, 17 October 2013, Siemens AG.

7 The specific avenues of individual and collective action in business, different from labor, were theoretically elaborated in Claus Offe and Helmut Wiesenthal, "Two Logics of Collective Action: Theoretical Notes on Social Class and Organizational Form," *Political Power and Social Theory* 1 (1980): 67–115. These insights can be applied to different territorial levels of business.

8 This issue is addressed at a general level in Mancur C. Olson, *The Logic of Collective Action: Public Goods and the Theory of Groups* (Cambridge: Harvard University Press, 1965). It is correct that larger members pay for small members but it is wrong to assert that the small exploit the large. The large members have significant benefits from working through representative associations.

9 Theory development of this perspective is needed but some ideas can be found in Kees van der Pijl, "Introduction: The World of Production and International Economy," in Kees van der Pijl, eds, *Handbook of the International Political Economy of Production* (Cheltenham: Edward Elgar, 2015), xxiii–xxxviii.

10 IFPMA, "Membership," www.ifpma.org/who-we-are/our-membership/ (accessed 12 September 2017).

11 This can be analyzed in a principal-agent perspective: Darren G. Hawkins, David A. Lake, Daniel L. Nielson and Michael J. Tierney, eds, *Delegation and Agency in International Organizations* (Cambridge: Cambridge University Press, 2006). This is mainly adapted to study intergovernmental bodies. A more varied perspective recognizing member asymmetries is offered in the corporate-actor model developed by James S. Coleman, *Foundations of Social Theory* (Cambridge: Belknap Press of Harvard University Press, 1990).

12 For a discussion of the administrative basis of associations: Karsten Ronit, "Organized Business and Global Public Policy: Administration, Participation, and Regulation," in Diane Stone and Kim Moloney, eds, *Oxford Handbook on Global Public Policy and Transnational Administration* (Oxford: Oxford University Press, 2018).

13 According to CEFIC, "The ICCA secretariat rotates every two years among ICCA members (usually CEFIC and the American Chemistry Council (ACC))," see: www.cefic.org/newsroom/More-news-from-2017/Cefic-and-ICCA-Supp

86 Industry associations

orting-responsible-chemical-management-across-the-globe/ (accessed 8 December 2017).
14 In recent years, this has led to a rich array of publications. See, for instance, John Gerard Ruggie, *Just Business: Multinational Corporations and Human Rights* (New York: W.W. Norton & Company, 2013).
15 BIMCO, "Why Join BIMCO?" www.bimco.org/about-us-and-our-members/why-join-bimco (accessed 10 October 2017).
16 For an interactive approach to INGO-NGO relations: Kenneth W. Abbott, Philipp Genschel, Duncan Snidal and Bernhard Zangl, "Orchestration: Global Governance through Intermediaries," in Kenneth W. Abbott, Philipp Genschel, Duncan Snidal and Bernhard Zangl, eds, *International Organizations as Orchestrators* (Cambridge: Cambridge University Press, 2015), 3–36.
17 For some treatises, see Tony Porter and Karsten Ronit, eds, *The Challenges of Global Business Authority: Democratic Renewal, Stalemate or Decay?* (Albany: State University of New York Press, 2010); Walter Mattli and Ngaire Woods, eds, *The Politics of Global Regulation* (Princeton: Princeton University Press, 2009); Tim Büthe and Walter Mattli, *The New Global Rulers: The Privatization of Regulation in the World Economy* (Princeton: Princeton University Press, 2011).
18 An overview is provided of this still expanding literature in: David J. Vogel, "The Private Regulation of Global Corporate Conduct: Achievements and Limitations," *Business & Society* 49, no. 1 (2010): 68–87.
19 There are different ways of defining these properties by means of induction and deduction. Both internal and external factors must be accounted for. See the design of Philippe C. Schmitter and Wolfgang Streeck, *The Organization of Business Interests. Studying the Associative Action of Business in Advanced Industrial Societies* (MPIFG: Cologne, 1999 [1981]).
20 Aynsley Kellow, "Privilege and Underprivilege: Countervailing Groups, Policy, and the Mining Industry at the Global Level," in Karsten Ronit, ed., *Global Public Policy: Business and the Countervailing Groups of Civil Society* (London: Routledge, 2007), 110–131.
21 ICMM, "10 Principles," www.icmm.com/en-gb/about-us/member-commitments/icmm-10-principles (accessed 8 December 2017).
22 ICMM, "Our Members," www.icmm.com/en-gb/members (accessed 10 November 2017).
23 For the composition of the leading body, the council, see ICMM, "About Us," www.icmm.com/en-gb/about-us/our-organisation/our-structure (accessed 6 November 2017).
24 There exists an International Food & Beverage Association, founded in 2012, which includes member associations from a few European countries as well as from a small number of Southeast Asian countries. This must not be confused with the International Food and Beverage Alliance (IFBA), which will be examined in the next chapter.
25 PMA, "Over 60 Years of Growth at PMA," http://pma.com/about-pma/history (accessed March 31 2017).
26 The FIO Network is based on the participation of large countries or regions. FIO, "Food Information Organization (FIO) Network," see: www.foodinsight.org/pages/food-information-organization-fio-network (accessed 12 October 2017).

Industry associations 87

27 ICC Commission on Marketing and Advertising, *Framework for Responsible Food and Beverage Marketing Communications 2012* (Paris: ICC, 2010).
28 ICBA, *International Council of Beverages Associations Guidelines on Marketing to Children* (Washington, DC: ICBA, 2015).
29 ITMF, *ITMF 100 Years. 1904–2004* (Zürich: ITMF, 2004).
30 ITMF, "Committee of Management," see: www.itmf.org/committees/committee-of-management (accessed 25 March 2017).
31 International Committee on Cotton Testing Methods (ICCTM), *Progress Report 2014. Proceedings of the ICCTM Meeting in Bremen* (18 March 2014).
32 Together with other UN organizations, ILO has developed the program "Better Work." ILO, "Better Work," https://betterwork.org/# (accessed 30 October 2017).
33 An example of a new organization getting involved in such problems is the SAC, initiated by leading brands and retailers, and later joined by stakeholders in civil society.
34 The organization was established as the International Iron and Steel Institute. For a glimpse of its history, worldsteel, "About Us," see: www.worldsteel.org/about-us/who-we-are/history.html.
35 worldsteel, "Membership," www.worldsteel.org/about-us/membership.html (accessed 8 December 2017).
36 worldsteel, "Our People," www.worldsteel.org/about-us/who-we-are/our-people.html (accessed 8 December 2017).
37 worldsteel, *Antitrust Compliance Guidelines* (Brussels: worldsteel, 2012).
38 In this process, a legal counsel from a recognized law firm is involved, and the leading bodies of the organization as well as member firms may consult with this counsel. worldsteel, *Antitrust Compliance Guidelines*.
39 Alberto Martinelli, ed., *International Markets and Global Firms: A Comparative Study of Organized Business in the Chemical Industry* (London: Sage, 1991).
40 Another organization going global is the International Chemical Trade Association (ICTA), established in 1992, reformed and presented under the new name in 2016. It represents chemical distributors.
41 ICCA, "Organizational Structure," www.icca-chem.org/about-us/ (accessed 4 June 2017).
42 ICCA, "Resources," www.icca-chem.org/resources/ (accessed 4 June 2017).
43 WSC, "Member Companies," www.worldshipping.org/about-the-council/member-corporations (accessed 6 July 2017).
44 Proshanto K. Mukherjee and Mark Brownrigg, *Farthing on International Shipping* (Heidelberg: Springer, 2013).
45 In the past, ISF was a more independent organization but has increasingly been absorbed by ICS. In the words of ICS, ISF "is the identity used by ICS when acting as the international employers' association for ship operators." ICS, *The International Chamber of Shipping (ICS). Representing the Global Shipping Industry* (London: ICS, 2013).
46 John Braithwaite and Peter Drahos, *Global Business Regulation* (Cambridge: Cambridge University Press, 2000), 418–437.
47 In labor relations, ILO is the key interlocutor. ICS has relations to an astonishing number of intergovernmental agencies. ICS, *The International Chamber of Shipping (ICS). Representing the Global Shipping Industry* (London: ICS, 2013).

48 ICS (and other organizations), *The Guidelines on Cyber Security Onboard Ships. Version 2.0* (London: ICS, 2017). Behind this work stood RT, one of the many alliances in global business.
49 IATA, "Early Days," www.iata.org/about/Pages/history-early-days.aspx (accessed 7 November 2017). Some aspects are also treated in: David MacKenzie, *ICAO: A History of the International Civil Aviation Organization* (Toronto: University of Toronto Press, 2010).
50 IATA, "The Economic Impact of Air Service Liberalization," see: www.iata.org/whatwedo/Documents/economics/liberalization_air_transport_study_30may06.pdf (accessed 22 May 2017).
51 Karsten Ronit, *Global Consumer Organizations* (London: Routledge, 2015), 119–120.
52 Remarks of Tony Tyler, director general of IATA, at the National Conference on Air Transport in Baku, Azerbaijan, 30 April 2013. See: IATA, "Pressroom," www.iata.org/pressroom/speeches/Pages/2013-04-30-01.aspx.
53 Russell W. Mills, "The Interaction of Private and Public Regulatory Governance: The Case of Association-Led Voluntary Aviation Safety Programs," *Policy and Society* 35, no. 1 (2016): 43–55.
54 At the same time as IATA offers various services, it is engaged in the co-production of services with different stakeholders through "strategic partnerships." IATA, "About," see: www.iata.org/about/sp/Documents/IATA-Strategic-Partnership-Brochure.pdf (accessed 13 March 2017).
55 Gerald A. Epstein, ed., *Financialization and the World Economy* (Cheltenham: Edward Elgar, 2005).
56 Tony Porter, "Tracing Associations in Global Finance," *International Political Sociology* 7, no. 3 (2013): 334–348.
57 Other entities operate with individual bank membership, for instance the issue-specific Wolfsberg Group that attends to anti-money-laundering problems. Gemma Aiolfi and Hans-Peter Bauer, "The Wolfsberg Group," in Mark Pieth, ed., *Collective Action: Innovative Strategies to Prevent Corruption* (Zurich/St Gallen: Dike, 2012), 97–112.
58 IBFed groups members into founding members (United States, Australia, Canada, EU, Japan and South Africa), and associate members (China, Brazil, India, South Korea and Russia). IBFed, "Members," www.ibfed.org/members (accessed 20 March 2017).
59 IBF, re: IBFed response to FSB consultation paper, "Guiding Principles on the Internal Total Loss-absorbing Capacity of G-SIBs ('Internal TLAC')" Letter to FSB, 10 February 2017.
60 The Institute of International Finance is also a key organization for finance and banking. It is a non-state actor and involves also central banks and thus is a mixed public-private entity. Heather McKeen-Edwards and Tony Porter, *Transnational Financial Associations and the Governance of Global Finance: Assembling Wealth and Power* (London: Routledge, 2013), 38–41.
61 The association continuously updates this information. IBFed, "Representing The International Banking Community," www.ibfed.org.uk (accessed 4 November 2017).
62 Richard Eccleston, *The Dynamics of Global Economic Governance: The Financial Crisis, the OECD, and the Politics of International Tax Cooperation* (Cheltenham: Edward Elgar, 2013).

63 Karsten Ronit, "Global Business Associations, Self-Regulation and Consumer Policy," in Achim Lang and Hannah Murphy, eds, *Business and Sustainability: Between Government Pressure and Self-Regulation* (Heidelberg and New York: Springer, 2014), 61–79. Furthermore, an interesting associational model is provided through the US-based Interactive Advertising Bureau (IAB). It specializes in digital and interactive marketing and has an IAB Global Network with affiliates in the form of more than 40 national associations. IAB, "Global Network," www.iab.com/global/ (accessed 20 November 2017).

64 International Advertising Association, "Organizational Members Directory," see: http://iaa-resources.org/resources/Organizational%20Members%20Directory%20May%202012.pdf (accessed 13 March 2017).

65 WFA, "Our Members," www.wfanet.org/about/our-members/#corporate (accessed 22 September 2017).

66 WFA, *WFA Statutes* (WFA: Brussels, 2015).

67 The organization has adopted a number of guidelines and best practices, for instance the *World Federation of Marketers' Media Charter*. Monitoring and enforcement are also delegated to other actors. www.responsibleadvertising.org/selfregulation.asp.

3

ALLIANCES OF CORPORATIONS AND ASSOCIATIONS

- Overview: the multiple *problematiques* of alliances
- Old roots or fresh initiatives?
- In or across industries?
- Temporary or permanent cooperation?
- Broad or narrow tasks?
- State- or market-related?
- Concrete alliances and major dilemmas
- Global Business Alliance for 2030
- Global Business Coalition for Education
- Family Business Network International
- The FIDO (Fast IDentity Online) Alliance
- International AntiCounterfeiting Coalition
- International Food and Beverage Alliance
- Conclusion

In a number of cases, peak associations and industry associations prove insufficient as vehicles of global business interests, and other forms of collective action are engineered. Some of these take the character of temporary or permanent alliances that are organized either as associations, and therefore may be hard to distinguish from the traditional entities, or as looser forms of cooperation based on other organizational principles. Variation is great, there is no single model applied, and the entities carry different names to mark the nature of their cooperation.[1] We find much semantic creativity, and these bodies are occasionally called councils, coalitions, clubs, platforms, networks or round tables, but today they are also frequently referred to as alliances. Their conceptual inconsistencies make it complicated to record the population of alliances, and it is difficult to theorize about them since we do not have a good grasp of their proliferation and pattern of activities. However, in line with how they are referred to in business, it is useful, from a research perspective, to build on an alliance concept that stresses the forms of cooperation that move beyond the boundaries of traditional industry and peak associations.[2] However, theories on peak and industry associations are not sufficiently helpful to guide a study on the special conditions of alliances. By adding global alliances to our study, we can not only present a more complete and precise picture of business and its organizations but also achieve a better understanding of how they evolve and challenge other actors in the business community. This gives us further theoretical insights into organized business.

The rationales for creating alliances that add to or replace existing peak and industry associations are manifold. Traditional associations cannot embrace particular issues because, for instance, these may only be of interest to a minority of members, or perhaps a majority cannot engage in particular questions without the consent of the whole constituency. Furthermore, traditional associations cannot cope with the tasks managed by alliances because these tasks cross several associational boundaries and require complex and costly coordination between associations. Indeed, traditional associations are often hard to reform, and new issues constantly arise and need swift action from business, and these are easier to accommodate with new platforms because it is demanding to provide the necessary expertise, expand tasks and formulate strategies in new issue areas.

Very often, the alliances organize and represent a small and particularly committed group of corporations and associations.[3] Consequently, the alliances are highly focused and do not have to wait for support from other firms in a given industry that are undecided or have other preferences. Examples of global alliances are the International Food and Beverage Alliance (IFBA), which unites leading corporations and addresses a range of issues relating to nutrition and lifestyle diseases, and the International AntiCounterfeiting Coalition (IACC), which works to protect the intellectual property rights of business. In both cases, existing organizations were not able to effectively represent businesses, and challenges needed to be addressed in a new framework.

In the following, we first provide an overview of theoretical challenges and discuss the major and variable properties of alliances as a unique form of cooperation, perhaps with a root in existing associations, perhaps on the way to the formation of new associations. We show that these entities tend to offer some advantages to business or, at least, to founder firms and associations and, thus, add to the landscape of organized business. We then study some examples of alliances that are found in different contexts and testify to the broad application and flexibility of the concept. In various ways, they handle the key dilemmas outlined in the following section and, together, typify the problems of alliances.

Overview: the multiple *problematiques* of alliances

There is clearly much cooperation in the global business community between firms in and across different industries, and also between associations that find common ground and liaise in new ways. To distinguish these forms of collective action, we need to emphasize that alliances, studied in this chapter, are organized as specific entities with the goal of improving the general reputation of the business concerned, of influencing relevant political institutions, and of influencing regulation in ways beneficial to the members of the alliance, potentially through formulating alternatives to public policy, such as self-regulation.[4] The alliances may share a number of the same tasks as traditional business associations at the peak or industry level, but they typically have selective membership. In this regard, they are somewhat similar to clubs, discussed in the next chapter, because they have clear commitment in markets and in politics, but they are, however, not supposed to bring social benefits to their members.

Theoretically, alliances emerge because there is at least one problem—out of several discussed below—that existing industry or peak associations cannot effectively cope with, and, in turn, complex and interrelated dilemmas shape the organizational and political profile of concrete alliances.[5] Thus, the alliances identify and carve out new niches,[6] and they adapt, utilizing experiences accumulated in the business community. Some of the perennial questions facing alliances are as follows: Should alliances be led by existing organizations or be guided by fresh initiatives? Should alliances be temporary or permanent? Should cooperation be nested in or across different industries? Should issue areas be narrow or wide? Finally, should cooperation address challenges in the market or in politics?

Old roots or fresh initiatives?

Some alliances are created by firms and associations that start building new entities on the basis of existing experiences, and some of the roots of these alliances are illustrated in Figure 3.1. Such developments are frequent because there is an advanced system of global peak and industry associations providing the basis for the branching out of new forms of collective action in the business community. Some established bodies will face situations in which they cannot represent some members or some concerns adequately,

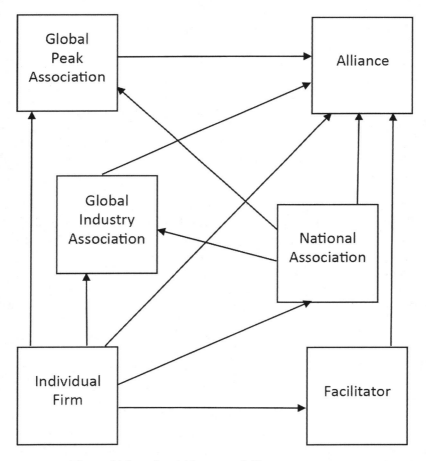

FIGURE 3.1 The multiple and variable roots of alliances

and with a background in established associations, members can draw on the social capital invested in these and find new opportunities.

Furthermore, the leadership of existing associations may play a very active role in the creation and administration of such alliances and officially delegate tasks. The new alliances will be able to draw members from the old associations alone or join forces with other firms and associations from the same industry or from industries unaffiliated with the existing association. As a result, measures are taken to effectively represent members through new platforms and in ways that were not possible before.

Other types of alliances have a different kind of origin. Some alliances are not so much offspring of existing associations but, rather, brand new entities without any significant institutional history attached to them.[7] This is the case, for instance, with the emergence of alliances representing new products, new firms or new principles, such as those relating to sustainable production. Here, alliances embody loose forms of cooperation that may eventually grow into industry or peak associations, but in such cases, fresh initiatives cannot build on previous experience of cooperation, and this lack of practice can, at least in the early stages, be a barrier.

Alliances sustain various types of relations with the old associations, whether related or unrelated in their formative stage. Alliances may become competitors, but they may also fill a void and manifest interests in areas hitherto neglected by associations. Indeed, firms and associations may find it relevant to maintain multiple memberships and rely on established industry associations in some areas and on alliances in other, usually specialized issues.[8] In such cases, alliances function as additions to established associations and engage in non-competitive relations. This may even be beneficial for traditional associations because they are relieved of some problematic areas of collective action that either temporarily or permanently are taken out of their portfolio.

In or across industries?

In many cases, members of alliances come from the very same industry where they have experienced rather similar challenges and feel the same need for action. Joint action, however, may be jeopardized by competition and by the fear of some firms and associations that future alliances may confer different costs and benefits to members and, thus, negatively affect incentives to launch such initiatives. However, industries are also a hub where social capital is produced, leading to a greater amount of trust without changing the competitive relations between members in the market. Certain barriers for cooperation have been overcome over time in business associations, and this shows that there are a number of ways to avoid or at least tame competition. Accordingly, an industry is a suitable point of departure for alliances, and such vertical alliances are relatively homogeneous.

Indeed, cooperation in existing associations may be a catalyst for the creation of new alliances, in cases in which members cannot find the necessary support for accommodating new initiatives within this already-known framework and instead build new industry-related bodies without necessarily abandoning membership in established associations. Given the industry basis of such alliances, initiatives may also be coupled with promotional ambitions on behalf of the member firms and, thus, help position members in a market context.

However, other avenues of alliance building may be envisaged. Firms and associations from different industries may, in spite of activity in different markets, experience some of the same challenges. If members probe potential interest and cannot find support for their cause in the different associations with which they are affiliated, perhaps because a problem only affects some segments of members, an option is to go outside these frameworks and find partners across industries. An important factor in such processes is that some large corporations are active in several industries and experience changes in markets and in politics sooner than others, sometimes facing these challenges before highly specialized associations.[9] Such firms become pioneers in the creation of alliances. Furthermore, and this can be the key driving force, coordination across different industries is much more powerful and demonstrates broad business support. Although in some respects more heterogeneous, broad alliances have opportunities to convincingly present their case in exchanges with governments, intergovernmental agencies and, sometimes, in a dialogue with relevant civil society groups.

Temporary or permanent cooperation?

A major issue in the formation of alliances concerns the lifetime of the cooperation. It is always hard to predict the time required for concerted alliance action and to gauge when a given problem is solved, but there is often an idea about the duration of an alliance, and this will most likely affect its design. There is, however, rarely a fixed date for its termination, and only experiences will decide this, but for reasons of simplicity, we may distinguish between temporary and permanent alliances. Their potentially temporary nature is an important feature of alliances, setting them apart from both peak and industry associations, which are generally created as permanent entities.

Many advantages are associated with forming temporary organizations.[10] The ambition to foster some temporary forms of cooperation via alliances may seem less controversial and not seriously questioning the authority of existing business associations. Often a concrete challenge can be identified and addressed, such as the adoption of a particular standard to facilitate production or the hindrance of a regulatory threat. Once problems are settled, and especially if battles are won, there is not necessarily a need for further business engagement through a given alliance. However, entities that are either designed to be temporary or which become redundant at some point may redefine their missions, discover new tasks and grow into permanent bodies. In this process, they can benefit from the social capital gained through the temporary cooperation of their participants.

If, however, an alliance is devised as a permanent body from the outset, and is therefore not related to a provisional task, other exigencies must be met. Thus, alliances may rather address some general themes facing a business or focus on a complex amalgamation of tasks that require perennial attention. In such cases, no immediate outcome of the alliance's efforts is in sight, so there is no immediate reason to fold the alliance. The perspective that the alliances are associations in the making has certain consequences. Indeed, the formation of permanent alliances can be a threat to existing associations because the alliance shows that theirs is not just an hoc task that needs relatively brief attention; instead, there are questions that require enduring consideration, and this is best done outside established peak and industry associations. The formation of permanent alliances, therefore, points to possible slack in business associations[11] and makes associations seem less likely to recapture the lost domains.

Broad or narrow tasks?

As with peak and industry associations, alliances have different domains, and they have to carve out relevant niches and define tasks in relation to other actors that either are or may become active in the same field. However, alliances also have to consider where members have a specific demand for cooperation that is not already covered, or at least not effectively managed. Alliances generally tend to be issue-specific and concentrate on a single concern or to engage in a few narrowly related problems,[12] but alliances emerge in institutional contexts and cannot freely define domains. It is preferable to establish cooperation around safe issues and keep transaction costs of negotiation at bay. If need be, cooperation can be extended later on, depending on member interests as well as on pressures from the institutional environment. In relation to competition from existing associations, this cautious approach seems feasible as alliances will not meet hard competition from initially more experienced organizations, and these organizations will more easily surrender tasks if members are not expected to leave and if new alliances are not seen as true competitors.

However, certain alliances have broader ambitions. From the outset, they define wider domains, again adapting to interests and expectations around themselves. Even these broader alliances, in terms of their issue coverage, will typically have far fewer tasks to manage than will peak and industry associations, but of course, the question arises as to when such alliances will evolve into peak or industry associations and strive to represent broader concerns. This is one of the possible pathways of alliances: their gradual development into future associations. The more issues that are covered, the more the alliances come to resemble traditional peak and industry associations. This is likely to have consequences as it will be accompanied by stronger secretariats and a more complex decision-making structure, a development that will go against some of the principal advantages of alliances, namely specialization, informal cooperation and an unbureaucratic working style. However, alliances can be understood as incipient associations, and historically, many established associations have started out through narrow ad hoc cooperation with very limited organizational infrastructure and later have become full-fledged associations. It is important to recognize these dynamics, some of which can, of course, only be observed over long periods of time and are not in any way planned.

State- or market-related?

Alliances have a variety of purposes. As a distinct task, many alliances leverage governments, intergovernmental agencies and other international institutions in an attempt to influence public policy, avoid regulation or drive it in directions beneficial for business. Sometimes an explicit goal is to take part in these policy processes and contribute knowledge that is not available at the public level so as to make potential regulation more legitimate and amenable in business. It is, therefore, possible that cooperation may be terminated once perceived threats have been warded off, but alliances may also be sustained and kept in reserve for future action. This kind of political activity is not exclusively directed at institutions of public authority but may also relate to civil society groups challenging businesses.

Other alliances are not so focused on political institution or traditional public policy. This does not necessarily suggest that they are less political but that their political goals are expressed in other ways. An important purpose of some alliances is simply to establish self-regulation and agree on certain rules and norms among members as an alternative to public regulation.[13] This is also a common practice of many industry and peak associations, but in the case of alliances, such self-regulation does not have to be supported by all firms in a given sector, where interest heterogeneity can be strong. Instead, it can rely on an already selected and particularly committed membership that has established the alliance, often with self-regulation in mind. Indeed, self-regulation may help members profile themselves in the market and distinguish them from firms not enrolled in the alliance.

In other words, self-regulation may be understood in a political context where a choice has to be made between public and private regulation, but there is usually also an important economic dimension of such alliance initiatives.[14] Additionally, the exact definition of rules and norms to be obeyed has an impact on competition between members of an alliance and, therefore, intricate negotiations are needed to sustain such schemes. In such cases, we should not forget that business may, in fact, involve interested civil society parties in a joint effort to establish a self-regulatory scheme without including traditional public regulators.

Concrete alliances and major dilemmas

There are various dilemmas associated with alliance building, including some of the major issues discussed above (i.e., use old roots or establish fresh initiatives, whether to form in or across industries, cooperate temporarily or permanently, undertake broad tasks or narrow tasks, and focus on state- or market-related issues). For heuristic reasons, these have been addressed as if they were isolated from each other, but they are actually entangled in intriguing ways, although they are not equally relevant in all alliances. The dilemmas all grapple with essential problems in the business community about when and how to organize interests and about the incentive structures for collective action among the participants of alliances.

However, collective action tends to be partial in alliances, and various limitations in time and space must theoretically be addressed in slightly different ways than when studying the more encompassing form of cooperation encountered in peak and industry associations. It is important to understand alliances, wedged between peak and industry associations, as occupying a place in the overall business community and, more particularly, in the associational system. Alliances come into competition with other entities when challenging their domains, but there is also the possibility that they will complement the activities of other actors and manage tasks that, for various reasons, are addressed by other bodies. Thus, we need a differentiated approach to the study of alliances.

Due to the less formal and somewhat fluctuating character of many alliances, their exact membership is somewhat harder to record, and, relatedly, there is a need for further conceptual clarification of alliances. The examples scrutinized below have been chosen to show that alliances are found in many areas of business and display many commonalities rather than thriving only in particular industries and issue areas.

In the following, we analyze alliances that have been active in recent years and decades. We begin with the alliances that are broadest in scope in terms of issues covered and move down to the most issue-specific. Such a "ranking" is not fully precise in characterizing entities that, in some sense, are all specialized, but there is, as yet, no established taxonomy to classify alliances, a problem requiring further research. However, issue coverage is a relevant starting point to group alliances into types and analyze their variations.

Global Business Alliance for 2030

The Global Business Alliance for 2030 (GBA) was founded in 2013 and born out of a process to give business a stronger position in the context of the UN resolution "Transforming our World: The 2030 Agenda for Sustainable Development." The alliance was initiated by the business world itself and welcomed by the UN as one of the major stakeholders with input in this process.[15] As the name suggests, this is clearly an alliance that will be terminated once the project is accomplished and relevant strategies are implemented, but it is possible that it will transform into another initiative or be absorbed by existing business associations.

Its goal is to coordinate interests on a grand scale, bring them into the UN system and partner in the implementation of the sustainable development goals of the UN expressed in the resolution. The proximity of the alliance to the UN processes emphasizes that its activity is, first and foremost, geared toward the development of public policy in a global context. It is not principally concerned with finding alternative private solutions through, for instance, self-regulation, as are a number of other alliances, and its style is not to confront these agencies but simply to participate in non-contentious ways.

Indeed, like many other alliances, the GBA program is quite broad and far from issue-specific. The broad nature of the alliance is reflected in its membership. Here, we find many of the big peak associations previously discussed (ICC, IOE, BIAC, WBCSD), which represent wide parts of the global business community and give the alliance a powerful voice.[16] Indeed, behind this fresh initiative are exceedingly established associations.

The peak associations are themselves large coordinators, but additional coordination is achieved through their cooperation. In the membership, we notice several industry associations (e.g., chemicals, pharmaceuticals, water, oil and gas, and mining and minerals), some of which lean toward environmental and sustainability issues, which is obvious given the agenda of the alliance. There is only a single firm. As none of the peak associations organizes industry associations, however, industry participation brings further interest into the alliance as well as experience and knowledge not already present.

This model indicates that the building of alliances is not necessarily something that is initiated by certain member groups in the associations, perhaps with support or consent from the associations. In this case, initiatives are undertaken by the associations in a more top-down manner, where they maintain considerable control of the alliances. The central role of the existing associations, and especially the peak associations, is also manifested in the management of the secretariat in the GBA. The ICC has taken responsibility for the secretariat and is a top coordinator in political and administrative terms. As this case demonstrates, it is also typical of some alliances that they do not have their own independent infrastructure but rely on that of their members and utilize existing resources.

Global Business Coalition for Education

Most alliances emerge in areas where specific concerns of corporations, industries or, occasionally, even a wider range of business interests are tabled, obviously with the goal of securing various benefits for alliance members.

However, there are different motives in the alliances, and some seek to profile themselves as contributing to the common good. One such alliance is the Global Business Coalition for Education (GBC-Education). It was founded in 2013 by a group of multinationals from different industries and, today, a number of large companies, such as Accenture, Chevron Corporation, Gucci, Intel, McKinsey, and Western Union, participate in the organization, which now totals more than 100 members.[17]

Education, at least as it is regarded within the alliance, is not a controversial issue that risks splitting members into different fractions and has dire consequences for the position of some firms in the market. Therefore, the adoption of a joint strategy seems relatively straightforward, a situation different from that of many other alliances, where major commercial interests are at stake. Accordingly, it has not been necessary to build up a larger apparatus to prepare and implement policies, and the secretariat in New York is minimal.

Membership does not affect the core interests of the business community and is, therefore, not compelling. Interestingly, this situation is different from that of many other alliances, where participation is needed and where alliance activities may have a great impact on members' competitiveness. Indeed, GBC-Education is one of many other corporate social responsibility initiatives aimed at branding contributing companies as not entirely self-interested actors, and in some ways, this enterprise is akin to those of entities, such as clubs, which will be treated in the next chapter. Indeed, the whole idea behind the alliance is not to educate a potential future workforce for these companies. Instead, the objective is to support education in poorer parts of the world—in Africa, Asia and Latin America—and, therefore, raise the standards of education through a diversity of projects.[18] This is clearly a key task for government in these countries as well as for IGOs active in education policy, but these actors do not provide sufficient support, and here the companies step in to bring about change and position themselves through philanthropy as well as through various partnerships and campaigns.[19]

Improving education does not give business any immediate and tangible benefits, but initiatives can be important for the betterment of welfare and stability in many countries, and it is from this perspective that the work must be seen. There is no convincing explanation based on self-interest for why the initiative has been able to attract the concrete members it has. In fact, large companies become involved in many issues, and reputational factors count—no doubt a reason why this activity has been chosen among a broad range of issues that will be of benefit to society.

Foregrounding societal goals offers GBC-Education many opportunities to interact with different partners in civil society and gain access to forums and communications platforms in which there is no strong tradition of business participation. However, given the pure business character of the alliance, it is not a multi-stakeholder initiative itself, although other parties are drawn into advisory functions. It is often difficult to determine why some alliances prefer to establish hybrid organizations involving several parties outside the business community or why they favor building on corporate interests alone, but it matters whether the original initiative is taken by businesses or other stakeholders, as this arrangement offers special opportunities to set new agendas. Thus, alliances are enabled to go into policy fields and forge cooperation in areas where they are not highly experienced and, thus, to extend their policy portfolios.

Family Business Network International

This organization is structured according to a special criterion not found in any of the other alliances in this chapter: the character of ownership. The Family Business Network International (FBN-I) has members from business but only from firms that are family owned and, thus, it represents a unique historical tradition in the business community that is still alive today. This principle cuts across all industries, but many other types of ownership are usually present in industry associations, and there are no frameworks for family business in these contexts. Under these conditions, it is relevant to have a forum to discuss the particular challenges of family ownership. Furthermore, family businesses are not restricted to particular countries and business cultures but are a global phenomenon, making it relevant to seek cooperation at the global level. Last, but not least, family-owned businesses are found across a wide range of firm sizes, from very small firms to large MNCs that are affiliated through the national sections of FBN-I.

A range of interests in family-owned firms can be taken care of through other business associations, but the social and legal aspects that are associated with this particular form of ownership need a particular forum. The network, founded in 1989, counts around 30 member organizations from different continents, most of them from Europe, where the organization is represented through national chapters. In addition, family businesses from other countries, and in this context individuals, are organized so that around

60 countries are covered, testifying to the rather broad coverage of the network.[20]

A major challenge for family-owned companies is the transfer to the next generation. To facilitate a smooth transfer, many conditions must be taken into account, and it is the goal of the organization to exchange experiences to help business-owning families, but it has set boundaries for its work. For obvious reasons, the issue of inheritance is crucial and requires political efforts, but as seen by the organization, "these issues are mostly ignored by general business networks."[21] It is clear that some of these challenges are related to governments and national legislation and, hence, cannot easily be managed by international organizations in business, such as the network in question.

However, cooperation between national chapters and firms can be important in helping each other and in achieving better conditions, for instance through regulation. Accordingly, it has a relatively low-key political orientation on the global stage,[22] but there is a huge variation between the various alliances and how they work to promote the interests of their members in markets and in politics, and whether they focus on attending to member concerns or on the broader interests in the business community. This profile is also stressed by the fact that, unlike many traditional business associations, it has no obvious intergovernmental body to relate to in the representation of interests, a factor that is usually important in the development and adaptation of political strategies.

Learning is given high priority. Much emphasis is on bringing members together to share various kinds of best practices. This effort to exchange experiences comes close to what we see in the clubs (discussed in the next chapter), where basic principles of confidentiality are applied. Different activities and events are launched to foster cooperation internally, and externally, the organization gives weight to cooperation with the consultancy business and with relevant parts of academia. With the assistance of donors, it is involved in the funding of certain research activities to examine particular problems of importance to its members with the overarching goal of improving the overall conditions for family business.

The FIDO (Fast IDentity Online) Alliance

The vast increase in communication via the internet, including financial transactions, has created new technologies, and new industries and organizations have emerged. One of the many new entities is the FIDO (Fast

IDentity Online) Alliance, which reflects pioneering developments that have taken place in the United States. The organization soon expanded and became ever more global. As with many other bodies governing different aspects of internet communication, its work is hardly noticed by the general public, but it has important functions that were not already covered by existing business associations.

FIDO was established in 2012 "to address the lack of interoperability among strong authentication technologies, and remedy the problems users face with creating and remembering multiple usernames and passwords."[23] Accordingly, the development of alternatives to replace these traditional forms of authentication and provide new standards for financial institutions and major online services will enhance security.[24] The idea is not to stop with the implementation of one particular authentication standard but engage in the adoption of new technologies, and several firms with this specialization have joined the alliance. Therefore, the alliance is not just a temporary effort to remedy current authentication problems but a more advanced form of cooperation the future format of which is difficult to predict. However, it involves members and participants in a range of different roles as illustrated in the organization's own scheme, Table 3.1.

The standard now defined is open for firms to adopt. These efforts may gradually become effective, especially because the initiative is supported by a range of key players of the internet, such as Google, Microsoft, Lenovo, Samsung, Alibaba Group, PayPal, Mastercard and Bank of America, which drive the implementation of standards.[25] Members go through a certification process enabling them to use the FIDO logo, showing that they comply with the alliance's standards.

Entailed in the setting of standards, however, is also an element of competition. The introduction of advanced standards may eventually exclude firms that cannot meet and comply with the new standards or are late in adopting them. Therefore, the alliance builds on a selective group of committed firms and is not designed to recruit members just to become more representative as this might have other consequences and bring too-diverse interests into the project.

To bring corporations from different industries, or even their associations, together and to involve businesses from different countries in addressing common concerns is a challenge often tackled by alliances. When a task is not within the domain of a particular association and, hence, sufficiently relevant for it to embrace alone, several associations and corporations can be mobilized and broader coordination can be called for. In the case of FIDO,

TABLE 3.1 Members, benefits and tasks in the FIDO Alliance

Membership benefits & dues by level		Board $50,000	Sponsor $25,000	Government** $15,000	Associate^ $2,500–$15,000
Leadership benefits	Eligible to serve as a Working Group Chair	•			
	Eligible to serve as a Working Group Vice Chair, Scribe or Editor	•	•	•	
	May propose the chartering of a new Working Group	•	•	•	
	May vote on the chartering of Working Groups	•			
	Sets the strategic direction of the Alliance	•			
Participation benefits	May participate in any Working Group	•	•	•	
	May vote in any Working Group	•	•		
	May participate & vote in Board meetings	•			
	May attend & participate in any Plenary meetings	•	•	•	
	May attend any one Plenary Meeting per calendar year				
	May participate in FIDO-sponsored events	•	•	•	•
	Eligible to serve as a Liaison Officer	•	•	•	•
	May contribute to specification requirements	•	•	•	
	May contribute to specification development	•	•	•	

Membership benefits & dues by level		Board $50,000	Sponsor $25,000	Government** $15,000	Associate^ $2,500–$15,000
	Eligible to be an Invited Participant in a Working Group by its Chair				●
Commercial benefits	May use the "FIDO Alliance Member" trademark	●	●	●	●
	Eligible to receive FIDO Executive quotes in your press release (subject to approval)	●	●	●	
	Eligible to be featured with a quote in FIDO announcements (subject to approval)	●	●	●	
	Priority eligibility to participate in FIDO Alliance marketing activities	●			
	May benefit from the non-assert IPR policy on Implementation Draft Specification	●	●	●	●
	Shall benefit from the non-assert IPR policy on Proposed Standard Specifications	●	●	●	●
	Shall have logo featured on FIDO Alliance website	●	●	●	
	Shall have logo featured in FIDO Alliance presentation materials and named in press releases	●			

Source: http://fidoalliance.org/participate/.

Notes: ★ Annual dues as of January 2016. Fee structure subject to change without prior written notice at the discretion of the FIDO Alliance. ^ Associate dues are $2,500 for organizations with 100 or fewer employees, and $15,000 for organizations with 101 or more employees. Board membership is open by application to current Sponsor-level members.

different US corporations independently identified a demand for new forms of authentication and began a dialogue to share experiences and define new standards. These corporations were already global players, but globalization was further amplified through the inclusion of many firms with backgrounds in other countries.

The FIDO Alliance is not highly political in the sense that it seeks to leverage key intergovernmental bodies supposed to regulate this cross-sectoral issue. Indeed, much governance of the internet is today provided outside governments and intergovernmental cooperation,[26] and therefore, the work of FIDO is not centered on these agencies but rather has taken on the character of self-regulation. This regulation, however, moves beyond pure industry self-regulation and embraces corporations from different industries, appealing to wider sections of business, and, as such, it can gradually fulfill public functions without involving governments.

International AntiCounterfeiting Coalition

IACC works to change regulations and achieve better protection of products and commercial interests, and it has been active in different national and international contexts since 1979.[27] When referring to the often temporary character of such alliances, this example shows that we should be very cautious about the time perspective of such forms of cooperation, and its relatively long history testifies to its role as a permanent entity in the business community, notably as an association working on a trans-industry basis. Its work is quite formalized, and it shares features with other peak and industry associations. Counterfeiting and piracy are familiar problems in many industries, and while single corporations and associations have tried to find ways to combat the ensuing problems, a general challenge to the protection of trademarks calls for coordination across a variety of industries. Hence, IACC involves corporations from industries including apparel, electronics, entertainment and pharmaceuticals. The alliance also involves a number of law firms and investigative firms that are busy with the challenge of counterfeiting and that contribute additional knowledge to the organization.[28] In fact, some of the actors analyzed as facilitators in a later chapter of this book are among IACC's members. Indeed, it is an interesting feature of some alliances that they seek to involve other parties than just businesses, a task that is harder within less flexible associations, where the ambition is to organize and represent industries in a more traditional sense.

Since industry associations whose members are somewhat affected by counterfeiting cannot handle the problem alone, IACC generates different experiences and formulates horizontal strategies in relation to a very specific issue. Resources are better harnessed at the alliance level, and IACC can bring stronger leverage on regulators. Although public regulation is central to the alliance, the organization is, at the same time, engaged in various programs of a self-regulatory nature to avoid counterfeiting, and it advocates for the combination of multiple public and private initiatives.[29]

However, other associations, namely peak associations, engage in horizontal issues. Interestingly, the "omnipotent" ICC that, in many areas, has strong legal expertise is also concerned with counterfeiting, and the peak association and the alliance, therefore, enter the same domain. The IACC organizes members in the form of corporations, and these have direct access to decision making in the alliance, channels that are not similarly available in the ICC given its other membership structure and the strong role of national chambers of commerce.

Based in Washington, DC, IACC has an American bias. Many of its activities are centered on events in the United States, and many of its members are of American origin. However, the alliance is also engaged in issues outside the United States and is active in various global contexts, which is logical given the transboundary character of counterfeiting. As IACC organizes a number of firms outside the United States that are affected by counterfeiting, it is justifiable to perceive the alliance as a global player. Nevertheless, this problem raises the question as to the territorial basis of the alliances. Obviously, alliances do not organize members from all countries, and members are not active in all countries, but at least IACC seeks to include members active in different contexts and seeks to represent these in interactions with various global institutions.

International Food and Beverage Alliance

IFBA was established in 2008, at a time when there arose an increasing focus on lifestyle diseases from IGOs, such as the UN and the WHO.[30] In this context, the food industry was, and still is, targeted as a serious contributor to the problem, and it was up to the industry to show that it could become part of the solution.

The alliance was initiated by a group of MNCs in the food and beverage industry. Among the founders were, for instance, the Coca-Cola Company, Nestlé and McDonald's. Instead of acting through the various industry associations with which these companies were affiliated, IFBA was established as a new platform. While the pertinent industry associations are themselves not market actors, do not represent any brands and are unknown to the general public, the food industry is often associated with individual producers that need special ways to communicate. However, the leading role of the firms cannot be seen exclusively from the stance of communication strategy. Overall, it can be difficult to find a joint strategy in business associations, and choosing other forms of collective action is a general option that can take issues out of existing associations or provide new avenues of cooperation where associations are not available.[31]

The creation of a new platform had the clear advantage that particularly committed firms could join and more quickly find ways to tackle the issue. Although very different in profile, the large companies are all global and could see the obvious global and trans-industry dimensions of the problem, which smaller firms operating in smaller markets were not geared to address. Furthermore, the corporations either come from different sectors of the food and beverage industry or have interests in several industries, so there is no association in the food and beverage industry that fully represents this group of firms. Indeed, the industry is generally characterized by a relatively high degree of fragmentation in the organization of interests. The niche that has now been taken by IFBA was not taken from a single association but is, rather, a kind of horizontal niche that none of the already existing organizations emphatically claim.

The emergence of IFBA was clearly related to potential public regulation, and the corporations feared that the tables could be turned on them. The large corporations, especially, preferred preemptive action to forestall public regulation, first at the European level and then on a broader international level. The formation of the alliance gave business an opportunity to influence developments but also signaled an intention to play an active role in fostering solutions. However, the efforts of IFBA have not only been directed toward the UN, the WHO and other intergovernmental institutions in an attempt to influence public regulation. To a high degree, important initiatives of self-regulation have been undertaken. The alliance has issued guidelines for the member companies to follow, involved third parties in monitoring compliance and issuing various reports on the performance of firms.[32] The alliance has further adopted a strategy committing its members to abandon the use of trans fats in their products.

These examples display the combination of different initiatives: political influence and self-regulation are not mutually isolated measures but are used with the intention to demonstrate that industry is capable of solving societal problems.[33] It is, at the same time, evident that the introduction of these measures can shield the food and beverage industry, and particularly the reputations of the firms in the alliance, allowing them to achieve a positive profile in the market and in the branding of their products.

Conclusion

Alliances perform some of the same functions as traditional peak and industry associations, but they also tend to embody other forms of cooperation. First, alliances are found both in and across industries, but they involve a selective membership. Second, they present fresh initiatives, but they branch out and typically emerge out of existing forms of cooperation. Third, alliances are often ephemeral, but some institutionalize and evolve into formal associations. Fourth, they usually have few issues on their agenda, and even those with broader commitments are very specialized. Fifth, they have political ambitions, but they often combine political activity with functions in the market and contribute to regulation.

As demonstrated by the cases in this chapter, there is significant variation among alliances, and they are difficult to capture because of their multidimensional properties. In some cases, they come close to traditional peak and industry associations: IACC, for instance, seems to have achieved a permanent status, FIDO has established many formal structures, and GBA has a relatively broad policy portfolio. It is also clear that these indicators, which need to be studied more profoundly, are subject to various dynamics. Mindful of these caveats, there is still reason to see the alliances as something unique, serving key purposes not managed by the traditional peak and industry associations. As such, they operate by a slightly different logic than these associations. These respective logics are both influenced by processes in the membership and the political environment.

With a relatively exclusive membership, we can expect stronger commitment from members of alliances, and most alliances will enjoy the benefits of collective action in small groups and find faster and easier means to agreement. There is a tendency for large firms with significant resources to dominate these processes, and with the absence of many other segments in business, there are interests that will not be considered in strategy formulation.

As far as the environment is concerned, IGOs and other institutions cannot expect alliances to manage the same kind of diversity as industry and peak associations do, and therefore, the pressures on alliances assume a different character. Under these circumstances, alliances are supposed to coordinate those interests involved in the alliance only, but still, alliances can represent very important interests, harness significant resources and offer alternative regulation that can contribute to public policy.

Alliances can be suitable complements to traditional associations at the industry and peak levels and take up questions not already covered or, at least, not sufficiently represented. However, competition is an inescapable factor when alliances enter the domains of established associations or seek to occupy niches that associations have in mind. In some cases, the risks of overlap can be reduced if existing associations become involved in the formative processes and an understanding is reached, but alliances also have their own dynamics. They can dissolve but can also become permanent entities that add to the associational system. In sum, alliances demonstrate that business finds many ways of creating new actors where existing bodies prove ineffective for its purposes, and both industry and peak associations must, for shorter or longer periods of time, learn to live with such organizations.

Notes

1 There are several motives to coordinate interests and form temporary or permanent alliances. Apart from classifying alliances, a major job remains in analyzing this form of cooperation. Recent advances have been made in understanding interagency coordination in international relations: Rafael Biermann and Joachim A. Koops, eds, *The Palgrave Handbook of Inter-Organizational Relations in World Politics* (London: Palgrave, 2017); however, business coordination beyond the market, manifested through alliances, is unaccounted for in research.
2 Alliances come in different hybrids. Some involve civil-society participation. Business can play a lead role in such arrangements, for instance demonstrated in SAC. However, it can be difficult to determine whether business is the key force, and hence qualifies as a business alliance, or whether it is rather a multistakeholder arrangement. These latter alliances are not dealt with in this chapter. Today, alliances may involve business as well as government. The Global Alliance for Trade Facilitation (GATF), presented as a public-private partnership, involves the peak associations WEF and ICC, together with the governments of Australia, Canada, the United Kingdom and the United States, http://tradefacilitation.org (accessed 7 June 2017).
3 There are also alliances that build on membership of individuals in their role as professionals and not as representatives of firms but the boundary is permeable. This is for instance the case in the Global Accounting Alliance (GAA).

112 Alliances of corporations and associations

4 Some of these forms enjoy strong legal backing whereas others are illegal, such as cartels, and can be punished and dissolved by law.
5 Institutional history can explain institutional change, and inspiration can he found here: James Maloney and Kathleen Thelen, eds, *Advances in Comparative-Historical Analysis* (Cambridge: Cambridge University Press, 2015). However, this tradition is not suited to expounding the emergence of new actors and evolution theory needs to be consulted.
6 Glenn R. Carroll and Michael T. Hannan, *The Demography of Corporations and Industries* (Princeton, NJ: Princeton University Press, 2000). Contributions on firms and industries can be usefully extended to embrace associations. For the complex concept of niches, see e.g. Jennifer A. Miller and Paul Holloway, "Niche Theory and Models," *The International Encyclopedia of Geography* 1–10 (2017).
7 In an evolutionary perspective new species, and in our case actors, will in principle have a background in existing entities: Ernst Mayr, "Speciational Evolution or Punctuated Equilibria," *Journal of Social and Biological Structures* 12 (1988): 137–158.
8 The multiple options of business action are discussed in Claus Offe and Helmut Wiesenthal, "Two Logics of Collective Action: Theoretical Notes on Social Class and Organizational Form," *Political Power and Social Theory* 1 (1980): 67–115. Further theory development is required to study multiple memberships in global associations.
9 Members can play different roles in interest groups, e.g.: Gordon C. Rausser, Johan Swinnen and Pinhas Zusman, *Political Power and Economic Policy: Theory, Analysis, and Empirical Applications* (Cambridge: Cambridge University Press, 2011), 125–146.
10 Martyna Janowicz-Panjaitan, René M. Bakker and Patrick Kenis, "Research on Temporary Organizations: The State of the Art and Distinct Approaches to Temporariness," in Patrick Kenis, Martyna Janowicz-Panjaitan and Bart Cambre, eds, *Temporary Organizations: Prevalence, Logic and Effectiveness* (Cheltenham: Edward Elgar, 2009), 56–85.
11 These organizational phenomena were systematically analyzed in Albert O. Hirschman, *Exit, Voice and Loyalty: Responses to Decline in Firms, Organizations and States* (Cambridge: Harvard University Press, 1970).
12 There is a considerable literature on "coalition building," part of it stemming from organization theory and inter-organizational relations. With the interest-group literature new entities were recognized: Marie Hojnacki, "Interest Groups' Decisions to Join Alliances or Work Alone," *American Journal of Political Science* 41, no. 1 (1997): 61–87. These perspectives are helpful to analyze the alliances studied in this chapter but we have to bear in mind that, e.g.: 1 members of alliances do not merely collaborate but create new organizations; 2 alliances become relatively stable entities and add new actors to the business community through evolution; 3 alliances bring not only interest groups but also single firms together in flexible frameworks; and 4 alliances fulfill important roles not only in politics but also in markets by adopting and policing rules.
13 Tony Porter and Karsten Ronit, "Implementation in International Business Self-regulation: The Importance of Sequences and their Linkages," *Journal of Law and Society* 42, no. 3 (2015): 413–433; Fabrizio Cafaggi, ed., *Enforcement of*

Transnational Regulation: Ensuring Compliance in a Global World (Cheltenham: Edward Elgar, 2012).

14 Approaches in economics and management study "strategic alliances" and "alliance capitalism" but mainly take an interest in behavior in the market. Michael E. Porter, ed., *Competition in Global Industries* (Boston: Harvard Business School Press, 1986); John H. Dunning, *Alliance Capitalism and Global Business* (London: Routledge, 1997); Stefanie Dorn, Bastian Schweiger and Sascha Albers, "Levels, Phases and Themes of Coopetition: A Systematic Literature Review and Research Agenda," *European Management Journal* 34, no. 5 (2016): 484–500.

15 GBA, "About GBA," www.gbafor2030.org/about.html (accessed 29 October 2016). There are other initiatives that could possibly be studied as alliances, for instance the private sector has an input to the sustainable development process through the Business and Industry Major Group, but this is rather a series of meetings than an organization. UN Department of Economic and Social Affairs, "Business and Industry," see: https://sustainabledevelopment.un.org/majorgroups/businessandindustry (accessed 8 November 2017).

16 GBA, "Participating Organizations," www.gbafor2030.org/organizations.html (accessed 13 April 2017).

17 GBC-Education, "Member Companies," http://gbc-education.org/our-members/companies/ (accessed 12 October 2017).

18 GBC-Education, "Mission," http://gbc-education.org/mission/ (accessed 12 October 2017).

19 GBC-Education, "Initiatives," http://gbc-education.org/initiatives/ (accessed 12 December 2017).

20 FBN-I, "Our Members," www.fbn-i.org/our-members/ (accessed 2 July 2017).

21 FBN-I, "Who We Are," www.fbn-i.org/who-are-we/ (accessed 2 July 2017).

22 It has, however, a rather vague pledge: FBN-I, *A Sustainable Future*, www.fbn-i.org/wp-content/uploads/2015/09/FBNSustainableFuture.pdf (accessed 2 July 2017).

23 FIDO Alliance, "IdentityX Joins FIDO Alliance Board," 6 March 2014, https://fidoalliance.org/identityx-joins-fido-alliance-board/ (accessed 13 March 2017). The organization distinguishes between when it was founded (2012) and publicly launched (2013). FIDO Alliance, "History of FIDO," https://fidoalliance.org/about/history/ (accessed 19 March 2017).

24 Some experiences from standard setting in the financial industries can be used to study online regulation, for instance: Sebastian Botzem, "Transnational Standard Setting in Accounting: Organizing Expertise-based Self-regulation in Times of Crises," *Accounting, Auditing & Accountability Journal* 27, no. 6 (2014): 933–955.

25 For the diversity of members, see: https://fidoalliance.org/participate/members/ (accessed 23 March 2017). Another initiative for payment cards is the Payment Card Industry Security Standards Council (PCI SCC) which builds on card vendors in the council plus other "participating organizations," see: www.pcisecuritystandards.org (accessed 8 November 2017).

26 Milton L. Mueller, *Networks and States: The Global Politics of Internet Governance* (Cambridge: The MIT Press, 2010); Laura DeNardis, *The Global War for Internet Governance* (New Haven: Yale University Press, 2014).

27 IACC, "History & Mission," www.iacc.org/about/history-mission (accessed 10 December 2017).

28 IACC, "Membership," www.iacc.org/membership/members (accessed 2 September 2017). Interestingly, there are also many facilitators involved in the coalition. The different facilitators will be analyzed in a separate chapter.
29 IACC, "Online Initiatives," www.iacc.org/online-initiatives/about (accessed 9 November 2017).
30 World Health Organization, *Global Strategy on Diet, Physical Activity and Health* (Geneva: WHO, 2004).
31 In lieu of a single encompassing body representing the global food industry there is also room for special transboundary initiatives. Other examples are, for instance, the International Agri-Food Network (IAFN) that is involved in poverty and food security issues, and the sustainability-oriented Global Agri-business Alliance (GAA) launched in 2016 and currently serviced by the WBCSD secretariat. GAA, "New agri-business alliance sets its sights on 2030 UN SDG targets to tackle global food security," see: http://globalagribusinessalliance.com/launch-press-release/ (accessed 31 October 2017).
32 See, for instance: Accenture, *2015 Compliance Monitoring Report for the International Food & Beverage Alliance on Global Advertising in Television, Print and Internet* (April 2016).
33 Studies on NGOs and IGOs usually limit the scope of analysis to participation and influence, e.g. Jonas Tallberg, Lisa M. Dellmuth, Hans Agné and Andreas Duit, "NGO Influence in International Organizations: Information, Access and Exchange," *British Journal of Political Science* 48, no. 1 (2018): 213–238; however, many business associations have other political tasks and are heavily involved in the governing of industries.

4

CLUBS AND THINK TANKS

- Overview: clubs in business
- Rotary International
- The Bilderberg Meetings
- The Trilateral Commission
- Caux Round Table
- Coalition for Inclusive Capitalism
- Overview: business-based and -oriented think tanks
- Carnegie Endowment for International Peace
- Brookings Institution
- Ford Foundation
- Open Society Foundations
- Bill & Melinda Gates Foundation
- Conclusion

There are many actors in the global business community that, in one way or another, purport to represent interests and set different agendas. In this chapter, we turn to two different but somewhat related types of actors in the form of clubs and think tanks that are built on other principles and have other purposes than classical business associations, be they at the peak, industry or alliance levels. These bodies do not necessarily have strong and irrevocable claims to speak for business in general or for specific sections of business, but some of them, at least, have certain association-like features.

To the degree that clubs and think tanks develop similar functions as traditional associations, they may come into competition with them without necessarily realizing or intending this. Their activities may further spill over into some of the service providers, which will be studied in the next chapter, because they offer various research-based activities, make certain forms of knowledge available to business and society, and foster social cohesion in the business community. Clubs and think tanks are, as a group, exceedingly varied, and it is difficult to pin them down in an overall scheme. They are found under a diversity of names, emphasizing their different backgrounds and commitments. This suggests that more conceptual and theoretical work has to be put into the analysis to understand their work and their complex role in the business community. Clubs and think tanks have received attention in separate literatures but have not been brought together and examined in relation to business associations.

Clubs and think tanks have in common that they attempt to set important global agendas from a general pro-business perspective,[1] and they accumulate, disseminate and utilize experiences and knowledge from both academia and practitioners. Yet, they are also remarkably different as, for instance, clubs are based on different forms of membership, a trait generally alien to think tanks, which have donors and other kinds of support structures. Some clubs use more informal channels or even secret means to influence politics while think tanks are, in principle, committed to more transparent forms of behavior. Although we find many commonalities and differences between these two major groups of actors, there are also important individual features of different clubs and think tanks showing the rich variation within these entities. Depending on the different individual profiles of clubs and think tanks, causes that always need to be observed, they are brought closer to or further from typical associations and alliances and assist or hamper their work, leading to mutual adaptations.

First, we offer a general overview of the two groups and add to the characterizations offered in the Introduction to this book. We show that clubs and think tanks engage in activities that are also found in a number of global associations or even among other organizations in business. Second, we move on to analyze specific clubs and think tanks. These are examples that display interesting variations across the two populations of actors. The selection of both clubs and think tanks is determined by the condition that they are founded by business-related people and organizations, are concerned with economic and political issues of importance to business, and undertake activities that are global in character.

Clubs such as the Bilderberg Meetings and the Trilateral Commission have been seen as iconic organizations of capitalism. They have a strong commitment to the market economy and to business, but their role must be studied in a broader institutional context, and their potential and limitations must be properly evaluated to arrive at clear understanding of their role as clubs. We also focus on some selected think tanks, such as the Carnegie Endowment for International Peace and the Open Society Foundation, both independent actors that emerged from business and work to advance certain business agendas, though typically, think tanks span much broader political issues of relevance to society.

Overview: clubs in business

The global clubs bring small and highly selected groups of business people together in their personal capacities. They apply a different category of membership than associations that are founded on firms as their basic units, sometimes represented directly, sometimes through associations. In that sense, clubs do not compete with associations for the same members. To become a member of a club, however, persons need to be rooted in business, either in their previous or current position, and thus, members are supposed to bring various types of business experience into clubs without necessarily representing firms in a strict sense.

Personal membership is meant to facilitate an open dialogue devoid of power relations. The social function is presented as a hallmark of clubs, where the building and maintaining of networks to exchange experiences between former and current leaders in an informal and confidential setting is central.[2] Therefore, clubs enjoy the advantage of small-scale collective action that will attract members. From the perspective of participants, a key motive for membership is the social benefits of meeting like-minded and knowledgeable people in a dialogue, taking part in events and deliberations, and having access to goods that non-members are denied.[3] It is an interesting feature of clubs that they are often initiated by wealthy and particularly networked people who have various material, intellectual and social resources with which to start brand-new organizations. Because the foundation and management of clubs to a large extent depends on the role of such individual entrepreneurs,[4] clubs are neither the planned offspring of established associations, nor are they a step toward new associations, although such developments are, in principle, imaginable.

Relatedly, clubs are maintained in a top-down process wherein different constellations of business people are co-opted into the organization. Because membership tends to be on an invite-only basis, existing members and clubs' management have important roles in identifying and recruiting new members. Recruitment is a complex process, however, because it is more difficult to find suitable individuals than, for instance, to identify prolific and leading firms.

This situation is unlike that of associations in the global business community, where membership is voluntary, emphasizing bottom-up principles in organizations. In these contexts, members can usually join if they fulfill certain criteria, such as representing relevant industrial activity, and it is often fairly straightforward who is eligible for membership. In associations, this does not rule out some scrutiny of applications, especially if the admission of a new member can damage the reputation of an association, but joining clubs is, in general, a different affair.

Clubs move beyond the social function and seek to influence the conditions set for business through the formulation of global strategies,[5] but it is important to note that participation in clubs is of a non-committal nature. Clubs are not mandated to represent specific interests, and decisions do not bind members. In principle, it is not a goal to speak for business in any formal way—in fact, other bodies, most typically associations, are instituted to represent interests; but despite this, the pro-business orientation of clubs indicates that they share some aims with associations. Moreover, clubs have certain functions that are connected with those of think tanks. Although some forms of knowledge building and investigations do not belong among the core functions of clubs, they also engage in research activities and communicate results to inform the public debate, and, hence, some activities overlap with those of typical think tanks.

The strategies adopted by clubs do not address the role of the private sector alone but can embrace a multitude of current economic, social and political issues. It is of great importance that many members have their background in business, and we restrict this study to the private sector, but a fair share of members may have other types of experience. Members are also drawn from other strata of global society, including government, media and academia, suggesting that some clubs have a hybrid character and multiple commitments.[6] This is yet another factor that reduces the potential of clubs to focus indiscriminately on business interests.

Rotary International

Rotary is the oldest of the clubs examined in this chapter. It started out as an American initiative in 1905 but soon globalized, long before more recent waves of globalization.[7] Today, it is at the same time very much centered on local activities and fixed on global commitments. It derives its highly decentralized structure from the thousands upon thousands of clubs across the countries and regions embraced by the organization, and it links and coordinates this local work through global strategies that facilitate a uniform approach. All dimensions of this work are highly formalized and overseen by a large secretariat in the United States that coordinates all international activities.

As in most other business clubs, the basic membership category is the individual person, not firms. Members generally have a background in the business community, broadly speaking, and are not linked to any particular industry. According to the constitution and bylaws of Rotary International, membership is derived from businesses, professions and communities, and it is even a goal to prompt "high ethical standards in business and professions,"[8] a self-regulatory tool to advance norms among members. Hence, joining is supposed to bring members a range of personal benefits through exchanges with like-minded people, especially business people, in the local community. Interestingly, the club is a large and global entity, but it is broken down into small entities that have a social value for participants.[9]

An important goal is to service business but also society in broader terms, and not just local societies where the clubs are located but also international society. Almost 100 years before corporate social responsibility became a fashion, efforts to define responsibility were central at Rotary clubs, not at the level of single firms but at the level of the business community. The organization is consequently involved in a number of projects to help solve economic and social problems, especially in third world countries, and it is very keen to cultivate a humanitarian profile, being engaged in policy areas such as climate change, the environment, education and health, and even hails peace as an overarching goal.

It is clear that these issues are, in one way or another, also addressed by many business associations. However, Rotary cannot speak for business as such and tends to be less occupied with influencing public policy and more focused on the practical implementation of already adopted policies with which it sympathizes. Advocating social values in a non-controversial fashion, rather than emphasizing commercial goals, Rotary is in a position to formulate softer goals than business associations usually do.

The political engagement is not new. The organization was active in promoting the idea of the UN and has since had a close relationship with it, and today, it enjoys consultative status with the UN's Economic and Social Council and has further relations with special agencies, such as UNESCO, UNICEF and the WHO.[10] It even organizes a joint UN-Rotary Day, showing its political and practical commitment to the UN.

Without having its own think tank, the organization is linked to various research activities and has set up a number of Rotary Peace Centers at universities in different countries. Work at these universities may, together with input from other research institutions, inform the strategies of Rotary and show that there is an interest in developing this arm of the organization. Such activities may be further augmented and institutionalized in future.

Rotary is very different from the other clubs examined in this chapter. It has a weaker political orientation or, rather, its activities seem less partisan and less geared toward influencing public policy. While avoiding a strict focus on the importance of free-market principles common to most of the other clubs analyzed in this study, it tends to emphasize a range of other issues that the other clubs discussed here tend to avoid.

The Bilderberg Meetings

Established in 1954 in the Netherlands, the Bilderberg Meetings, frequently referred to as the Bilderberg Club or Bilderberg Group, is the oldest of the organizations with more distinct political ambitions treated in this chapter.[11] It is a private organization with a considerable business flavor, and with strong participation from MNCs, its agenda is unmistakably pro-business. However, it also has a strong political component through the involvement of former and current politicians, often of the statesman or -woman type, from Europe and North America in particular, stressing its Atlantic tradition. Participation from beyond these two regions is minimal, involving only occasional attendance from a few other countries, so in many ways, the club has interesting similarity with, for instance, the Transatlantic Business Coalition (TBC), which is a transcontinental peak organization covering business in the United States and in Europe but without global aspirations to expand.[12] Furthermore, the Bilderberg Club is not tied to the negotiations between the United States and the EU, and does not deliver an input into these processes.

It is noteworthy that the club does not have members in a traditional sense. However, we may consider the invited participants of annual

FIGURE 4.1 Hotel de Bilderberg—the first meeting place of the club
Source: www.bilderberg.nl/oosterbeek/hotel-de-bilderberg/.

meetings as proxy members that come together for shorter or longer periods of time to deliberate current societal problems essential to the governance of business and society. Therefore, the shifting agendas are concerned with economic, social and political stability essential to the business community, but business leaders are also challenged to discuss issues that are sometimes only narrowly related to business and not addressed by, for instance, associations. However, certain topics may, in the long run, become of crucial importance to business, and there are a good deal of foreign-policy issues tabled for dialogue. Adhering to the Chatham House Rules, deliberations at meetings are confidential and are not reported outside the club context, a factor stressing the primacy of the social dimension of exchanges where selected individuals act in their personal capacity. This norm is important in preserving a confidential atmosphere, and it is no doubt one of the reasons why the club has often been seen as a secretive and even conspiratorial body of world capitalism.

Its major activity is the annual meeting, held in different locations in Europe and North America. Much time is spent preparing these meetings, finding topical themes and selecting participants, tasks managed by the secretariat. No real activity is organized between these meetings. Actually, the club takes pride in not publicly disseminating ideas from its meetings, limiting activity to a minimal press release stating the major themes to be discussed at the meetings. Although a number of ideas can be generated and eventually be filtered into business, this process is unclear, and it is not a stated goal.

Obviously, the club is quite different from the other clubs that have emerged over the last decades to deliberate more or less the same problems from the perspective of global business, and its style is more reticent. In that sense, the Bilderberg Meetings strongly reflect the time of their inauguration, the 1950s, when there were fewer institutions to coordinate international cooperation in business and politics, and when there were other expectations as to what such actors should do to further their agendas and achieve greater impact. New styles of club engagement have emerged to adapt to a changing institutional framework in business and in politics, and a more proactive communication approach has developed to match other actors in society.

The Trilateral Commission

A club reflecting some of the same concerns as the Bilderberg Meetings is the Trilateral Commission, which was established in 1973 in the United States in a process where David Rockefeller was a leading figure.[13] Again, we are on the edges of the business community. The strategic orientation of the commission is unequivocally pro-business, but the ultimate goal is not only to bring leading business figures together in the joint deliberation of important issues but to gather key decision makers from across the public and private sectors.

Originally, the focus was on the United States, Europe, and Japan, at a time when Japan became recognized as a key industrial power, but membership has expanded considerably, and there is today an explicit strategy to involve members from different continents. In fact, there is a rule regarding the balanced distribution of membership, and it gives weight to different regions. Today, it embraces the European Group, the North American Group, and the Asia Pacific Group, each hosting a secretariat.[14] Africa and South America are not represented in the commission, and there does not seem to be an ambition to expand participation to these regions. It has not adapted fully to recent trends toward globalization, and emphasis on the old post-war axis between the United States, Europe and Japan is maintained.

The organization is exceedingly event driven, with an annual meeting and regional meetings at the centers of activities. Membership is by invitation only, and this emphasizes the elite nature of the organization. Because the group is relatively small and has strict selection criteria, members can also benefit from the social character of the meetings, which is typical of clubs. In a strict sense, members are not expected to represent particular interests and are not given any mandate to do so, so personal qualities are important. The profiles of business-related members also suggest that there is no ambition to gather people who represent important subsets of the business community, such as associations.

However, the working style of the commission is very different from the Bilderberg Club, as the commission puts a huge emphasis on the dissemination of its work, and it has a clear ambition to gain influence through its meetings, research activities and general communications. Although meetings are confidential, the commission has gradually developed a public face, but it was not fully designed from the beginning. However, like the Bilderberg Club, the Trilateral Commission has been perceived as an elite network and a challenge to democracy,[15] and they are lumped together as sinister forces of capitalism, but its real power is difficult to assess and tends to be exaggerated. It is important to note that the organization is, after all, a fairly heterogeneous entity, and business coordination is just one of its several tasks.

An important feature of its profile is its research engagement. It is not only a club but also has functions typical of think tanks. Right from the beginning, it was intended to perform analyses that could inform leaders in the public and the private sector on topical issues and facilitate change. These think tank activities do not suggest that publications are the result of negotiations between members but must rather be understood as the output of an independent research arm of the organization. They indicate that this work is similar to research done in organizations that consider themselves full-blooded think tanks, and this illustrates the hybrid character of the Trilateral Commission.

Caux Round Table

As with a number of other round tables, the Caux Round Table (CRT) was initiated by business in cooperation with politicians. The Dutch company Philips and the Japanese corporation Canon were the major entrepreneurs in setting up the round table, but the involvement of former French President Olivier Giscard d'Estaing added political support. Today, it is entirely driven by business and has chapters and members in 13 countries and secretariats in both Caux (Switzerland), where it was founded, and in Saint Paul, Minnesota (United States).[16] It involves business leaders from the Western world, but Russia and China are also included, and it has even engaged in defining how its principles are compatible with the Quran, though it has been unable to form chapters in Arab countries. It is backed by various business-friendly organizations, for instance in research, and enjoys other forms of support from like-minded institutions in the private and public sectors, such as the UN Global Compact. However, its own knowledge base and related dissemination of ideas are relatively thin and do not qualify as think tank activity.

According to its statutes, its goal is to gather a network of "business leaders" for the formulation and implementation of a "moral capitalism."[17] Typical of business round tables, a major event is the annual meeting where leaders have opportunities to exchange experiences and address joint concerns. This social aspect is very important in the management of the organization, but it is not limited to being a forum for the select few as some clubs are, and it is also active between the meetings.

Since it was founded in 1986, many voices in global business have advocated for greater social responsibility, and the CRT is not alone in promoting this agenda. Many corporations have adopted programs to signal corporate responsibility in different economic, social and environmental fields, and many business associations have defined schemes for smaller or larger sections of the business community. Amid this abundance of statements and programs, the CRT has adopted its own tools to advance "moral capitalism." Unavoidably, it comes into direct or indirect competition with many other actors in global business as this niche is densely populated and not as vacant as it was decades ago. This does not suggest that the CRT has become obsolete, as it caters to its own community, but it indicates that positions are often challenged and difficult to maintain without adapting to new circumstances.

Originally focused on avoiding trade wars, especially between Europe and Japan, it has expanded to address many other matters and, for instance, also embraces development, poverty and investment issues. A major policy document is the CRT Principles for Business from the middle of the 1990s, but this has been followed by a number of statements, best-practice standards and even Principles for Government,[18] and with these activities, it comes invariably into competition with many other actors in business who seek to formulate rules and norms for responsible business conduct. It has spread its activities to include training and education in business, and in such areas, it links up with other institutions in and beyond the business community. However, its service program is modest compared to those of the facilitators studied in the next chapter.

Coalition for Inclusive Capitalism

In many ways, the Coalition for Inclusive Capitalism bears some resemblance to the CRT, although founded in a different institutional context many years later, in 2014 with E.L. Rothschild as a major force.[19] Its flagship is also its annual conference where luminaries are invited to attract broader attention, address key themes in global business and bring their own experiences into the conference. Likewise, a major purpose of the conference is to bring important CEOs together to deliberate which efforts are needed to change existing practices of business and relate better to societal concerns. Hence, its remit is not just the exchange of experiences between participants in a closed forum; the spread of key messages is central.

It was founded in the wake of the financial crisis, which challenged capitalism at a profound systemic level and required convincing initiatives in the business community to improve trust. The Coalition was a reaction to serious problems that were widely considered in global business community but, to some extent, also required actions and solutions, or at least deliberations, involving institutional investors and asset managers as well as interested parties beyond business. The Coalition seems particularly intent on encouraging the changing of investment strategies and bringing these in line with the expectations of society, thereby alluding to problems leading to the financial crisis. Advocating for an inclusive capitalism is, of course, a rather broad task and, in principle, it encompasses a range of complex issues, but it is essentially a revisionist strategy that challenges purely self-interested behavior, and the Coalition calls for some kind of enlightened corporate conduct.[20]

It is a strength of the business clubs, however, that they do not have to put their strategies into action in the same way that peak and industry associations and alliances are compelled to. Associations have to agree on strategies in a formal way, and they usually hammer out their policies at a concrete level with potential consequences for their members, but clubs are in a different situation. The agenda and working style of the Coalition are rather akin to the work done by the World Economic Forum, but, in comparison, the Coalition is a very small initiative.

Nonetheless, it is interesting to note that the organization at least harbors an ambition to move beyond general ideas and launch concrete activities to educate business leaders and stimulate government action. Indeed, the Coalition has an active life between the conferences and runs a small secretariat in London to develop advisory functions and facilitate learning processes; it refers to itself as a "movement,"[21] but this seems wildly exaggerated given its scope of activities and impact.

Overview: business-based and -oriented think tanks

There is a large population of think tanks, and a subset of them form part of the wider business community. Typically, these entities are founded by highly successful businessmen, a practice also found among several clubs. They engage in philanthropy and use resources for driving think tank activity of various sorts, and they engage in policy fields of importance to business and society and, thus, reach competence in issues potentially tackled by some of the business associations or other actors in business. Obviously, they rely on different sources of funding, especially from private foundations that fund selective activities and specific projects or support a given think tank in more general terms.

Therefore, it can be difficult to distinguish between foundations as important donors and as important research institutions, and determine precisely what separates some foundations from dedicated think tanks. Legal criteria, as they are applied in different countries, may not prove helpful in understanding their global work and, especially in this context, examining how they are related to associations. Examples covered in this chapter, therefore, embrace the whole spectrum of think tanks and their business-related activities.

Business-oriented think tanks can today be found in many countries and have several purposes reflecting different traditions.[22] The profile of think tanks varies enormously, but the majority of think tanks tends to have a domestic departure without being located in, drawing resources from and being managed by people from a multiplicity of countries around the globe. When they have a mainly domestic base, they come into less competition with other organizations in business that already have or aspire to reach real global coverage.[23] However, some actors globalize in the sense that they increasingly address global issues, seek to reach global audiences and aim to set global agendas. This evolution gives them ample opportunities to take up a number of tasks similar to those found among other organizations in global business. In addition, a number of think tanks globalize even further by moving activities to other countries and by establishing offices in new locations, a development that has accelerated in recent decades.[24]

TABLE 4.1 Location of think tank offices and entities

	North America	Latin America	Europe	Africa	Asia-Pacific
Carnegie Endowment for International Peace	Washington, DC		Brussels		Beijing, Beirut, Moscow, New Delhi
Brookings Institution	Washington, DC				Beijing, Doha, New Delhi
Ford Foundation	New York	Bogotá, Rio de Janeiro, Mexico City		Nairobi, Cairo, Johannesburg, Lagos, New Delhi, Jakarta	Beijing
Open Society Foundations	New York, Washington, DC, Baltimore	Rio de Janeiro, Bogotá, Port-au-Prince	Brussels, Budapest, London, Tirana, Sarajevo, Pristina, Skopje, Belgrade, Barcelona, Chisinau, Kiev	Luanda, Kinshasa, Conakry, Nairobi, Monrovia, Abuja, Dakar, Freetown, Cape Town, Johannesburg, Juba, Dar es Salaam, Kampala, Jakarta, Tunis	Ulan Bator, Yangon, Yerevan, Tbilisi, Kabul, Almaty, Amman, Islamabad, Dushanbe, Istanbul, Bishkek
Bill & Melinda Gates Foundation	Seattle, Washington, DC		London	Addis Ababa, Johannesburg, Abuja	Beijing, New Delhi

Source: Carnegie Endowment for International Peace, http://carnegieendowment.org/#beyond-sunni-and-shia-the-roots-of-sectarianism-in-a-changing-middle-east; Brookings Institution, "Brookings, Research Programs, Centers, and Projects," www.brookings.edu/programs/; Ford Foundation, www.fordfoundation.org/people/erika-wood/; Open Society Foundations, www.opensocietyfoundations.org/about/offices-foundations; Bill & Melinda Gates Foundation, www.gatesfoundation.org/Who-We-Are/General-Information/Contact-Us.

All these different versions of research-based and research-promoting organizations do not need to bring different actors together to mediate interests, as with associations, or deliberate issues of common concern, as with clubs, and, hence, they do not act for business in any conspicuous way. As firms, think tanks are not built on collective action, and they do not globalize through extending their membership base but by means of market operations, network building and strategic cooperation. In terms of their organizational logics, they share a number of the same features as facilitators (which we will study in the next chapter) because they are organized as firms and not as collective bodies.

To varying degrees, think tanks claim an independent status and offer research-based analyses more or less in the same way as traditional research institutions, although driven by particular interests and generally with a strong focus on political impact. Indeed, they may forge various links with firms, associations and other actors in business, but occasionally also in civil society, and their general activity or specific projects may rely on private funding from business, especially when contracted to undertake specific studies. However, think tanks have traditional profiles and obligations that they still need to observe to maintain their reputation as independent institutions.

The basic role of think tanks, in so far as they are related to global business, is to help create a business-friendly climate in global politics and stress the positive role of free markets. This is a job that many different organizations, associations and other actors have in common. As discussed in an earlier chapter, an organization like WEF shares a number of features with designated think tanks.

Some think tanks relate this broader principle to specific issues on economic, competition and trade policy. However, business perspectives are also offered on other topical issues, such as the environment, climate change and human rights, where there is not necessarily a uniform and coordinated interest in business. Interestingly, think tanks may serve the purpose of enlightening the business community and raising questions that confront business or particular industries without necessarily offering an answer, and they are in a position to recognize and scrutinize problems that associations cannot examine with the same profoundness. Sometimes, associations avoid addressing certain sensitive issues because an engagement may risk splitting constituencies or does not serve any immediate purpose, and here, think tanks may come in handy as they can take up problems that are of broader concern in society and that have a much longer time horizon.

Carnegie Endowment for International Peace

Founded by the steel magnate Andrew Carnegie in 1910, this organization is one of the oldest in the landscape of American think tanks.[25] While its origin in business is indisputable and shows how wealth amassed in the market may be employed to position firms in new ways and influence society through research programs, the current profile of Carnegie is not strictly focused on business. Far from it.

A major goal is to promote the value of peace, as indicated in the name. This is of crucial importance to business; without peaceful relations among nations, it is difficult for business to prosper, at least in most industries, a fact that is easily forgotten in times of prosperity. A major effort is made in the field of foreign policy, an area covered by many other think tanks, and many general international issues in democracy and development are addressed.[26] It would be quite unusual for a business association, even the peak associations occupied with a number of broader agendas, to engage in such problems, although business depends on peace and development. A range of problems are approached in ways that are important in foreign policy and international relations and, thus, inform government strategy and decision making, and such analyses and recommendations are not so easily picked up by corporations and other business actors. However, this research and the debates surrounding it may be useful for corporations in making choices in relation to the global economy and also in specific regional contexts, such as Russia, the Middle East, or India.

However, the organization is also active in political and economic issues that seem to have a more direct impact on business. Again, many issues are approached in general ways, such as economic stability and free trade, based on a conviction that pro-market policies can ultimately improve business conditions. Also, policies of relevance to specific sections of business, such as climate and energy policy, are included, but here and in other areas, research is done in ways that are not purely business driven and cannot provide business-particular tools in policy development. There is clearly a distance between what associations need in an operational context and what Carnegie can offer as a think tank.

Carnegie started out as an entirely American think tank, but its profile has changed considerably. Over the last decades, it has become a global actor with stronger competence in different areas of global politics. This expansion is further manifested through the opening of new offices outside the United States (Beijing, Beirut, Brussels, Moscow and New Delhi), and this may help Carnegie in further developing its global profile and moving beyond American biases.[27] In this way, Carnegie is a good example of the encompassing process of globalization inherent in the business community.

Brookings Institution

Founded in 1916, the Brookings Institution dates back more than 100 years. A prominent businessman of his time, Robert S. Brookings, embarked on a philanthropic strategy and was instrumental in setting up the Brookings Institution in the United States.[28] With a historical background in the business community, the overall goals of the organization are largely similar to those of Carnegie, and today, business-related think tanks are geared toward solving a range of problems in society. However, the concrete emphasis of its work is phrased in somewhat different terms than Carnegie's. Global economic and political problems are central to its programs, but these tend to be less clad in the language of international peace and are addressed, instead, from the perspective of cooperation and governance.

General perspectives on economy and politics, rather than views on particular industries, are focused upon, and Brookings has an ambition to formulate "ideas to achieve broad-based economic growth, a strong labor market, sound fiscal and monetary policy, and economic opportunity and social mobility. The research aims to increase understanding of how the economy works and what can be done to make it work better."[29] Such general objectives, which always need further specialization, are shared by many forces in society, including the business community, and they are, to a large extent, also advanced by global business associations.

However, it is the distinct mission of think tanks like Brookings to document conditions and substantiate policies through research, a task not taken up by the associations, although they engage in many of the same issues. This type of work intersects with many other actors, such as universities and IGOs, that have commitments in broad areas of the economy, and Brookings, therefore, belongs to a much larger chorus of voices in the global arena.

Like a number of other think tanks, the Brookings Institution has outgrown its original American context. In recent decades, it has established offices in other parts of the world, namely in Qatar, India and China. These initiatives do not seem to be an attempt to better serve the business community[30] but must, rather, be interpreted as a response to the general globalization of politics and to the initiatives of other comparable think tanks that expand the scope of their work. This has enhanced the regional competence of Brookings and given it a further global outlook, although the majority of its activities are still centered on the United States. As with many other think tanks, it is less visible in global contexts, but recognition may, to some degree, spill over to the international realm. However, it is not an immediate challenge or partner for global business.

Ford Foundation

Established in 1936, the Ford Foundation is a bit more recent but still belongs to the older generation of think tanks. The picture here is rather similar to previous and later formations of think tanks: money to run the Foundation came from an extremely profitable sector, the car industry—or to be more precise, the Ford Motor Company—and its owner, Henry Ford, was the key figure in creating the Ford Foundation, turning himself into a philanthropist.[31] As in many other cases, the original ties between the corporation and the foundation gradually loosened and have now disappeared, furnishing the Foundation with a more independent status. This gives the organization a more autonomous role vis-à-vis the business community and other institutions in society.

Although the Ford Foundation has its background in the business world, it has today a broad scope of activities. Its main objective is directed toward addressing general problems in society, not just those of interest to business, but one of its program committees is explicitly concerned with "Economic Opportunity and Markets."[32] The promotion of research on economic and democratic development, including diverse aspects of inequality and human rights, of course incredibly comprehensive themes, are at the center of the Foundation's priorities, while trade- or environment-related problems, often linked to economic progress and democracy, are not so central to its agenda. This is a profile shared with many other think tanks, including those discussed above, and this direction is not surprising.

There is a deep-seated ambition among philanthropists, coming from profit-seeking corporations, to engage in non-profit activity and do something demonstrably good for society. Of course, business has a key interest in stable conditions and societal peace, although these basic values are given different emphasis in different parts of the business community. These overarching goals can more easily be addressed and knowledge can be provided about these conditions by think tanks. These issues are also important to business associations and their members as well as to other actors in business, but they tend not to avoid such general themes; instead, they are engaged in more immediate concerns, or at least link public and private goals in different ways as we have seen in the debate on corporate social responsibility. The Ford Foundation is one of the numerous American think tanks with an original focus on the United States but with later extensions to other countries, and this has broadened its scope of knowledge building.[33] Furthermore, it has globalized by expanding to many other countries. Today, it is represented on several continents (excluding Europe) and addresses issues that are important in local as well as in global contexts, and this globalization strategy was adopted earlier than by most other think tanks that have adopted a global profile. This process seems mainly driven by an ambition to take up real-world concerns and display a global commitment but also to place the Foundation in the context of the wider think tank landscape and match other think tanks with similar agendas.

Open Society Foundations

This organization both conducts its own think tank activities and funds those of other actors, but all aspects of its work cannot be characterized as think tank oriented. It was founded in 1993 by the Hungarian expat-turned-US citizen George Soros, who has used large sums of money gained from currency speculation to fund activities that should be of benefit to society more broadly.[34] It is, today, engaged in institutions and projects in many parts of the world, and as the plural "foundations" suggests, it has offices and branches in many countries.

Unlike the other examples of think tanks presented above, the Open Society Foundations were not originally confined to the United States. From its inception, the organization took an international outlook and defined its own work in much broader international terms. It was in an era when, for instance, the emergence of new democracies in Eastern Europe was drawing attention. Since then, this region has been given high priority by the Open Society Foundations, the special profile of which sets it apart from other think tanks, but by no means are its operations restricted to these countries. In addition, globalization has increasingly come on the agenda of many think tanks and other private organizations, and therefore, it was quite natural to adapt to this development when defining the goals of the organization.

The Open Society Foundations have their origin in business, but their ambitions are much broader, although not unrelated to the business community. A primary goal is to foster democracy and further ideas about free societies, a mission that is directed toward the public as well as private sectors. This implies, for instance, the introduction of the rule of law, free and fair elections, freedom of speech and accountable governments, all goals that may seem basic but have still not been achieved in many parts of the world. In some cases, this program has made Soros a controversial figure as different perceptions of these objectives and their concrete implementation surround them.[35]

Inherent in this ideology is an ambition to align values of democracy with values of the market economy and, in this way, guarantee that "people are free to participate fully in civic, economic, and cultural life."[36] Yet, at the same time, people must be secure in the notion that participation in economic life follows certain democratic rules and standards. In other words, the organization advocates for some kind of civilized capitalism. This is an important and highly general objective that many other entities in the global business community, including a number of clubs and think tanks, seek to advance to provide the necessary foundation for business. It is, however, also a concern of many business associations, especially peak associations with broad agendas, but this work tends to be integrated in many other and specific issues, and the efforts to promote general democratic values in society are not styled in the same way as in some of the think tanks.

Bill & Melinda Gates Foundation

Like the Open Society Foundation, the Bill & Melinda Gates Foundation is a recent initiative, founded in 2000, and while at least some of the older businessmen behind think tanks may have been largely forgotten by the public, Bill Gates is, for modern generations, a household name.[37] The Foundation testifies to the constant renewal of the population of think tanks that emerges from corporations and, in one way or another, contributes to the engagement of business in global affairs. The new organization follows a long and established tradition in American business of philanthropy. In this case, it transfers substantial funds from a corporation—not from old industries, such as steel or cars, but from the branch of modern computer software—to address current societal challenges.

The Foundation does not operate in the same fashion as some of the typical think tanks discussed above, and it is difficult to draw an exact line of division between foundations and think tanks. It has its own programs and defines, to a considerable extent, a number of research projects. Therefore, it is not just an important funder, although it contributes significant amounts to initiatives hosted by other actors, such as universities, NGOs and international agencies. To refurbish the conditions of business is not a proclaimed ambition. It is a global player in the sense that it has several offices located outside the United States, where it is headquartered. It has, furthermore, a clear global profile, with several programs focusing on global problems, and provides significant donations to organizations in various countries[38] while specific American issues are given far less attention. It has, therefore, followed a different globalization strategy than those think tanks establishing new offices abroad, which shows that there are different ways for think tanks to achieve globalization. This may affect how other actors perceive the Foundation and adapt to its expansion.

Apart from a specific territorial orientation in the form of global issues, the organization also has a unique policy focus. Trade and economic policy are not central policy fields, and the Foundation does not seem to engage in or support work that is of general relevance to the business community and those global business associations that pay attention to these issues. Instead, the Bill & Melinda Gates Foundation is highly prolific in health policy, especially in combating diseases in third world countries.[39] These efforts are, today, important in influencing agendas and assisting in implementing global health policy, and consequently, they have special relevance for those sections of business that are active in that field. This includes, for instance, the pharmaceutical industry and those global industry associations that, in one way or another, are involved in global health policy.

Given its basic role as a not-for-profit organization, the Foundation highlights ideas and public goals in ways not feasible for industry, and, furthermore, it has been innovative in designing new forms of partnership in ways that are challenging for industries in the health sector. As a consequence, the Foundation has come to undertake tasks that are too difficult or complex for business to embrace, and in this way, it can play a positive role in the division of labor in the business community. However, the activity of such think tanks can also overlap with those of designated business associations and other actors in business and may, therefore, give rise to instances of competition.

Conclusion

Global business consists of a fairly heterogeneous population of actors, in which clubs and think tanks occupy a special place, but closer inspection reveals that they are not always purely business actors, involving a smaller or larger fraction of political leaders and academic experts as members. They are on the edges of the business community. The actors examined in this chapter, however, have a sufficiently strong business core—more visibly in the case of clubs, less in the case of think tanks—to qualify them as actors in the global business community.

While the clubs have key business people as members, think tanks link up with business through donors. However, we have seen that club constituencies also consist of participants at annual meetings, blurring the membership category, and we also find certain intermediate structures, such as regional groups or national chapters, that assist in recruiting and finding members. The work of clubs and think tanks centers on identifying new issues, setting bold agendas and evaluating policies, and the study of these actors can be an important addition to agenda-setting theory.[40] They engage in agenda setting in competition with other private and public actors in global politics, and this work may augment or sometimes conflict with the efforts of associations in the business community. However, neither clubs nor think tanks represent corporate interests in any formal sense, and they are not authorized to represent interests in exchanges with their institutionalized environment, such as IGOs. Neither are supposed to coordinate strategies in the same way as associations, and all of the actors reviewed in this chapter have their own stock of members and donors with very little overlap.

Free from commitments to represent interests, they operate in a more independent and dynamic fashion, generate ideas and disseminate them in the business community or filter them into the broader public debate, sometimes in ways that would be impossible or problematic for traditional associations. As such, they share a number of features with some of the facilitators, as will be discussed in the next chapter. However, the research content of clubs and think tanks varies, with far better analytic resources behind the think tanks and more explicit communication strategies.

In terms of style, there is variation between clubs, between think tanks, and also between the two categories of actors. All adapt to changing environments, but the focus of their work tends to reflect the time in which they were created. The early clubs tend to be more secretive while recent clubs have adopted a more transparent style and give more consideration to the responsibility of business in society in an attempt to reform capitalism. The older and more established think tanks seem to keep a greater distance from business while the new entities, or at least some of them, tend to be more ideological.

The mission of clubs and think tanks is not to assist in enhancing the competitiveness of firms by addressing specific pieces of regulation, like associations do. However, the cases examined in this chapter show that they are inclined to address issues that have a bearing on the general position of business in society, and that often they are advocates of ethical values and a reformed capitalism. As such, they tend to work in a long-term perspective, recognizing that changes in the perceptions of business in society take time. Together, these features indicate that some club and think tank activities resemble the efforts of certain peak associations that, to different degrees, address these wide-ranging agendas in addition to many immediate concerns. As we shall see, consulting firms may also engage in similar types of analyses and investigations. In this respect, relations become competitive, but neither the clubs and think tanks nor the associations and consulting firms seem to discuss this challenge, tending to concentrate on their own work without observing the parallel efforts of other actors.

Notes

1 Clubs and think tanks are both active in policy development and some have a background in business. That several actors in global politics produce knowledge and bring this into the policy process, and especially agenda setting, is analyzed in Diane Stone, *Knowledge Actors and Transnational Governance: The Private-Public Policy Nexus in the Global Agora* (Houndmills: Palgrave, 2013).
2 This is in line with James M. Buchanan, "An Economic Theory of Clubs," *Economica* 32, no. 125 (1965): 1–14. The benefits are distributed to club members only and, in this case, individual persons. They come from firms, but in the clubs they tend not to represent these.
3 For a classical treatment of selective/club goods: James M. Buchanan, "An Economic Theory of Clubs," *Economica* 32, no. 125 (1965): 1–14; Mancur C. Olson, *The Logic of Collective action: Public Goods and the Theory of Groups* (Cambridge: Harvard University Press, 1965). In this sense, also associations are categorized as clubs, but such a broad category is not used in this chapter. Attempt has been made to distinguish clubs and associations as separate entities in the general governance of business: Philippe C. Schmitter, "Sectors in Modern Capitalism: Modes of Governance and Variations in Performance," in Renato Brunetta and Carlo Dell'Aringa, eds, *Labour Relations and Economic Performance* (London: Macmillan, 1990), 3–39.
4 Robert H. Salisbury, "An Exchange Theory of Interest Groups," *Midwest Journal of Political Science* 13, no. 1 (1969): 1–32.
5 Those clubs that are most relevant in a study on business associations and related entities aim to influence different aspects of public policy. However, there are other entities that do not have this as an explicit purpose and lack transparent structures and policy styles. This applies, for instance, to Freemasons.
6 Georgina Murray and John Scott, eds, *Financial Elites and Transnational Business: Who Rules the World?* (Cheltenham: Edward Elgar, 2012). The elite concept

often refers to a combination of private and public sector elements, whereas clubs referred to in this chapter are a private sector phenomenon. The World Economic Forum also has some club features: Jean-Christophe Graz, "How Powerful are Transnational Elite Clubs? The Social Myth of the World Economic Forum," *New Political Economy* 8, no. 3 (2003): 321–340.
7 Rotary International, "History," www.rotary.org/en/about-rotary/history (accessed 14 December 2017).
8 Rotary International, *Constitution of Rotary International*, n.d., www.rotary.org (accessed 9 May 2017).
9 A similar model is applied in Lions International. Paul Martin and Robert Kleinfelder, *Lions Clubs in the 21st Century* (Bloomington: AuthorHouse, 2008).
10 In the case of WHO see, for instance: WHO, "Global Health Organizations Recognize Rotary International's Unprecedented Role in the Fight to End Polio Worldwide," www.who.int/mediacentre/news/releases/2005/pr28/en/ (accessed 20 October 2017).
11 Ian Richardson, Andrew P. Kakabadse and Nada K. Kakabadse, *Bilderberg People: Elite Power and Consensus in World Affairs* (London: Routledge, 2011). Also others have analyzed the Bilderberg meetings, often from a highly critical perspective.
12 TBC was established in 2013, bringing the TransAtlantic Business Dialogue (TABD) and the European-American Business Council (EABC) together. Laurie Buonanno, Natalia Cuglesan and Keith Henderson, eds, *The New and Changing Transatlanticism: Politics and Policy Perspectives* (London: Routledge, 2017).
13 On the early years of the organization: Dino Knudsen, *The Trilateral Commission and Global Governance: Informal Elite Diplomacy, 1972–82* (London: Routledge, 2016).
14 The Trilateral Commission, "About the Trilateral Commission," http://trilateral.org/page/3/about-trilateral (accessed 12 September 2017).
15 Holly Sklar, ed., *Trilateralism: The Trilateral Commission and Elite Planning for World Management* (Boston: South End Press, 1980); Stephen Gill, *American Hegemony and the Trilateral Commission* (Cambridge: Cambridge University Press, 1990).
16 Caux Roundtable, "How to Participate?" www.cauxroundtable.org/index.cfm?&menuid=20 (accessed 4 April 2017).
17 Its leader has published a book to create a foundation for its work: Stephen B. Young, *Moral Capitalism: Reconciling Private Interest With the Public Good* (San Francisco: Berrett-Koehler, 2002).
18 Caux Roundtable, "Principles for Business," www.cauxroundtable.org/index.cfm?&menuid=8 (accessed 13 December 2017).
19 Another body with a somewhat similar program was the International Business Leaders Forum which ceased its activity in 2013 but, based in London and Moscow, was carried on under the name International Business Leaders Forum Global (IBLF Global). The original name of the initiative was The Prince of Wales Business Leaders Forum (PWBLF).
20 Diana Fox Carney and Chrystia Freeland, eds, *Making Capitalism More Inclusive. Selected Speeches and Essays from Participants at the Conference on Inclusive Capitalism* (London: Coalition for Inclusive Change, 2014).
21 Coalition for Inclusive Capitalism, "About Us," http://inc-cap.com/about-us/ (accessed April 2, 2017).

22 James G. McGann, *2016 Global Go To Think Tank Index Report*. https://repository.upenn.edu/cgi/viewcontent.cgi?article=1011&context=think_tanks (accessed 14 December 2017). This annual report records the development of think tanks and their profiles from different comparative perspectives. There is a modest ambition to place think tanks as part of the wider business community.
23 Thomas Medvetz, *Think Tanks in America* (Chicago: Chicago University Press, 2012).
24 Diane Stone, "Think Tank Transnationalisation and Non-Profit Analysis, Advice and Advocacy," *Global Society* 14, no. 2 (2000): 153–172; James G. McGann with Richard Sabatini, *Global Think Tanks: Policy Networks and Governance* (London: Routledge, 2011).
25 Inderjeet Parmar, *Foundations of the American Century: The Ford, Carnegie, and Rockefeller Foundations in the Rise of American Power* (New York: Columbia University Press, 2012).
26 Carnegie, "Foreign Policy," http://carnegieendowment.org/topic/1296 (accessed 22 September 2017).
27 Carnegie, "Experts," http://carnegieendowment.org/experts (accessed 22 September 2017).
28 Donald T. Critchlow, *The Brookings Institution, 1916–1952: Expertise and the Public Interest in a Democratic Society* (DeKalb: Northern Illinois University Press, 1985).
29 Brookings Institution, "Economic Studies," www.brookings.edu/program/economic-studies/ (accessed 12 September 2017).
30 In domestic contexts, the Brookings Institution can be an interesting ally for business in general and for particular business groups but this would push our examination toward the domestic scene of American politics. Eric Lipton and Brook Williams, "How Think Tanks Amplify Corporate America's Influence," *The New York Times* (7 August 2016).
31 Inderjeet Parmar, *Foundations of the American Century: The Ford, Carnegie, and Rockefeller Foundations in the Rise of American Power* (New York: Columbia University Press, 2012).
32 Ford Foundation, "Board of Trustees," www.fordfoundation.org/people/board-of-trustees/ (accessed 15 May 2017).
33 Ford Foundation, "The Latest," www.fordfoundation.org (accessed 22 August 2017).
34 Michael T. Kaufman, *Soros: The Life and Times of a Messianic Billionaire* (New York: Alfred A. Knopf, 2002).
35 Diane Stone, "Transnational Philanthropy or Policy Transfer? The Transnational Norms of the Open Society Institute," *Policy and Politics* 38, no. 2 (2010): 269–287.
36 Open Society Foundation, "Missions and Values," www.opensocietyfoundations.org/about/mission-values (accessed 22 August 2017).
37 Business, and especially American business, tends to produce ever-new philanthropists who engage in activities beyond or in relation to the business community. The most recent is the founder of Facebook, Mark Zuckerberg. David Gelles, "Giving Away Billions as Fast as They Can," *The New York Times* (20 October 2017); David Callahan, *The Givers: Wealth, Power, and Philanthropy in a New Gilded Age* (New York: Alfred A. Knopf, 2017).

38 Bill & Melinda Gates Foundation, "Foundation Fact Sheet," www.gatesfounda tion.org/Who-We-Are/General-Information/Foundation-Factsheet (accessed 13 December 2017).
39 Bill & Melinda Gates Foundation, "What We Do," www.gatesfoundation.org/What-We-Do (accessed 13 December 2017).
40 Studies on think tanks and studies on agenda setting have flourished in recent decades, while research into business clubs has not. However, think tanks have not been well integrated into agenda-setting research: Nikolaos Zahariadis, ed., *Handbook of Public Policy Agenda Setting* (Cheltenham: Edward Elgar, 2016).

5
FACILITATORS

- Overview: the general functions of facilitators
- Public affairs and public relations bureaus
- Self-regulators
- Law firms
- Security and crime protection
- Consulting firms
- Accounting and auditing firms
- Rating agencies
- Business media and information services
- Conclusions

Many actors in the global business community provide services on a commercial basis—often to individual firms—to facilitate market operations. But they also provide services to other actors generally not active in the market, such as associations. Depending on the various profiles of the associations, the facilitators may encroach on their established domains, but associations also expand and engage in activities typically managed by facilitators and offer selective goods in the form of various services.[1] Either way, associations and facilitators come to address a number of the same issues and produce some of the same services. As a peak association, the International Chamber of Commerce (ICC) is highly active in the production of services, and at the level of industry, an organization such as the Baltic and

International Maritime Council (BIMCO), has a strong record as a service provider in shipping. The role of facilitators in the business community is therefore complex, influenced by different ambitions and dynamics, and with important impacts on associations.

Facilitators is a broad term covering a variety of actors and services. In many cases, they are rooted in specific professions[2] that have undergone a significant process of globalization in which MNCs are central, but in other cases they are not built on a strong institutional history. The actors analyzed so far—the various associations but also clubs and think tanks—produce various kinds of services as part of their profile, but the facilitators include a mixed category whose core function is market facilitation.[3] It is important to bear in mind that the different facilitators are characterized by specialization and often concentrate on a single activity that they master, but there are also opposing trends, and, as conglomerates, some firms engage in several activities.

In this chapter, we first provide an overview of the theoretical challenges in the analysis of facilitators. Indeed, the task here is not to treat the various facilitators in their own right (a different and much wider undertaking), but relate them to the part played by traditional associations. We then analyze major groups of facilitators whose chief goal is to thrive as individual businesses by servicing other firms and actors in areas where they need special knowledge and skills. It is analytically difficult to establish a particular order in the treatment of these actors, but the role and profile of the groups of facilitators are examined according to their ambitions to enhance the performance of business in politics and in the market, recognizing that there are many gray areas.

Following this principle, facilitators include a number of actors: public affairs bureaus, which help individual firms or, occasionally, particular industries that are entering the domain of politics to influence public regulation; self-regulators define norms and rules for business that are communicated to signal compliance with certain standards, and they are often adopted in areas where traditional public regulation is weak or missing; law firms which dispense expert legal knowledge in many areas and can help individual firms in the global market in their transactions with other firms, and, sometimes, when in conflict with different judicial systems or international regulation; rating agencies, which scrutinize the performance of firms and evaluate their creditworthiness, an essential parameter in the adoption of loans but also in the creation of reputation; accounting firms, which monitor many kinds of corporate activity and examine the compliance of firms with public regulation and sometimes self-regulation and communicate this information to firms and various stakeholders; consulting firms, which provide different forms of advice and offer a range of services to improve the overall performance of firms and adopt organizational changes to these ends; security firms, which are active in many areas to guard the physical safety of firms but also provide systems that protect property in a much wider sense; and finally, business media and information services, which are involved in analyses of business, and disseminate important information on companies and industries to the business community and the public.

Overview: the general functions of facilitators

In this chapter, the goal is to understand the role of associations and how they meet competition from facilitators that are active in some of the same areas and engage in some of the same issues. Before we begin a description and analysis of the major facilitators and their inherent properties, a broader view of facilitators is warranted. Essentially, facilitators are important in enabling market transactions and, thus, assisting firms in optimizing their performance. Tasks that are neither possible to manage efficiently within the firms themselves, nor are carried out fully through the different types of business associations available, are accomplished by a range of other actors: the facilitators.

Different literatures, especially those of institutional economics, economic history and economic sociology, have addressed such actors and their functions in the economy—without, however, relating them to business associations. From the micro-perspective of the individual firm, there are a number of options for increasing performance and for reducing transaction costs.[4] In other words, delegation of tasks to and purchasing of services from entities outside a firm can be more cost efficient than if carried out internally by a firm. This transaction-cost perspective is also useful in our context because it can help us explain the presence of many actors beyond the firm level and the necessity of drawing on external resources. From the macro-perspective of the economy, a primary task of facilitators is to enable exchanges between actors in the market and to help them make informed choices, although the institutions created for this purpose are sometimes characterized by various power asymmetries and can, therefore, be exploited by firms. Today, a range of private institutions produce rules and norms, showing that the regulation of the economy is not only accomplished by public regulation.[5] This research is helpful because it recognizes the huge complexity of the business community and identifies and categorizes some of these facilitators. Thus, the literature gives us some clues as to why individual firms draw on external institutions and how concrete institutions foster exchange, but they are not well suited to examine the specific role of associations and the role of various facilitators in the business community. When drawing on theories predominantly related to individual firm behavior and market processes, we should be careful when applying such insights to our field. Some caveats are due.

First, it is important to remember that only in some cases are members of global business associations firms, and, thus, request the typical kind of services offered by the facilitators dealt with in this chapter. Other members, such as national associations, may request various services from global associations with which they are affiliated without being present in the market, and in this context, facilitators could merely develop activities that might as well unfold within global associations. Indeed, different groups of members may raise demands on global associations, and, in turn, these demands may, to different extents, be met by facilitators.

Second, the objective of facilitators is not only to enhance the performance of member firms in the market but also to address a range of political issues. Thus, several facilitators actively assist in the development of political strategies to leverage governments and IGOs, and they further provide a number of regulatory functions, all activities that in principle could be handled by business associations, and, to some extent, also pose viable alternatives to public regulation.

In sum, we need a differentiated approach to the study of facilitators. Facilitators offer various knowledge-based services that enhance the performance of their clients (firms, associations and other entities) in the market and in politics. Some of these services are closely related to each of these domains, but some facilitators and some services cross these boundaries, have both an economic and political dimension, and are intrinsically interwoven. Tentatively, we can try to separate them, and Figure 5.1 shows that various fields of associational activity are challenged—some relating to markets, some to politics, and some to a combination of markets and politics.

In terms of taxonomy, it is possible to distinguish major types of facilitators on account of their services and functions in the business community, although we have to recognize that these are not laid out in a neat order but are subject to evolution.[6] They are anchored in industries characterized

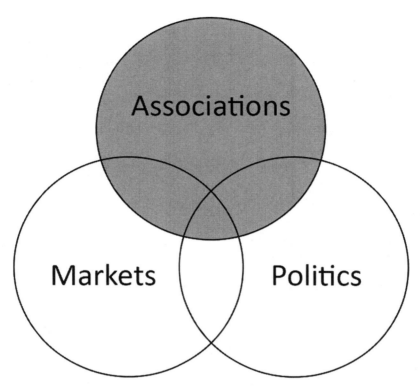

FIGURE 5.1 Tasks managed by facilitators in markets and politics overlapping partly with those of associations

by constant development and strong globalization. First, the profiles of the various facilitators overlap, and in some cases, they compete with each other because some firms engage in multiple activities and because certain activities are managed by several facilitators. The consultancy business is a clear example as consultancy services are today offered by many facilitators. Second, facilitators are characterized by interesting dynamics, whereby old activities often become embraced by facilitators who integrate a number of tasks, and the emergence of new services leads to the creation of new facilitators that offer associations and their members a series of services that, in the past, were poorly developed or did not exist. Indeed, many of the facilitators can draw on a long institutional history—for instance, law firms—while some facilitators, such as public affairs bureaus, have become important mainly in recent decades. Indeed, many aspects deserve attention in the analysis of the complex group of facilitators, but in this chapter, the emphasis is on their role in relation to global business associations, which are sometimes competitors. They are relevant to draw on in cases when associations need input from competent professionals in areas where knowledge is missing, and they become a challenge when associations and facilitators share some of the same ambitions.

Public affairs and public relations bureaus

The consultancy business has grown enormously in recent decades, and today, many activities are covered.[7] As a special branch, but in many cases integrated into broader consulting firms, we find the public affairs and public relations business, which, in one way or another, help firms, and perhaps even entities such as business associations, which communicate with government and various important stakeholder groups.

Part of their work is very much accomplished in the political realm, but an important and related goal is to improve the general reputation of their clients. In many ways, this activity comes close to the work of global business associations because the bureaus dispose of special knowledge not readily available to single corporations, can draw on broader knowledge and, in some cases, understand the relevant political machinations far better than do individual firms.

Yet, a number of significant distinctions must be made to underline the qualitatively different character of these actors. First, the bureaus assist business on a commercial basis, and firms and other entities consequently pay for the services delivered according to a contract; meanwhile, members of associations pay general fees and remunerate associations for efforts to influence political decision making. Second, the work done by the bureaus is limited in time and scope, and generally has an ad hoc character, while the activities of associations do not cease with a single task but are designed to assist members on a permanent basis and within a variety of fields. Third, the public affairs bureaus give professional advice to their clients but, to varying degrees, also act on their behalf in various domestic and international settings, while associations are bodies that represent collective interests and, therefore, can speak with more weight. The public affairs bureaus can help individual clients and discuss potential strategies without involving other parties in business, while the efforts of business associations are crucially dependent on internal decision processes, including negotiation and compromise between competing business interests, and hence, they are more complex.

This kind of consulting can be highly useful for associations because public affairs and relations companies may offer assistance in cases when associations and their members lack experience and need strategic advice; however, it can also be harmful, for example, if associations fail to develop relevant capacities and always must refer to and even draw on external advice, and it can damage their membership bases severely if members prefer these services to those offered by the associations. Occasionally, member firms may have incentives to requisition such services because they are more flexible and benefit a single firm rather than a whole industry or a larger part of business.[8]

However, services offered by the public affairs and public relations branch must be understood in their proper institutional framework. While the role of public affairs firms has been highlighted in different domestic contexts,[9] emerging in the United States where they have a track record of representing different types of clients in business, and then later transferring to other countries, the same conditions for these kinds of companies may not apply in a global context simply because we find different political institutions and rules for interacting with private interests.

Indeed, many intergovernmental agencies have carved out relatively standardized strategies for handling relations with NGOs, including organized business. As a general guideline, they consult with representative bodies in business and civil society, such as global associations, an important factor of legitimacy in their work.[10] Indeed, there are no instructions that encourage direct relations and contacts with the public affairs world or the individual clients they advise, and this would, in principle, violate some of the general rules formulated by intergovernmental agencies.

Furthermore, the relatively slow globalization of this kind of facilitator, for instance in terms of ownership, coordination and operation of activities, is no doubt an important barrier for (especially) public affairs firms to proliferate and become more important in the global realm.[11] However, the public affairs and public relations companies may, in principle, enhance capacities and, to a greater extent, help associations form their strategies and tactics when exchanging with IGOs or various stakeholders without in any formal way trying to represent these interests. They may further help them by improving their public relations functions when interacting with relevant civil society groups and with the public in general, and devise campaigns to augment their general reputation.

Self-regulators

Much global regulation is adopted in the context of intergovernmental agencies, but we would not have a full picture of global regulation if we only studied traditional public regulation.[12] Indeed, many actors in the business community today are active in rule-making, either through associations or through other bodies,[13] and some of the facilitators treated below may, together with other tasks, engage in self-regulation.

We have already paid some attention to self-regulation as it is adopted and implemented in peak associations, in industry associations and in alliances. Indeed, associations are some of the most potent self-regulators because they already organize a substantial group in business, harness relevant informational resources and accumulate important experiences. Members are also more likely to acquiesce to rules, when they have been involved in negotiating and endorsing them. Also, if they risk being expelled from associations in case of non-compliance, they have strong incentives to stick to the rules and, thus, sustain membership. These organizational properties are of great value when designing and implementing a scheme, as rules of representative organizations are likely to govern behavior in business and therefore may be a valid alternative, becoming accepted, or at least tolerated, by states and intergovernmental agencies and, in some cases, even encouraged by public authority.

Various forms of self-regulation in business, however, are managed by other bodies, and separate consideration of their work is needed. These private bodies are, to varying degrees, formed in processes involving different interactions with public authority. Some initiatives are encouraged by governments and IGOs, but some emerge quite independently without prior contacts with the public sector. We also see interesting variations concerning relations with civil society: some initiatives taken by business deliberately involve civil society groups that have relevant expertise to closely follow business and act as a countervailing power, whereas other initiatives emerge more or less in civil society and are then presented to firms which are invited to join on a voluntary basis. Some of these are labelled multi-stakeholder arrangements, and some notable examples are the well-studied stewardship councils: the Forest Stewardship Council (FSC), Marine Stewardship Council (MSC), and Aquaculture Stewardship Council (ASC).[14] They offer certification of firms, products and processes in so far as they are in compliance with the rules and standards of these councils.

In general, the voluntary element seems to be stronger in self-regulation adopted outside the associations simply because decisions to join and comply with independent schemes are not related to an existing membership. In such cases, firms are not bound by any norm or social pressure in the association, but there can always be important functional imperatives or normative expectations in an industry that compel firms to join a self-regulatory scheme and follow its rules.

For technical, economic, social and political reasons, firms sometimes need licenses to operate because this is considered best practice in an industry and crucial to a firm's reputation in the business community and in the broader environment. In some industries, the DNV GL Group, formerly known as Det Norske Veritas, offers a range of highly specialized services on a commercial basis, and a major task in its classification activity is to inspect and certify firms that comply with its own and other agreed-upon standards in the maritime industry, in various energy sectors, and in food and healthcare.[15]

In a number of fields, the necessity to comply with rules is even more compelling. In areas of the financial industry, for instance, firms have to follow certain practices set by independent self-regulatory bodies; stock exchanges and credit card companies provide interesting examples. Obviously, arrangements to govern their behavior cannot be seen as soft and truly voluntary because independent self-regulatory bodies are so strong that firms simply need to comply if they want to trade and stay in business.

There is a plethora of stand-alone bodies whose tasks are mainly concentrated on self-regulation. They can be found across different stages of the policy process; they set agendas, make rules and implement them.[16] A number of specialized entities are also involved in arbitration and alternative dispute resolution and function as private courts. ICA is closely related to ICC as a leading business association (as was discussed in a previous chapter), but we find additional, independent and autonomous entities, such as the London Court of International Arbitration (LCIA), and various adjudication functions are also built into self-regulatory organizations that do not present themselves as courts *per se*.[17] This indicates that there can be complex relations between bodies administered by associations and independent bodies. As already established players, associations can often take the lead in creating relevant schemes, but if this is not feasible, initiatives may be taken by others. However, there is always a potential risk of overlay and competition.

Law firms

Unlike management consulting, accounting and auditing firms, global law firms rely primarily, if not solely, on the provision of legal expertise and, therefore, build on a single profession with a strong tradition and identity.[18] Such firms are consequently embedded in a much larger legal community with a rich variety of activities of professional, educational and social character, and they contribute actively to this environment by further globalization of the legal world, from fostering more general ideas to the implementation of concrete practices. This does not imply that law firms are the only providers of legal advice, however. Many other service organizations will include certain legal advice, and in some cases, they will even emphasize this service, a factor reflecting profile overlap and competition across the many service industries.

The activity of law firms is intuitively much easier to grasp than most other services. Following professional norms, it consists of giving legal advice to clients, avoiding or promoting lawsuits and, if necessary, taking cases to court. They represent their clients or otherwise present their case in institutional contexts to which they have special access. Although some general associations, in particular ICC, are recognized for their legal expertise, and many industry associations dispose of industry-specific knowledge with a legal component, services offered by law firms tend to have another character than the assistance provided by business associations. The associations must take broader concerns of their membership into account when developing their legal services, and they cannot represent their members (for instance, in relation to courts) in the same way as law firms.

With increasing transboundary activities, there is a growing demand for special legal services, and a number of law firms have become internationalized and globalized to meet such demands in business. Internal drivers in the industry have also propelled these processes. However, law firms, bound to different jurisdictions and legal systems, have not globalized with the same speed as have, for instance, auditing and accounting.

There is a strong bias in this kind of globalization, however: it is entirely dominated by US and UK law firms,[19] although other firms in other parts of the "Anglosphere" are included. These law firms either work through subsidiaries or partners in other countries to extend their territorial scope of operation, and many less globalized firms seek an advantage in linking up with these giants. However, many other forms of cooperation have evolved at the global level, bringing independent law firms together in more network-like constructions to provide services.[20] In some cases, these networks specialize in certain policy fields and areas of regulation; in other cases, networks consist of full-service law firms that cover a wide array of legal challenges.

Interestingly, these networked and often top-tier law firms are sometimes referred to as associations. Their purpose seems primarily to foster cooperation between the many independent entities, benefit from professional contacts and suggest referrals rather than to represent members in public-policy contexts. The ambition of this type of association, however, is not to organize law firms comprehensively and, thus, enhance their representativeness in relation to political institutions,[21] a hallmark of business associations. In some cases, however, single networks and associations of law firms may share their opinions on various regulatory issues, especially when it comes to the regulation of law firms, but also with regard to regulation of other businesses. In such cases, they engage in some of the same activities as traditional industry and peak associations.

Instead, the goal of these networks, whose admission criteria are often strict, is to rally major firms around mutual interests and, hence, improve their standing through a uniform profile. Evidently, reputational matters are of great concern.[22] To secure and enhance reputation, the firms agree on a number of standards in exchanging with their clients, and compliance with these standards is policed by the network itself, with those that are non-compliant running the risk of expulsion. One of the world's leading networks of law firms, Lex Mundi, has developed its own service standards.[23] In promoting corporate norms and standards, the networks and organizations engage in governing relations in the legal community but also in fostering practices in business in general or in specific industries, regulatory tasks that, to varying degrees, may be lifted by traditional business associations or through traditional public regulation.

Security and crime protection

To carry out global business activities, security is needed in a variety of contexts: property must be protected against fraud, theft and, in an even wider sense, against violent actions that threaten not only the properties of firms but also the lives of staff. The basic provision of security and combatting of crime have generally been seen as the obligation of states toward their citizens. Indeed, this is a classical public good. In a broader context, designated IGOs also bear such responsibilities—for instance, the protection of patents and other intellectual properties through the World Intellectual Property Organization (WIPO). However, the centrality of public authority does not rule out initiatives taken by various private actors,[24] especially in areas where the security of states is not affected but where different dimensions of corporate security are defied, although it can be difficult to draw a sharp line between these. The problem of public versus private solutions is often cast as a choice between governments or firms providing security, thus entirely sidestepping the role of intermediary institutions and the solutions available beyond state and market. This is where business associations come into the picture.

In fact, business associations can also play a crucial role in assisting the general business community as well as their own members in taking relevant security measures, and in some cases, such efforts are demanded and expected from members. Consequently, a key objective of many associations is to build and maintain a strong competence in relevant security matters, and such tasks are not readily surrendered to firms that intend to provide similar services in a commercial background. Thus, relations between associations and different alternative private facilitators vary strongly, and research is needed to map and analyze these, but in our context, it suffices to stress that the provision of security in its various dimensions is a contested field crossing the domains of associations and facilitators. This can lead to different forms of competition but also open up avenues of specialization and division of labor.

Obviously, associational commitment in security matters varies considerably; in some cases, it has a high priority while, in other cases, it is completely missing from the agenda. Furthermore, these efforts are very much adjusted to the specific character of the challenges: in the financial industries, the combatting of fraud plays a significant role, and we find rich examples of associations involved in the development of a lot of technical systems that will, for instance, guarantee the safe transfer of money or protect the bank accounts of clients, and the introduction of new financial products constantly requires the enactment of new measures. In shipping, there is a strong tradition of focusing on the physical security of ships but also, of course, on the safety of crews and passengers. Especially in relation to piracy, associations have stepped up already existing policies,[25] and in recent years, new dimensions have been added to these efforts in order to counter terrorism.

Interestingly, finance and shipping are also areas where facilitators are abundant, indicating that these industries are ridden by many serious security problems. Numerous companies have sprung up to assist ship owners both in analyzing risks and installing effective procedures; in finance, we have seen private companies offering services in relation to, for instance, the combatting of money laundering.[26]

It seems that the various facilitators and associations may have some of the same services to offer in gathering relevant intelligence and in analyzing developments, but associations tend to be less effective when it comes to operations on the ground. This may be attributable to the fact that facilitators can provide specialized assistance to single firms while associations are strong in analyzing business in general or concrete industries and providing solutions at these levels. Indeed, many areas of business have their own specialized firms that are involved in different aspects of security and provide services not managed by associations. With the globalization of markets, new mechanisms are constantly needed to solve problems that, in the past, were mainly addressed at domestic levels. Security issues related to the internet are a clear example, being linked to cybercrime, hacking and the stealing of intellectual property rights.

The combatting of crime and, hence, the improvement of security conditions for firms, entails a variety of steps. The prevention stage, where businesses take measures to avoid being exposed, are crucial, but additional efforts are launched to investigate committed crimes and breaches of security. Different private organizations are involved and contribute intelligence at this stage; these include general detective bureaus such as Pinkerton, and highly specialized bodies such as the Association of Certified Anti-Money Laundering Specialists (ACAMS).[27] Here, investigation may overlap with law firms, another major facilitator in the business community, and acquire a stronger political dimension.

Consulting firms

Consulting firms accomplish a broad category of analytical and advisory activities aimed at assisting the public and private sectors in improving economic, technical, organizational and political performance. Clearly, these activities are somewhat difficult to isolate from services offered by other facilitators (for example, accounting firms or public affairs bureaus). Indeed, the large firms that today dominate management consulting, such as McKinsey & Company, the Boston Consulting Group, Bain & Company, Deloitte Consulting, PricewaterhouseCoopers, Ernst & Young, and Accenture (see Figure 5.2), are conglomerates that master several functions,

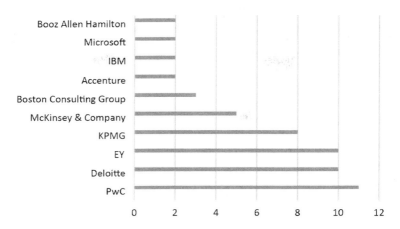

FIGURE 5.2 The major consulting firms and their global market shares in percent (2016)
Source: www.consultancy.uk/news/14018/the-10-largest-consulting-firms-in-the-world.

giving smaller or greater weight to traditional consultancy. As with many other kinds of facilitators in the business community, we cannot perceive these firms only as single entities with unique philosophies. We have to grasp their broader properties as an industry and relate them to other categories of facilitators as well as other forms of organized business.[28]

Many consulting firms have established a global basis and offer services in many countries, assuming the role of global actors. This applies, for instance, to McKinsey, a major player and pioneer in the development of the industry.[29] McKinsey offers a range of services to its clients, some of them similar to those offered by business associations to their members, although services in associations tend not to be tailored in the same way to individual members and are not based on specific contracts. The consulting business also has business associations as clients; tasks that could be handled by associations independently are instead bought as services by associations. Economics of scale is an important factor, and it can be an advantage for many businesses to purchase these services instead of investing resources in their own organizations.

In general, consulting firms are not dedicated to serve any particular industry but have clients in many sectors of business and typically list wide groups of industries in which they have expertise. This accumulation of knowledge and advice suggests that they can address a range of general business themes as well as specific areas of production. The official missions and values of the organizations are to advance the performance of their clients in a broad sense, help them improve their positions in the market and shape their relations with other actors in their environment, including public authority.[30] In this way, aspects of economic and political behavior are combined.

Although the consultancy business is not distinctly partisan, it is clearly based on pro-market organizations, and this permeates all its activities. This general aspect can be difficult to distill from a business's many concrete activities, but it is obvious that such an expanding and important industry as management consulting also has an important power. Individual companies represent important business interests and, at the same time, the industry holds an important position in relation to other sectors of business.

McKinsey, for instance, not only serves clients in a reactive manner by responding to requests but also takes initiative by setting agendas and by examining and evaluating the implementation of policies: "We continuously invest in research on some of the biggest issues facing society. We hope that our insights on these topics help to frame and open up debates, bring new thinking and identify potential solutions."[31]

Of course, such aspirations are also harbored by many other actors in global business, including associations, which attempt to influence public policy by mobilizing knowledge and by setting agendas. However, consulting firms do not have representative functions and can neither speak for specific industries nor for business in general, but as discussed in the previous sections, many firms or functions are devoted to assisting firms and associations in politics. In addition, consulting firms may, in their own right, perform various investigations and offer analyses of pertinent issues, initiatives that sometimes will have a bearing on politics in the global realm. Depending on the character of the advice offered by consulting firms, certain joint norms and standards can be promoted in business, especially among large corporations and other global actors who are among their major clients.

Accounting and auditing firms

Auditing and accounting are very often confused, and they are, indeed, closely related and often hard to separate, and clients may refer as much to auditing firms as to accounting firms or management consulting, depending on specialization.[32] However, auditing tends to be seen as a broader activity done by specialized external reviewers while accounting is also handled internally, and typically, the major activity of accounting lies in the examination, evaluation and presentation of (especially) financial data to internal and external stakeholders. Partly coming out of the consultancy business, this activity relies on professional communities. Accounting and auditing business have today become a growth industry with a high level of economic concentration, leading to the emergence of a few global players. Often nicknamed the "big four" (Deloitte, PricewaterhouseCoopers, Ernst & Young, and KPMG), a few companies today dominate the global market for these professional services, and to varying degrees, they engage in advisory activities, including management consulting, tax and risk management.

These firms often date their existence back several decades or even a century, when early founders, whose ingenuity and wisdom they claim to build on, created smaller firms. In recent decades, however, their businesses have expanded enormously, leading to many mergers, but, in spite of the general branding, local subsidiaries are said to have some independence while forming part of a larger network.

A major activity of accounting and auditing firms is to analyze whether clients comply with relevant norms and expectations, including, of course, national and international regulations adopted by the International Accounting Standards Board (IASB), and the International Financial Reporting Standards (IFRS) used in many countries. They also assist in the interpretation of rule systems and test various boundaries of regulation.

However, the firms are also active in creating various norms and standards to guide clients.[33] Thus, experiences from different sectors—and the big four and other companies are involved in many industries—are used to create certain general recommendations for corporate behavior. In this way, they shape behavior and communication where this task is not appropriately handled by governments and IGOs or, for that matter, business associations. However, there is also variation across accounting and auditing firms. It cannot be taken for granted that advice always goes in the same direction or leads to a greater homogeneity in accounting and auditing practices.

An important field of activity is, for instance, "tax planning," where clients are assisted in understanding tax rules but also are advised on how to circumvent them and avoid paying taxes or at least reduce taxes considerably.[34] Although the major accounting and auditing firms are engaged in such activity, this does not necessarily suggest that they provide exactly the same kind of advice or that they are immune to changing demands inside and outside the business community. Increasing pressure is on businesses to respond to demands among different stakeholders, and this political development is also a challenge for the accounting and auditing business. Business associations have important advisory functions, some of which overlap with accounting and auditing firms, and associations can assist their members in many ways. As with other kinds of services, assistance tends, in one way or another, to be offered as an integral part of their general relationship with members, and services are not obtained on a special-contract basis as with selected accounting and auditing firms. Because associations have to take broader concerns into consideration, they cannot target individual members in the same areas and to the same degree as specialized accounting and auditing firms, and great care is needed not to privilege certain members. In itself, this is a serious factor inhibiting service engagement.

Rating agencies

Through different kinds of rating systems, market actors—consumers as well as other businesses—are given access to information that may inform their choices, but since this information is also related to actors beyond the marketplace, rating may serve broader purposes. For instance, civil society groups can, on the basis of ratings, better evaluate who to target with campaigns, and government may be better equipped to determine where regulation is needed and which tools to apply. Rating agencies are often firms themselves, and they are found in many areas of business. They are both linked to the private sector in general and to specific industries.[35] Moreover, not all of them carry out their activities under the title of "rating agency" or other homogenized concepts and, hence, they are difficult to identify and understand as a general phenomenon in the business community. Nevertheless, they share many of the same features by consistently monitoring and rating businesses according to selected criteria and indicators, and as such, they represent a kind of self-regulation administered by special bodies.

At a very general level, we find rating agencies that evaluate the creditworthiness of different institutional debtors, and paradigm cases are the credit rating agencies that are dominated by three players: Moody's Investors Service, Standard & Poor's, and Fitch Ratings. The three big companies that are important in a global context all come from the United States and indicate an exceedingly high concentration among this very special kind of service provider,[36] but many other credit rating agencies exist across the world. They provide information and statements to different types of investors in the business community but also to governments, and they have introduced gradation systems that classify debtors and debt instruments. Their activities are especially relevant for and affect the financial sector but also relate to business in general as ratings, in various ways, influence the general business climate.

Other agencies rate the performance of business in specific policy areas. In some cases, they tend to be both a part of the global business community and the global civil society community because they need the legitimacy of both communities. Transparency International, for instance, focuses on improving the performance of business in selected areas,[37] through better access to information and avoidance of corruption, which, if not mended, are detrimental to business operations around the globe. Analyses can be an important factor in fostering change, although a number of the organization's activities tend to be related to the performance of business at the level of countries and are not focused on the global dimension. Nevertheless, this kind of information can propel learning processes and have an impact on business behavior in global contexts.

We also find examples of industry-specific rating, and the list is in no way exhaustive. A major classical example is the film industry, where films, producers and stars are rated, and important information is signaled to the industry itself, to critics and to the general audience. There are several organizations and prizes involved in this rating system, but the Academy Awards are probably the most prestigious of them all. In relation to restaurants, we find similar systems. The most recognized is, no doubt, the Michelin Guide, which honors high-ranking restaurants but also distinguishes between this already selected faction of outstanding firms according to specific criteria. More recently, have we seen global rating schemes develop in the hotel business. Although there is an established tradition of rating hotels, new rating systems have been created through the internet, where search machines, such as Booking.com, accumulate information on the preferences of consumers and advise new customers.

Business associations must be very careful regarding all sorts of ratings.[38] In principle, many associations have profound insight into an industry and the performance of their members, but by singling out winners and losers, they run an imminent risk of alienating members. The associations may be well informed about differences in the membership, but this information must be handled carefully. Indeed, associations are interested in promoting the overall reputation of their members, and they communicate, for instance, the compliance of members with rules and norms adopted by the associations, and this may set rule-abiding members apart from recalcitrant free-riders. This is a different kind of rating exercise, of course, and it is usually a part of self-regulation administered by associations that endeavor to portray a coherent and supportive membership.

Business media and information services

The last kind of facilitators to be scrutinized in this chapter is the global business press, which consists of an exceedingly amorphous set of actors and is, consequently, hard to nail down. Essentially, the task of the business press is to disseminate information from the business community, and yet, at the same time, critically investigate business news and make analyses available to expert segments in business and to the broader public. Media and news services have a very important function and enable business transactions by providing updated and realistic information to inform choices.

Some of these tasks are shared with global business associations, whose information strategies serve internal and professional demands in business. In addition, the associations seek to reach a broader audience to convey a positive image of corporate initiatives and events but with an emphasis on common issues in business or industries rather than on individual corporations. The latter is primarily a job for single firms.

To varying degrees, we find press sections in associations or press functions that are integrated into other activities. Indeed, it can be important for associations to control certain aspects of communication, or at least maintain a responsive capacity, and that they avoid surrendering this completely to the business media, whether these are driven by commercial motives or are engaged for other reasons. There are areas and issues that are potentially addressed by the business press as well as by associations and, for that matter, other entities in business, but many tasks cannot be undertaken cost-effectively by associations, so associations tend to refrain from expanding their domains in these directions.

There are both general media and specialized business media, but some general media include business issues of various kinds in special sections. Some of the business-directed media are committed to business in general and go into broader economic, financial and legal issues, and here, Thomson Reuters and Bloomberg L.P. are exceedingly important conglomerates with a foot in many areas of business news. They are also important financial data vendors and provide technologies and solutions in data processing and communication to help firms manage their own information strategies. Some of these tasks can, in principle, be managed by associations in business or in the financial industries. Other media concentrate on the conditions in particular industries and are not known beyond specialized communities, such as Drewry, a key consulting firm that collects and provides information in the maritime field.[39] Starting with the monthly bulletin *Shipping Insight* in 1975, it has added several other informational activities to its profile in market research and expanded in different directions in the maritime field. It further sets important standards for presenting and analyzing data, an example being the development of the Container Spot Market Freight Rate Index. Another example in specific industry information is the Independent Chemical Information Service (ICIS), whose goal is "to give companies in global commodities markets a competitive advantage by delivering trusted pricing data, high-value news, analysis and independent consulting, enabling our customers to make better-informed trading and planning decisions."[40] It is active in relation to chemical, energy and fertilizer commodities and, in addition, it provides a variety of consulting services and issues various newsletters, magazines and reports. Other business media can draw on such activities and reach a broader audience beyond the often relatively narrow industries where specialized news media thrive.

The ambitions of these comparatively small entities vary considerably and encompass everything from more formal news publications to more modest newsletters, and again, these are activities that can be managed at the level of industry associations. It is always a challenge for associations to define the scope of these efforts and weigh them against other tasks.

Media and news services disseminate various news items, undertake analytical investigations and provide services to firms and industries to develop their information strategies. Taken together, the selection and priority of news, and the development of relevant tools can also have a normative value and contribute to self-understanding in the business community. Indeed, the media are platforms for the exchange and testing of ideas in business, and, eventually, they assist in the setting of new agendas. In addition, the way news and information strategies are designed can have a regulatory function—for instance, the ordering of information through statistics—and this is necessary to record developments in the market. Provided by some business media, financial data vendors will have a standardizing effect and shape perceptions of professional performance and effectiveness in a given business sector. As with many other facilitators, the business media therefore manage multiple tasks.

Conclusions

Facilitators constitute a highly diverse group of actors in the business community, theorized under different concepts. This chapter has identified and analyzed major categories of facilitators: some of them independent bodies and some of them trades unto themselves, but they all help others doing business, and, as such, they form an essential part of the environment of global business associations.

From the perspective of associations, facilitators can be exceptionally useful and solve tasks that associations are unable to perform or do not give sufficient priority, but they can also engage in activities that associations keenly want to specialize in. Therefore, the relations between business associations and the facilitators are complex, but they are of a quite different nature than relations between the different associations, because facilitators do not strive to take over associations' core functions. Since facilitators are a heterogeneous group, relations with associations are not the same: some are mainly characterized by competition while cooperation is dominant in other areas, and these relations change over time.

As service providers and third parties establish rules for business, they offer a mixed bag of assistance. Although it is difficult and problematic to make a clear-cut separation, we may distinguish between facilitators that primarily help associations in carrying out either economic or political functions, and hence position them along a continuum. In general, facilitators risk coming into competition with associations when they engage in activities that in some way resemble those of the associations, such as activities performed by public affairs bureaus and self-regulators, while facilitators, such as rating agencies and media, are less inclined to challenge the principal domains of associations. Obviously, this pattern is related to the key mission of associations to represent their members in the political realm, and this in a very broad sense. However, we must be careful not to perceive associations as entities narrowly specialized in political affairs, and acknowledge the many other activities carried out in these organizations, including the provision of various legal and technical services, the dissemination of specific knowledge to members, to the business community and to society in general, and the assistance to members in the implementation of rules and norms.

A special challenge to associations comes from the various dynamics of facilitators. In almost in every field, we can note two interrelated developments: first, strong economic concentration among the service providers; and second, enhanced globalization in terms of ownership and operation. These trends are particularly strong in consulting and accounting but are also found elsewhere. This evolution is interesting in itself and deserves independent scrutiny, but what is important here is that these trends have consequences for the organization of business interests. The facilitators grow bigger and bigger, and facilitators embrace and combine multiple activities and build up experiences in relation to different sectors of business. Under these circumstances, it becomes increasingly difficult for business associations to match these capacities and maintain or build up a profile in contested areas. Eventually, this evolution may have repercussions on their status as business associations and challenge established divisions of labor in the global business community.

Notes

1 We can study associations as "producer," "employer" and "market associations," where the latter category is active in the market, for instance, through coordinating behavior and providing services: Ernst-Bernd Blümle and Peter Schwartz, eds, *Wirtschaftsverbände und ihre Funktion* (Darmstadt: Wissenschaftliche Buchgesellschaft, 1985).
2 Yves Dezalay and David Sugarman, eds, *Professional Competition and Professional Power* (London: Routledge, 1995). In recent years, much has been written on professions, especially in the financial industries where experts side with different groups in society and become important in politics, e.g. Leonard Seabrooke and Duncan Wigan, "Powering Ideas Through Expertise: Professionals in Global Tax Battles," *Journal of European Public Policy* 23, no. 3 (2016): 357–374.
3 Certain functions, but not all the facilitators examined in this chapter, are summarized under the concept of "coordination services firms": A. Claire Cutler, Virginia Haufler and Tony Porter, "Private Authority and International Affairs," in A. Claire Cutler, Virginia Haufler and Tony Porter, eds, *Private Authority and International Affairs* (Albany: State University of New York Press, 1999), 3–28. Some functions are also treated in: Avner Greif, "Commitment, Coercion and Markets: The Nature and Dynamics of Institutions Supporting Exchange," in Claude Ménard and Mary M. Shirley, eds, *Handbook of New Institutional Economics* (New York: Springer, 2005), 727–788.
4 Oliver E. Williamson, "The Economics of Organization: The Transaction Cost Approach," *American Journal of Sociology* 87, no. 3 (1981): 548–577. Today, this perspective is applied in many institutional contexts but work is needed to apply this to associations and other actors performing functions overlapping with associations.
5 Karsten Ronit and Volker Schneider, "Global Governance Through Private Organizations," *Governance* 12, no. 3 (1999): 243–266; Tim Büthe and Walter

Mattli, *The New Global Rulers: The Privatization of Regulation in the World Economy* (Princeton: Princeton University Press, 2011).

6 For an evolutionary perspective applicable to our field: Ernst Mayr, "Speciational Evolution or Punctuated Equilibria," *Journal of Social and Biological Structures* 12 (1988): 137–158. This has some affinity with historical institutionalism; see: James Mahoney and Kathleen Thelen, eds, *Advances in Comparative-Historical Analysis* (Cambridge: Cambridge University Press, 2015).

7 Phil Harris and Craig S. Fleisher, eds, *The SAGE Handbook of International Corporate and Public Affairs* (London: Sage, 2016).

8 Amy J. Hillman and Michael A. Hitt, "Corporate Political Strategy Formulation: A Model of Approach, Participation and Strategy Decisions," *The Academy of Management Review* 24, no. 4 (1999): 825–842; Duane Windsor, "Theoretical Lenses and Conceptual Models for Understanding Public Affairs," in Phil Harris and Craig S. Fleisher, eds, *The SAGE Handbook of International Corporate and Public Affairs* (London: Sage, 2016), 40–55.

9 Public affairs tends to unfold in different national settings rather than as a concerted global activity: Phil Harris, "Across the Continents: The Global Reach of Public Affairs," *Journal of Public Affairs* 16, no. 2 (2016): 107–110.

10 Peter Willetts, *Non-Governmental Organizations in World Politics* (London: Routledge, 2011).

11 The integration of public affairs and public relations in professional firms has varied across countries, with stronger integration in the United States: John Mahon, "Public Affairs in North America," in Phil Harris and Craig S. Fleisher, eds, *The SAGE Handbook of International Corporate and Public Affairs* (London: Sage, 2016), 388–404.

12 A special case is ISO. In the literature, this is seen as public, private and a hybrid between the two. Members come from the public as well as private sectors. ISO negotiates and adopts a rich variety of standards and is important for business. Craig N. Murphy and Joanne Yates, *The International Organization for Standardization (ISO): Global Governance through Voluntary Consensus* (London: Routledge, 2009).

13 Tony Porter and Karsten Ronit, "Self-Regulation as Policy Process: The Multiple and Criss-Crossing Stages of Private Rule-Making," *Policy Sciences* 39, no. 1 (2006): 41–72; Kenneth W. Abbott and Duncan Snidal, "The Governance Triangle: Regulatory Standards Institutions and the Shadow of the State," in Walter Mattli and Ngaire Woods, eds, *The Politics of Global Regulation* (Princeton: Princeton University Press, 2009), 44–88; David Levi-Faur, "Regulation and Regulatory Governance," in David Levi-Faur, ed., *Handbook on the Politics of Regulation* (Cheltenham: Edward Elgar, 2011), 1–25.

14 Stephen M. Maurer, "The New Self-Governance: A Theoretical Framework," *Business and Politics* 19, no. 1 (2017): 41–67.

15 Gard Paulsen, Håkon With Andersen, John Peter Collett and Iver Tangen Stensrud, *Building Trust: The History of DNV 1864–2014* (Oslo: Dinamo Forlag, 2014).

16 Tony Porter and Karsten Ronit, "Implementation in International Business Self-Regulation: The Importance of Sequences and their Linkages," *Journal of Law and Society* 42, no. 3 (2015): 413–433.

17 Yves Dezalay and Bryant G. Garth, *Dealing in Virtue: International Commercial Arbitration and the Construction of a Transnational Legal Order* (Chicago: Chicago University Press, 1996).

18 Yves Dezalay and Bryant G. Garth, eds, *Lawyers and the Rule of Law in an Era of Globalization* (London: Routledge, 2011). For changes in relations between law firms and consulting firms: David B. Wilkins and Maria J. Esteban Ferrer, "The Integration of Law into Global Business Solutions: The Rise, Transformation and Potential Future of the Big Four Accountancy Networks in the Global Legal Services Market," *Law & Social Inquiry* (2017) (online version).
19 Marie-Laure Djelic and Sigrid Quack, eds, *Transnational Communities: Shaping Global Economic Governance* (Cambridge: Cambridge University Press, 2010).
20 The Legal 500. See www.legal500.com/assets/pages/networks/network_listings. html (accessed 12 September 2016); www.legal500.com/assets/pages/networks/ network_listings.html.
21 For law firms and the law profession, these tasks are managed by associations such as the International Bar Association (IBA), and the International Association of Lawyers (UIA).
22 These practices are, for instance, dealt with in club theory: Todd Sandler and John Tschirhart, "Club Theory: Thirty Years Later," *Public Choice* 93 (1997): 335–355.
23 Lex Mundi, "Lex Mundi Service Standards," www.lexmundi.com/lexmundi/ Service_Standards.asp (accessed 18 September 2016).
24 Research on private security companies has flourished over the last decades, e.g. Rita Abrahamsen and Michael C. Williams, *Security Beyond the State—Private Security in International Politics* (Cambridge: Cambridge University Press, 2011). However, the role of these companies is not discussed in relation to the tasks of business associations.
25 ICS, "Piracy," www.ics-shipping.org/free-resources/piracy; ICC, "Maritime Piracy," https://iccwbo.org/global-issues-trends/trade-investment/maritime-pira cy/ (accessed 19 December 2017).
26 Carolin Liss and Jason C. Sharman, "Global Corporate Crime-Fighters: Private Transnational Responses to Piracy and Money Laundering," *Review of International Political Economy* 22, no. 4 (2015): 693–718.
27 ACAMS, "What is ACAMS?," www.acams.org/what-is-acams/ (accessed 20 September 2017).
28 Christopher D. McKenna, *The World's Newest Profession: Management Consulting in the Twentieth Century* (Cambridge: Cambridge University Press, 2010); Glenn Morgan, Andrew Sturdy and Michal Frenkel, "The Role of Large Management Consultancy Firms in Global Public Policy," in Diane Stone and Kim Moloney, eds, *Oxford Handbook of Global Policy and Transnational Administration* (Oxford: Oxford University Press, 2018). Some of this debate is related to exchanges between consulting firms and public sector organizations, while other parts of research discuss the role of these firms within business; see Colin Crouch, *The Knowledge Corrupters: Hidden Consequences of the Financial Takeover of Public Life* (Cambridge: Polity, 2016), 32–65.
29 Walter Kiechel III, *The Lords of Strategy: The Secret Intellectual History of the New Corporate World* (Boston: Harvard Business Review Press, 2010).
30 McKinsey, "About Us," www.mckinsey.com/about-us/social-impact (accessed 2 September 2016).
31 McKinsey, "About Us," www.mckinsey.com/about-us/social-impact (accessed 17 December 2017).

32 Again, we have to do with specific professions where various rules and norms apply, and where overlaps exist. Michael Power, *The Audit Society: Rituals of Verification* (Oxford: Oxford University Press, 1997).
33 Jochen Zimmermann, Jörg R. Werner and Philipp B. Volmer, *Global Governance in Accounting: Rebalancing Public Power and Private Commitment* (Houndmills: Palgrave, 2008).
34 Lyne Latullipe, "Tax Professionals and the Demand for Aggressive Tax Planning," in Richard Eccleston and Ainsley Elbra, eds, *Paying a Fair Share? Business, Civil Society and the "New" Politics of Corporate Tax Justice* (Cheltenham: Edward Elgar, 2018).
35 Timothy J. Sinclair, *The New Masters of Capital: American Bond Rating Agencies and the Politics of Creditworthiness* (Ithaca: Cornell University Press, 2005); Andreas Kruck, *Private Ratings, Public Regulations: Credit Rating Agencies and Global Financial Governance* (Houndmills: Palgrave, 2011).
36 Herwig M. Langohr and Patricia T. Langohr, *The Rating Agencies and Their Credit Ratings: What They Are, How They Work, and Why They are Relevant* (Chichester: Wiley, 2008).
37 Sandra Waddock, "Creating Corporate Accountability: Foundational Principles to Make Corporate Citizenship Real," *Journal of Business Ethics* 50, no. 4 (2004): 313–327.
38 Associational engagement may hail some members and damage the reputation of others, and IATA, for instance, refrains from issuing ratings on safety matters: www.iata.org/policy/Documents/safety-ratings-position-paper.pdfairplines (accessed 12 May 2017).
39 Drewry, "About Us," www.drewry.co.uk/about-us (accessed 16 June 2017).
40 ICIS, "Press Release," www.icis.com (accessed 16 June 2017).

6
CONCLUSION

- **Different associational formats**
- **Beyond associations**
- **Multiple forms of competition and cooperation**
- **Moving beyond existing theories: ways forward**

Global political activities of business are often equated with the stern efforts of large corporations, especially from the Western world, and their ambitions to control markets and ward off regulation challenging their operations while the empirical scrutiny and theoretical development of the collective organization of business interests are sidestepped. It is a strange irony, however, that global business is highly organized and abounds with a rich variety of associations and other collective entities.

It is, indeed, possible for not only large corporations but also many other groups of firms to rally around issues of mutual concern, build associations and sustain them over time. This does not rule out, of course, that corporations seek a number of highly individual goals, but it shows that global business has a rich repertoire and is able to permanently direct resources to organize and represent business.

The abundance of global associations further illustrates that business associability is by no means restricted to national domains. Business operations are transboundary, and it would only be logical if these economic activities were accompanied by parallel efforts to organize interests.

Business-government relations are very important at domestic levels, and down through history, economic interests of business and political interests of states are interwoven. There is a strong tradition of analyzing various "capitalisms," and in the "variety of capitalism research," the organization of business interests is one out of several variables used to describe and analyze different economic systems. It is important, however, that business is not understood exclusively in national contexts, and that further and more encompassing global forms of collective action are recognized, although all sectors of business are not equally globalized.

These findings have broader implications for the study of international affairs. Instead of perceiving business as an overly fragmented interest category, where collective action is missing and uncoordinated at the global level, we need a revised approach that elevates business to a stronger role in global politics. Prevailing theories on the dominance of states or the moral power of civil society groups in the international system need to be confronted with analyses that give the global business community a central place. Indeed, organized business is not just another group that deserves scholarly attention but should be ascribed a major role as a mobile and driving force in globalization and as a force that is both able to contribute to policy and adopt regulation to govern the market, yet at the same time is able to evade control.

Global business associations, together with a number of related organizations, in the business community provide many opportunities for contributing to global governance. Essentially, business associations are self-interested actors whose goal it is to represent the core economic interests of their members, but this does not exclude that they can engage with other public and private actors and sometimes provide solutions to intricate global problems. As such, associations are in a qualitatively different position than single corporations who can only engage on an individual basis and not on behalf of wider groups in business.

However, this situation does not suggest that associations can always be a stabilizing element. Neither is unitary action fostered with ease in global business, nor is social order brought into society with the effect that the different institutions provide an equilibrating system.[1] This also has consequences for the role of business in the broader context of global governance. Indeed, many economic, social, environmental and political crises cannot be properly remedied, and the strong and systematic tradition of organizing business in a collective framework does not in itself lead to better problem-solving or global order.

There are many factors that can prevent organized business from fully exhausting its potential as there are risks that firms and national associations will free-ride and avoid investing time and resources and, thus, make associations less representative than otherwise supposed. Also, the process of decision-making in global associations is highly complex, requiring the ability to reach compromises between stronger and weaker parts in business and avoid the dominance of large corporations or leading economies. Inside the associations, it is not always possible to unify interests, and powerful actors struggle for influence in the formulation of strategy. Between global associations, there can be many conflicts in defining and representing interests and they all work to stand their ground and position themselves. Finding an adequate division of labor between the many associations and between these and the many other entities present in the global business community are goals that must be worked for on a continuous basis. Notwithstanding these barriers, which influence the character and speed of collective action, there is a strong documentation of the diversity of associational action in the global business community but also theoretical arguments that explain these patterns of coordinated behavior.

In the following, we will discuss four major themes to synthesize the experiences from this book. First, the problems of dividing labor between the three types of associations, namely peak associations, industry associations, and alliances. Second, the management of tasks by entities outside the formal associational system and which both diverge from and overlap with traditional associations. Third, the different forms of competition and cooperation that characterize the relations between the many actors in the global business community. Fourth, the major shortcomings in existing theories to map and theorize organized business at the global level, how they can be mended, and how global business associations and related entities can be approached in future studies.

Different associational formats

Different business interests are organized and represented in the global arena, many of them through formal associations. The global business associations accommodate such diverse members and properties as, for instance, firms, product groups, industries, national businesses, single-issue-driven concerns, functions (producers and employers), and legal statuses (chambers of commerce). In some cases, associations build entirely on a single type of member while, in other cases, associations can have several types of members. Management of member relations is precarious, and we need further theoretical tools to analyze this problem.

Associations also respond to quite different institutional environments as some businesses are heavily regulated while others meet few political challenges and, in some cases, define a number of private rules and even have the capability to implement policy.[2] It is also of great importance that some areas are characterized by considerable globalization while other areas are mainly addressed at national levels and require other forms of coordination through the associations.

Revolving round a little more than a handful of organizations, the cluster of peak associations is quite small, and they all have to forge broad compromises and speak on behalf of exceedingly broad sections of the global business community. At first glance, they may seem rather similar and perhaps even too numerous to represent the general interests of global business, but a closer investigation shows that peak associations are not one thing. They are characterized by a significant degree of specialization as they cover different functions (employers and producers), legal statutes (chambers), and members (national associations and corporations), and there are also some differences in their global foundations and orientations toward IGOs, all factors that diminish competition between these bodies. Furthermore, they have strong and different historical roots, and nonetheless there is room for experiments, and new bodies have emerged.[3]

Yet, we find some overlap as some share certain member groups and engage in similar policy fields, although from slightly different perspectives and without the same clout. The associations try to avoid significant intersections, and, in some cases, they engage in coordination so as to use scarce resources effectively, but certain cases of duplication can be found. Efforts have been made to diminish overlap and even discuss amalgamations but, so far, initiatives have not been crowned with success, and there is no agreement on the desirability and feasibility of such projects. In the evolution of these associations, adaptation is not through a grand scheme but achieved by means of gradual adjustments.

The second cluster is constituted by global industry associations and is, indeed, populous.[4] The much narrower interests of industries shape their profiles, but industry associations are varied and cover a huge variety of organizational types, depending on their membership structure, governance and relations with other bodies in business as well as with regulatory authorities. There is usually a clear lead association that is able to speak authoritatively for an industry as a whole, and it is able to coordinate the interests of different national industries and member corporations, but their contributions to the global association tend to vary significantly.

Industry associations are comparatively close to markets and mirror changes in the industry more strongly and rapidly, such as the disappearance or introduction of new products and the crises or prospering of corporations.[5] Such material factors tend to have an immediate impact on industry associations and can ultimately foster their rise or decline. Moreover, global industry associations are exposed to developments in their political environments. Here, we may distinguish between industry associations that have a single and dominant interlocutor, such as shipping and airlines, and associations that have relations with a variety of intergovernmental agencies, such as chemicals and textiles. Formal recognition and unified pressure from key agencies seem to propel an especially high degree of coordination in business, fostering clear lead associations.[6] These mechanisms, however, need further scrutiny.

Alliances stand out as the third major avenue of organizing interests through global business. They are often significant, yet fluctuating, amorphous and hard to capture both empirically and theoretically. Alliances can mean many different things: cooperation between selected corporations in an industry, cross-industry cooperation, cooperation between peak associations, and a combination of these and other principles. Flexibility is key. This also applies to the life-cycle of the alliances. They are often formed to provide ad hoc cooperation in a new or neglected field and can be dissolved once tasks have been addressed, but there is also the possibility that alliances become permanent and eventually evolve into industry or peak associations.

The role of alliances in relation to peak and industry associations is complex. On the one hand, the formation of alliances may indicate that existing associations are not in a position to take on board certain pertinent issues, and therefore have to surrender a niche to the alliances. On the other hand, alliances may ease the burden on existing associations in cases where they find it difficult to manage new or difficult issues dividing members, and hence accept or even find it worthwhile to engage in some kind of labor division with relevant alliances. Our cases show that it is primarily the latter understanding of alliances that is most promising, but our knowledge is too limited to draw any final conclusion.

Action through business associations is an exceedingly common practice in global business, with many organizational formats available. Clearly, it was useful to establish three fundamental and complementary categories (peak, industry, and alliances). They are typical manifestations of collective action for different groups in business, but it was also evident there were interesting variations within each of these three categories. We need to establish a taxonomy that captures how different formats have evolved over time and how they are currently related, an independent and important task that must not be halted by demands to examine the influence of business, which is a recurrent theme in the study of politics and business. Reflecting varied approaches in different sections of the business community and unifying various national practices at the global level, it is evident that it is difficult to place the many organizational formats in a clear and strong taxonomy, and much more work has to be put into such an endeavor to better appreciate variation.

Beyond associations

The organization of interests in the global business community is not limited to associations. We find other actors that, in one way or another, share some of the multiple functions managed by associations or otherwise affect their work.[7] Several actors in the global business community are not organized as associations proper, and hence, they are not compelled to demonstrate any kind of representativeness on behalf of business in general or to speak for specific industries. It is not only useful, but necessary to combine different scholarships.

Essentially, these actors are of a qualitatively different character than associations. They seek various forms of support and need to attract resources in the market, and economic performance is essential. They do not all recruit members to become active in political affairs, and, as a consequence, they are not engaged in the burdensome coordination of heterogeneous member interests and in the adoption of consolidated opinions, and, hence, are not exposed to the same kind of collective-action problems.[8]

Although they are distinctly different from global associations, there is no agreed-upon order that defines the tasks of these different entities in the business community, and overlap is therefore not unusual. Moreover, many associations and the related entities studied in this book become involved in a number of similar functions over time by means of expansion. Indeed, we find numerous examples of actors engaging in the production and dissemination of knowledge and in the marketing of various forms of services.[9]

There are entities that come rather close to associations, especially different clubs that often have a broad profile and do not appeal to particular segments of business, such as industries. Clubs are typically based on various groups of business executives, and a significant income accrued through membership fees. Some are highly exclusive, even secretive, and only recruit a few people in business, often by invitation, while other clubs are very open and aim to enlist as many members as possible. As such, there are many similarities with the typical business associations, but unlike associations, the clubs tend to emphasize social benefits for their members, and many clubs prefer to keep a relatively low profile in political matters. Such an understanding carries much of their work. Clubs do not represent their members in any strict and binding sense, and do not become involved in regulatory issues to define or implement policy, but, again to varying degrees, they convey a number of general messages to the business community and to political institutions in their environment.

Another entity that, at least in certain respects, comes close to associations, are the various think tanks that today thrive in global politics. What associations and think tanks may have in common is that they engage in the production of various forms of knowledge that they, like many other actors, bring into politics, and knowledge is an important factor in the representation and legitimation of business interests. However, think tanks are much easier to distinguish from associations than are clubs. Think tanks generally put great emphasis on conducting independent research and, in principle, avoid becoming directed by any particular group, although some adopt business-friendly strategies. Today, most think tanks are not fully geared toward the global realm and do not encroach on the domain of global business associations to any significant degree.

In addition to clubs and think tanks, a number of other entities, together labelled facilitators, have been analyzed in this book. This category embraces a rich diversity of organizations, such as public affairs bureaus, consultancy firms, self-regulating bodies, law firms, credit rating agencies, accounting and auditing firms, business and information services, as well as firms providing security. At first glance, these facilitators may seem quite distant from associations: they do not have members, they do not engage explicitly in the representation of any interest, and their scene is the market where they provide different services on a commercial basis to clients. Nonetheless, there are interesting parallels in the work of associations and facilitators.

In fact, business associations develop some of the same services and make these available to their members and, under specific conditions, also to non-members. To keep members and attract new ones, it is important that global business associations have something to offer and do not leave these activities to other actors. Indeed, business associations need different sources of income to boost their resources and provide a solid background for their political work. With profound insight into business and into particular industries, the provision of various services is an organic extension of other activities. Of course, there is a huge variation in the extent to which associations and facilitators engage in similar activities, a pattern that needs to be analyzed in each case, but a general conclusion suggests that the profiles of associations and facilitators are not always sharply demarcated.

If we limit our analysis of organized business to formal associations, which have unique tasks to perform, we only get a partial understanding of the complex population of business actors in global politics. Actors beyond associations create norms and values that are important in the global business community, and these actors constitute an exceedingly diverse group where an equally diverse set of theories are needed to capture activities. Available theories, however, rarely take an interest in how these actors can be related to the role of associations.[10] Efforts must be made to better understand this relationship. Without challenging the core political work of the associations, a number of other actors have parallel functions and may either assist the performance of associations or take important activities away from them in ways that can ultimately threaten their existence.

Multiple forms of competition and cooperation

To understand the conditions facing the many different associational and non-associational actors in the global business community, concepts of competition and cooperation are pivotal as these principles govern not only the relations between members of associations but also relations between the various categories of actors analyzed in this book. In analyzing the different organizations' profiles, we have briefly discussed certain aspects of competition and cooperation as they apply to the member levels (i.e., primarily firms and national associations), and as they affect associations and various cognate entities, and in the following, we give greater weight to the application of these principles. However, competition and cooperation are between highly aggregated actors, some of which are active in politics and some of which are active in markets, factors that complicate the analysis to a significant degree.

The few peak business associations that exist today in the global realm have fairly well-defined domains, but at first glance, they seem rather identical in their ambition to organize and represent general business

Conclusion 173

interests. They are, however, quite diverse in terms of membership. Members—national associations and corporations—are simply too varied to gather in a single and coherent organization. In addition, their policy focus is different. Some are relatively narrow in scope while others address a huge number of issues. While there is clearly encouragement from individual IGOs to organize business through unified associations (for instance, BIAC in the context of the OECD, and IOE in the context of the ILO), there is no overarching body that compels the world's businesses to become represented through a single encompassing association. This division of labor does not suggest that competition is absent but that competition is between associations with somewhat different profiles, or in other words, all the organizations are subspecies of peak associations and display variation in membership base and in policy focus.[11] Yet, these relations are not settled once and for all. For instance, the associations tend to expand into new policy areas and come to address a number of the same issues, leading to gradual changes in the character and degree of competition, but competition hinges on their adaptive behavior and ability to avoid clear overlaps.

The general situation among global industry associations is rather different with their comparatively clear focus and circumscribed niches. In the cases reviewed in this book (and the many more that exist across industries), there is typically a major organization that represents the broad interests of the industry concerned, but several organizations in its surroundings may manage specific tasks and sometimes even encroach on its domain.[12] Competition, therefore, tends to be moderate. This is, in many cases, both the result of an internal historical process within an industry and the effect of external recognition granted by specific intergovernmental agencies that can be found in relation to several industries.

Our knowledge of the various alliances is still too limited to arrive at any solid conclusion. The alliances are created in many different ways that bring evidence of their relations or lack of relations with existing associations, be they at the peak or industry level. Further insights will help us identify potential elements of competition. However, the formation of alliances is, for instance, attributable to the inattention of associations, the active delegation to alliances or the surrendering of tasks, and new alliances can, therefore, become competitors or partners to existing associations. They may build on some of the same members, and they may address identical issues, but alliances can also fill important gaps and be welcomed.

Competition also exists between associations and all related entities. This is, however, not competition between the same kind of actors, and we can therefore label this interspecific competition to stress these different conditions.[13] If actors beyond associations were to represent the same section of business and concentrate on the same tasks as associations, we would expect fierce competition, eventually leading to hard selection, but that is not the case here. In fact, associations have other jobs to perform than clubs, think tanks and service providers of different kinds. Yet, it would be a mistake to deny any kind of competition. Obviously, some activities and some of these non-associational actors are more likely to come into competition with associations but not necessarily to the same extent with each of the three associational categories discussed here. Ultimately, only a differentiated analysis on specific associations and specific, related entities can map and characterize the exact patterns of competition, but competition will, of course, be strongest where associations and kindred actors host more or less the same ambitions. Some associations will, for instance, find it natural to pay significant attention to self-regulatory matters and involve their members in such activities while other associations are committed to particular forms of information and press activity on behalf of an industry. If independent bodies, including the many facilitators, engage in similar activities, competition may be profound.

Another pertinent issue is whether the management of certain activities is important to the survival of associations. If there is competition around some activities that are of minor importance to the profile of associations and to their income, we can expect that this will take a moderate form. On the contrary, where some of the many related entities pose a serious challenge to associations, competition will be much stronger, even if the entities' goal in no way is to replace associations but "only" to win some market segments important to their own survival.

Moving beyond existing theories: ways forward

Businesses and business associations are recognized as important factors in studies on domestic politics and the changes it undergoes,[14] although there is strong variation in the role of associational action. Business, a transboundary actor, extends its various organizations and increasingly connects national and international associations, but it is not correct that business is relatively organized in domestic contexts while lacking or fragmented on the global scene. Indeed, business associations and other organizations in the business community are abundant in the real world of global politics and involved in many policy fields, but they are not equally recognized in research.

It is important that research on global business associations stands on its own feet, but many links can be forged with existing and often mutually divided theories. Several theories have grappled with aspects of politics and business in a global context but tend to eke out business associations and their diverse manifestations of collective behavior. There is obviously a preference for either studying the macro-structures (social classes or states as bodies representing the ruling classes), or the micro-structures (corporations, especially MNCs), if the really active role of business in politics is not entirely ignored in international studies.

This absence is probably related to the various disciplinary backgrounds that explicitly or implicitly inform research, where states (in political science and international relations), or individual corporations (in economics, management and business administration), seem to spill over into studies on global politics and business. Also, international political economy, a transdisciplinary set of approaches, stresses the role of "states and markets," but these categories are too crude to capture the involvement of business in global politics. In this research, intermediate structures, such as associations, are less attended too. However, there is nothing that prevents a number of traditions, such as international political economy, international political sociology, economic sociology and INGO studies, from embracing and integrating the role of associations into their various approaches. Indeed, the integration of business associations into these different strands of research could, in many ways, give them a much stronger platform and potentially boost their influence among other theories on international affairs.

Orthodox theories on comparative politics and international relations keep insisting on the dominance of states, but some schools and approaches seek to integrate a business dimension: corporate preferences may inform the international behavior of states, and states may represent business as part of their foreign policy.[15] Also, certain IGOs, such as the WTO and the OECD, can be seen as promoting business-friendly agendas, formulating ideas, and adopting rules that meet the expectations of business. These studies emphasize important dimensions of international affairs, but they inadequately capture the role of organized business in the global arena. A major problem is that agency in business is lacking. Business interests cannot be properly taken care of by various proxies, either at domestic or at international levels, but need their own independent organizations. Other actors cannot identify and define interests on behalf of business and speak with the same kind of zest and authority, and business needs various forums to bring its own experiences and priorities into deliberation, negotiation, and action.

However, global business is not a unified actor, and agency is complex. Obviously, a general recognition of the intermediate structures that we find between the macro-structures and micro-structures is only a starting point. The population-ecology approach that, in recent years, has been employed to study IGOs, also has an interesting and, as yet, unexploited potential for the study of private organizations.[16]

While states are the basic units behind these intergovernmental agencies, business is a far more diverse category behind the business associations and other entities in business, and organizational variation in business is important. This makes the study on the evolution of associations, as well as other organizations of business, more complex because several factors have to be taken into account. First, business is not represented through single national associations in global business associations but through several functional associations (for instance, producer, employer, and chamber organizations), and this brings stronger diversity into the organization of private business interests than into the organization of public organizations, such as agencies. Second, members of global associations are not only constituted by various national associations but also include corporations that enjoy direct membership, and corporations can be represented on their own and through multiple national associations. In sum, this brings comparatively strong diversity into the composition of business associations and new thinking on global business associations as part of an organizational ecology is consequently needed.

Furthermore, diversity is also manifested in special ways in the different levels of organizations, and we have identified three basic categories, namely peak associations, industry associations, and alliances. These organizational levels cannot be defined through insights from general population ecology, but must be established on the basis of the concrete empirical situation in business. These levels do not produce a complete and final taxonomy, and further studies can reveal other relevant categories, and, by all means, new dynamics can foster additional forms of organization.

To recognize the full variation in the business community, a population-ecology approach has to take account of the many actors that are organized beyond the associations and do not always have explicit political purposes. It is important to define populations of associations and their various subcategories because different conditions apply to these different levels of collective action, but at the same time, it is necessary to adopt a flexible strategy and recognize the porous boundaries between associations and related entities in a broader population ecology when studying the global

Conclusion 177

business community. Indeed, many other actors have similar functions, and they have proliferated over recent decades. On a commercial basis, they offer services that appeal to the members of associations or to the associations themselves, suggesting that associations are being challenged in their established domains or when adding new activities to their portfolio. This evolution is likely to continue in the future and lead to greater and more subtle forms of complementarity between actors, but there is also a risk that such changes will erode the resource basis of global business associations and, eventually, jeopardize their role as actors in global politics. A variety of scenarios will be in store.

Notes

1 Wolfgang Streeck, *How Will Capitalism End?* (London: Verso, 2016).
2 This suggests that business associations are not merely "pressure groups" that from the outside seek to influence IGOs, but that these agencies make strong and systematic efforts to structure their environment. Kenneth W. Abbott, Philipp Genschel, Duncan Snidal and Bernhard Zangl, "Orchestration: Global Governance through Intermediaries," in Kenneth W. Abbott, Philipp Genschel, Duncan Snidal and Bernhard Zangl, eds, *International Organizations as Orchestrators* (Cambridge: Cambridge University Press, 2015), 3–36. This argument is strongly reminiscent of the neo-corporatist debate in the 1970s and 1980s where exchanges were mapped and theorized. The discipline of comparative politics was faster to recognize these patterns than were international relations studies.
3 Karsten Ronit, "Global Employer and Business Associations: Their Relations with Members in the Development of Mutual Capacities," *European Review of International Studies* 3, no. 1 (2016): 53–77.
4 UIA, *Yearbook of International Organizations* (Leiden: Brill, n.d.).
5 Material approaches can provide important explanations for associational life and many basic inspirations can be found. Fernand Braudel, *The Structures of Everyday Life* (Vol. 1), *The Wheels of Commerce* (Vol. 2), *The Perspective of the World* (Vol. 3) (Berkeley: University of California Press, 1992).
6 An interesting exemption to this "rule" is the food industry which has many specialized associations but one major IGO in the shape of FAO. Cooperation is highly institutionalized, see FAO, *FAO Strategy for Partnerships with Civil Society Organizations* (Rome: FAO, 2013).
7 All these actors belong to a complex system and can, in part, be analyzed with the help of concepts in population ecology: Joel A.C. Baum and Andrew Shipilov, "Ecological Approaches to Organizations," in Stewart R. Clegg, Cynthia Hardy, Thomas B. Lawrence and Walter R. Nord, eds, *The Sage Handbook of Organization Studies* (London: Sage, 2006), 55–110.
8 Clubs are related to networks but network theory is generally too abstract to capture the empirical phenomenon of clubs. For an attempt to discuss the role of clubs: J. Rogers Hollingsworth and Robert Boyer, "Coordination of Economic Actors and Social System of Production," in J. Rogers Hollingsworth

and Robert Boyer, eds, *Contemporary Capitalism: The Embeddedness of Institutions* (Cambridge: Cambridge University Press, 1997).
9 Max Weber referred to these kinds of association as "wirtschaftender Verband" and "Wirtschaftsverband," i.e. associations doing business themselves and business associations: Max Weber, *Wirtschaft und Gesellschaft* (Tübingen: J.C.B. Mohr) (Paul Siebeck, 1985 [1922]), 37–38.
10 J. Rogers Hollingsworth, Philipppe C. Schmitter and Wolfgang Streeck, "Capitalism, Sectors, Institutions, and Performance," in J. Rogers Hollingsworth, Philippe C. Schmitter and Wolfgang Streeck, eds, *Governing Capitalist Economies: Performance and Control of Economic Sectors* (Oxford: Oxford University Press, 1994), 3–16; Avner Greif, "Commitment, Coercion and Markets: The Nature and Dynamics of Institutions Supporting Exchange," in Claude Ménard and Mary M. Shirley, eds, *Handbook of New Institutional Economics* (New York: Springer, 2005), 727–788.
11 Basic insights from biology in analyzing taxonomic ranks, such as subspecies, can be utilized to classify associations, and in this case peak associations. Ernst Mayr, "Working on Classifying Species and Subspecies" (39/150), YouTube (accessed 24 August 2017).
12 ICS, *Representing the Global Shipping Industry* (London: ICS, 2013), 4.
13 Just referring to competition would miss the qualitatively different forms of competition. Applying scientific advances in biology, we can distinguish between intraspecific and interspecific competition: Ernst Mayr, *This is Biology: The Science of the Living World* (Cambridge: The Belknap Press of Harvard University Press, 1997), 212–214.
14 Wolfgang Streeck, Jürgen R. Grote, Volker Schneider and Jelle Visser, eds, *Governing Interests: Business Associations Facing Internationalization* (London: Routledge, 2006).
15 Recognizing domestic forces has always been one of the keys to understanding the role of business in global politics: Peter Gourevitch, "The Second Image Reversed: The International Sources of Domestic Politics," *International Organization* 32, no. 4 (1978): 881–912; Robert D. Putnam, "Diplomacy and Domestic Politics: The Logic of Two-Level Games," *International Organization* 42, no. 3 (1988): 427–460.
16 Rafael Biermann and Joachim A. Koops, eds, *Palgrave Handbook of Inter-Organizational Relations in World Politics* (London: Palgrave, 2016).

BIBLIOGRAPHY

The overwhelming part of business-association studies is devoted to domestic and comparative politics emphasizing cross-country variation, and to a smaller degree cross-industry differences. Given the strong globalization of business, this situation is rather strange. However, certain aspects of this literature have the potential to inform the study on global business associations as well, for instance when linkages between national and international activities are addressed, when similar problems are examined, or when generic issues are discussed with an ambition to foster general theory on business associability.

Of course, reasons are more compelling to review literatures on the organizations of global business, but contributions are relatively few and research is fragmented. Given the apparent scarcity of research into global business association, the search must be extended to a somewhat broader interpretation of global politics and business interests, and to studies that also grapple with domestic, comparative or generic issues.

Various classics in political science, sociology and business administration deal in incisive ways with business and politics, and we find interesting studies on some global associations, such as organizational monographs, from the past. However, an inclusion of such a vast body of research would expand the boundary for what a select bibliography permits. The select bibliography, here presented in alphabetical order, offers suggestions for further reading, but only work from recent decades is included, and only book-length studies. In the bibliography, I have omitted my own work but references to this can be found in the individual chapters.

John Braithwaite and Peter Drahos, eds. *Global Business Regulation* (Cambridge: Cambridge University Press, 2000).

This big volume covers a multiplicity of industries and how they are regulated, and it provides analyses on the historical background of regulation. Different analytical approaches are developed, and industries are put into economic and political contexts. The book is particularly strong on public policy and regulation, but it also addresses the work of a number of international associations and how they are involved in various forms of global problem-solving. Associations are not central in the analysis but seen as one group out of many players in the business community.

Doris Fuchs, *Business Power in Global Governance* (Lynne Rienner, 2007).

This book does a good job addressing a range of issues on business and political power at a more generic level and discusses how business contributes to governance at the international level. Transnational corporations occupy the central role, but the many themes of the book also embrace associations, although their role is not carved out. However, the book offers many useful perspectives to the study of global business associations, and is particularly strong in taking up the perennial issue of power, not specifically dealt with in this volume. Fuchs's book has certain affinities with studies done back in the 1960s and 1970s in Germany and continental Europe, some of which are completely redundant, some of which could be revisited. To some extent, this shows that the power of business is a classic issue, and that research has not moved so much forward in recent decades.

Justin Greenwood and Henry P. Jacek, eds. *Organized Business and the New Global Order* (London: Macmillan, 2000).

This book moves beyond the traditional national and comparative focus and sees business as organized at the global level through associations. As an anthology, it brings many different authors and approaches together, its clear strength, but it is less precise in offering a coherent theoretical perspective. It covers different sectors, highlights the role of associations and offers explanations of why studies of business and international relations are not integrated. Although published almost two decades ago, many arguments found in the book are still valuable.

Avner Greif, "Commitment, Coercion, and Markets: The Nature and Dynamics of Institutions Supporting Exchange," in C. Ménard and M. Shirley eds., *Handbook of New Institutional Economics* (The Netherlands: Springer, 2005), 727–786.

This chapter, written in the tradition of economic history and new institutionalism, identifies a number of intermediary institutions between state and market that play important roles in norm and rule building. Business associations are not the key object of scrutiny, but they assume certain roles in the regulation of the economy and thus compete or cooperate with other institutions that the chapter seeks to classify. As such, the chapter includes some of the related entities, for instance some of the facilitators, treated in this volume.

Bibliography 181

Jürgen R. Grote, Achim Lang and Volker Schneider, eds. *Organized Business Interests in Changing Environments* (Houndmills: Palgrave, 2008).

This work reports some of the findings of larger research projects, and it provides interesting reflections on the adaptation of business associations to internationalization, in particular to Europeanization. It sees associations as a key form of business representation, and it utilizes different concepts and ideas from studies on evolution and adapts them to particular cases. Some of these reflections are also useful in the study of global business associations.

Heather McKeen-Edwards and Tony Porter, *Transnational Financial Associations and the Governance of Global Finance. Assembling Wealth and Power* (London and New York: Routledge, 2013).

This book does not study business in broad terms but is a rather specialized volume on the organization of the financial industry. There is a rich tradition of IPE studies on finance but few highlight the role of associations. One of the strengths of the book is that it goes through various sectors of the financial industry and is not limited to, for instance, banking. It identifies various types of tasks lifted by the associations but mainly inductively, and based of the self-presentation of organizations.

Philippe C. Schmitter and Wolfgang Streeck, *The Organization of Business Interests. A Research Design to Study the Associative Action of Business in the Advanced Industrial Societies of Western Europe* (Cologne: MPIFG, 1999).

This study was originally published in 1981 to guide comparative research on the "Organization of Business Interest," dubbed the OBI-Project, in Western Europe and North America (especially Canada). It provides interesting discussions on relevant classics in political science, sociology and management that have something to say about the part played by business associations in markets, societies and politics. It develops a design identifying the different and contradictory demands that business associations must confront in the organization and representation of interests. With associations as the key unit of analysis, primary weight is on the internal processes of associations as well as on their institutional environments, and it is still a key work on "business association theory" that researchers can draw on.

Christian Tietje and Alan Brouder, eds. *Handbook of Transnational Economic Governance Regimes* (Leiden: Brill, 2009).

The book has many entries and lexicographic articles that portray a number of relevant associations, some of them also analyzed in this book. It traces some of the major developments in selected organizations and offers quick insights into their historical roots and traditions, but the book is not focused on associations *per se*. It is not always clear what have been the criteria for the selection of concrete entries, and both public and private bodies are included. The analytical side is therefore weaker, but this challenge is also difficult in a handbook of this kind.

Kees van der Pijl, *Transnational Classes and International Relations* (London and New York: Routledge, 1998).

This book sees capital as organized at the international level, not necessarily at the global stage, and recognizes that business is not just acting through multinational corporations. The book traces historical developments and offers interesting interpretations of various classics and their relevance for transnational classes. The material basis of business provides the foundation for political action, and the role of social class, a highly aggregated and abstract concept, is central. However, attention is also given to associations as important entities that coordinate interests, and also other organizations in business are reviewed.

INDEX

Page numbers in *italics* refer to figures; page numbers in **bold** refer to tables; 'n' after a page number indicates the endnote number.

Academy Awards 157
ACAMS (Association of Certified Anti-Money Laundering Specialists) 152
ACC (American Chemistry Council) 73
Accenture 101, 152–3, *153*
accounting and auditing firms 141–2, 154–6, 161; *see also* facilitator actor 115; business actor 7, 14, 135, 172; collective actor 7; global actor 24, 129, 153, 154
advertising industry 81–2; ICC and 34, 68, 82; *see also* industry association
airline industry 58, 72, 76–9, 169; *see also* industry association
Alibaba Group 104
alliance of corporations and associations 13, 90–2, 110–11, 112n12, 169, 176; advantages of 13, 92, 111; building of 93–5, 98, 100; challenges/dilemmas 92–9, 104; civil society and 95, 102; collective action 93, 98–9, 109, 110, 169–70; competition and cooperation 94–5, 97, 99, 100, 111, 169, 173; diversity 90–1, 103, 110; global alliance 91, 108, 109; goals 92, 97; hybrid membership 102, 111n2; IGOs and 95, 97–8, 110; in/across industries 94–5, 110; membership 91, 92, 110; MNCs 91, 95,102, 104, 107, 108, 109; multiple and variable roots of alliances *93*; niche 92, 96, 109, 111, 169; old roots/fresh initiatives 93–4, 110; overlapping 111; population of 91; public regulation 108, 109, 110; rationales for creating alliances 91, 92, 169, 173; self-regulation 92, 98, 100, 107, 108, 109; state/market-related 97–8, 110; tasks: broad/narrow issues 96–7, 110; taxonomy of 99, 111n1; temporary/permanent cooperation 95–6, 107, 110, 169
ASC (Aquaculture Stewardship Council) 147

B20 (Business 20 Coalition) 43–4, 50n14, 54n53; *see also* GBC
Bain & Company 152–3

184 Index

Bank of America 104
BBC (BRICS Business Council) 29, 45–7, *46*; BRICS countries 45; BRICS institutionalization 28, 46; BRICS summits 45, 46; Council and chapters 46–7; market orientation 25; membership 24, *30*, 45; origins 44–5; policy field 25, 47; roles 46; secretariat 47; service provision 27, 47
BDI (Bundesverband der Deutschen Industrie/Federation of German Industries) 54n53
BIAC (Business and Industry Advisory Committee to the OECD) 38–9, 100; market orientation 25; membership 24, 25, *30*, 38, 39; OECD and 28, 38, 39, 50n10, 173; origins 38; policy field 25–6, 38; resources 39; roles 38; secretariat 39; service provision 27; unions and 29
The Bilderberg Meetings (Bilderberg Club) 120–2, *121*; capitalism 117, 121, 123; political ambitions 120, 123
Bill & Melinda Gates Foundation **127**, 133–4
BIMCO (Baltic and International Maritime Council) 62, 76, 77, 140–1
BIS (Bank for International Settlements) 80
Booking.com 157
Boston Consulting Group 152–3, *153*
BRICS (Brazil, Russia, India, China, South Africa) 25; *see also* BBC
Brookings, Robert S. 130
Brookings Institution **127**, 130–1, 138n30
BUSA (Business Unity South Africa) 54n60
Business Africa 52n29
Business and Industry Major Group 113n15
business/business community 115, 134–5, 140, 165, 174; business actor 7, 14, 135, 172; collective action 2, 4, 6, 10, 14, 15; complementarities in 11–12; global business association and 4, 11, 15; global governance and 14–15, 166; global politics and 166, 174; IGOs and 9; state and business 9, 19n30, 166
Business Europe 44, 52n29
business media and information services 142, 158–60; *see also* facilitator

CAPE (Confederation of Asia-Pacific Employers) 52n29
capitalism 10, 117, 121, 123, 135, 166; capitalist class 7–8, 11; civilized capitalism 133; inclusive capitalism 125; moral capitalism 124
Carnegie, Andrew 129
Carnegie Endowment for International Peace 117, **127**, 129–30
CCI Russia (Chamber of Commerce and Industry of the Russian Federation) 54n60
CCOIC (China Chamber of International Commerce) 54n60
CCPIT (China Council for the Promotion of International Trade) 54n60
CEATAL (Business Technical Advisory Committee on Labor Matters) 52n29
CEFIC (European Chemical Industry Council) 73, 85n13
chemical industry 72–4, 83, 169; *see also* industry association; pharmaceutical industry
Chevron Corporation 101
civil society 1, 15; alliance of corporations and associations and 95, 102; facilitator and 146, 156, 157; global business associations and 14, 15; industry association and 57, 64, 73; peak association and 27, 31; self-regulation 147; think tank and 128; *see also* NGO
club 13, 101, 115–17, 134–6, 170–1, 177n8; agenda-setting 116, 135, 136n1; association-like features 115–16, 136, 136n1; clubs/associations distinction 118, 125, 136n3; clubs in business 117–26, 139n40; clubs/think tanks common features 116, 118, 123; collective action 117; diversity 116, 135; elite nature of 123, 171;

Index

membership 116, 117, 118, 119, 120–1, 123, 134; MNCs 120; policy and 13, 119, 120, 136n5; social function/benefits 92, 117, 119, 121, 123, 136n2, 171; tasks 11, 13, 118, 135, 136
CNI (National Confederation of Industry) 54n60
Coalition for Inclusive Capitalism 125–6
Coca-Cola Company 67, 108
Codex Alimentarius Commission 68
collective action 1–2, 4, 6, 12, 61, 90, 166, 167, 176; alliance of corporations and associations 93, 98–9, 109, 110, 169–70; business and 2, 4, 6, 10, 14, 15; club 117; industry association 57, 58, 65, 67, 73, 75, 80, 169–70; peak association 24, 35, 36, 40, 42, 44, 48, 49n1, 169–70
Commission on Global Governance 14
comparative politics 10, 175, 177n2
competition and cooperation 12, 172–4; alliance of corporations and associations 94–5, 97, 99, 100, 111, 169, 173; associations/related entities competition 12, 173–4; IATA 78, 79; industry association 58, 59–60, 61, 65, 78, 83, 173; interspecific competition 174, 178n13; peak association 13, 23, 25, 48, 49, 168, 173
consulting firm 136, 142, 144, 145, 152–4, 161; *see also* facilitator
Container Spot Market Freight Rate Index 159
corporate social responsibility 26, 101, 119, 124, 132
CRT (Caux Round Table) 123–5; CRT Principles for Business 124; Principles for Government 124

Deloitte Consulting 152–3, *153*, 155
democracy 129, 131, 133
developed country 5, 24, 78
developing country 24, 35, 69
division of labor 12, 45, 134, 151, 166, 167–70; peak association 25, 26, 48; *see also* niche; overlapping domain

DNV GL Group (Det Norske Veritas) 148
Drewry 159

EABC (European-American Business Council) 137n12
ECOSOC (Economic and Social Council, UN) 51n19, 120
Ernst & Young 152–3, *153*, 155

Facebook 40, 83, 138n37
facilitator 14, 140–2, 160–1, 171–2; association-like features 171–2; civil society and 146, 156, 157; definition 141; facilitators/think tanks common features 128, 135, 136; functions and tasks 14, 141, 142–5, *144*, 160; globalization of 146, 149; IACC 113n28; IGOs and 143, 146; market facilitation 141, 142; overlapping 144, 149, 152, 156; political issues 143, 145, 152; public regulation 14, 141, 142, 143, 150, 155, 159; reputational matters 14, 141, 145, 146, 148, 150, 158; research/knowledge-based tasks 135, 136, 143; *see also* accounting and auditing firms; business media and information services; consulting firm; law firm; public affairs and public relations bureaus; rating agency; security and crime protection; self-regulator
FAO (Food and Agriculture Organization, UN) 68, 177n6
FBN-I (Family Business Network International) 102–103; family ownership 102
FICCI (Federation of Indian Chambers of Commerce and Industry) 47, 54n60
FIDO (Fast IDentity Online Alliance) 103–107, 110; goal 104; membership 104, **105–106**
film industry 157
finance industry 79–81; banking 79; globalization and 79; security problems 151–2; *see also* industry association

FIO Network (Food Information Organization Network) 68, 86n26
Fitch Ratings 156
food industry 66–8, 108–10, 114n31, 177n6; *see also* industry association
Ford, Henry 131
Ford Foundation **127**, 131–2
Ford Motor Company 131
FSB (Financial Stability Board) 80
FSC (Forest Stewardship Council) 147

G5 (Group of Five) 44
G7 (Group of Seven) 54n53
G20 (Group of Twenty) 29, 44, 50n14, 72, 80; GBC and G20 summits 26, 28, 43, 45
GAA (Global Accounting Alliance) 111n3
GAA (Global Agri-business Alliance) 114n31
GAN (Global Apprenticeships Network) 35
Gates, Bill 133
GATF (Global Alliance for Trade Facilitation) 111n2
GATT (General Agreement on Tariffs and Trade) 70
GBA (Global Business Alliance for 2030) 99–100, 110
GBC (Global Business Coalition) 24, 25, 29, 43–5; B20 Coalition 43–4, 50n14, 54n53; collective action 44; G20 summits 26, 28, 43, 45; leadership and structure 44–5; membership *30*, 44; Russia and China 44; secretariat 45; service provision 27; tasks 43
GBC-Education (Global Business Coalition for Education) 100–102
GFMA (Global Financial Market Association) 79
GIRN (Global Industrial Relations Network) 35
Giscard d'Estaing, Olivier 123
global business association 1, 165–6, 169–70; business community and 4, 11, 15; civil society and 14, 15; concept 2–3; diversity 2, 8, 14, 47, 166, 176; global governance and 14, 166; global level of 5, 17n11, 29, 168; globalization and 1, 5, 6, 19n26; history of 1, 5–6, 48; IGOs and 15, 177n2; importance of 1–2; market and 14, 15; membership 3–4, 5, 10, 49n3, 167–8, 176; niche 16n7; organizational properties 3–5; policy fields 3, 4, 5, 10, 15, 168; political orientation 3, 4; private nature of 4, 6; research on 2, 7–11, 174–7; roles and tasks 2, 12, 14, 15; service provision 171–2; state and 14, 15; territorial levels 3, 4–5; *see also* alliance of corporations and associations; industry association; peak association; related private entities
global governance 14–15, 166
globalization 56, 83, 119, 166; facilitator, globalization of 146, 149; finance industry and 79; global actor 24, 129, 153, 154; global business associations and 1, 5, 6, 19n26; internationalization and 5; think tank, globalization of 126, 128, 130, 132, 134
Google 40, 83, 104
GOSH (Global Occupational Safety & Health Network) 35
Gucci 101
Gurría, Ángel 28

IAA (International Advertising Association) 81
IAB (Interactive Advertising Bureau) 88–9n63
IACC (International AntiCounterfeiting Coalition) 91, 107–108, 110, 113n28; membership 108; public regulation 107, 108
IAFN (International Agri-Food Network) 114n31
IASB (International Accounting Standards Board) 155
IATA (International Air Transport Association) 63, 76, 78–9, 88n54, 164n38; competition 78, 79; IGOs

and 78; membership 58, 76, 78; service provision 79, 88n54
IBA (International Bar Association) 163n21
IBCC (International Bureau of Chambers of Commerce) 52n31
IBFed (International Banking Federation) 80–1, 88n58
IBLF Global (International Business Leaders Forum Global) 137n19
ICA (International Court of Arbitration) 34, 51n17, 148
ICAO (International Civil Aviation Organization) 63, 78
ICB (Industry Classification Benchmark) 84n2
ICBA (International Council of Beverages Associations) 59, 67; International Council of Beverages Associations Guidelines on Marketing to Children 68
ICC (International Chamber of Commerce) 6, 24, 31–4, 37, 148; advertising 34, 68, 82; arbitration 34, 51n17; GBA and 100; headquarters 32, 33, 37; ICC Framework for Responsible Food and Beverage Market Communication 68; IGOs/ other actors and 28–9, 32; legal expertise 149; market orientation 25; membership 30, 32, 51n20; national chambers 32–3, 37; origins 31–2, 34; policy field 25, 26, 28; resources 33–4; role 32, 37, 50n7; secretariat 34, 37; self-regulation 25, 34; service provision 26–7, 34, 140; shipping and 76; sustainability issues 53n46; UN observer status 51n19; WCF and 36–7
ICCA (International Council of Chemical Associations) 59, 73–4; Responsible Care Programs 74; secretariat 62, 73–4, 85n13
ICCIMB (International Maritime Bureau) 76
ICIS (Independent Chemical Information Service) 159
ICMM (International Council of Mining and Minerals) 65–6

ICS (International Chamber of Shipping) 6, 63, 74–6, 87n45; Cyber Security Onboard Ships 76, 77; IGOs and 76, 87n47; maritime policy 74, 75; piracy 76; secretariat 75; service provision 75–6
ICTA (International Chemical Trade Association) 87n40
IDC (International Diamond Council) 65
IFBA (International Food and Beverage Alliance) 86n24, 91, 108–109
IFPMA (International Federation of Pharmaceutical Manufacturers and Associations) 60, 63, 73
IFRS (International Financial Reporting Standards) 155
IGO (intergovernmental organization) 101, 108, 176; alliance of corporations and associations and 95, 97–8, 110; business and 9; crime protection 150–1; facilitator and 143, 146; global business associations and 15, 177n2; IATA 78; ICC 28–9, 32; ICS 76, 87n47; industry association and 13, 56, 60, 63–4, 68, 70, 72, 74, 76, 83, 84, 169, 173; IOE 27, 34–5; peak associations and 27–9, 31, 48, 168, 173; public regulation and 147; research on 9, 114n33, 176; think tank and 130, 135; WBCSD 28, 29, 43; WCF 28–9; WEF 28, 29, 41; *see also* state
IIBCC (International Information Bureau of Chambers of Commerce) 52n31
IIF (Institute of International Finance) 58, 79–80, 88n60
IISI (International Iron and Steel Institute) 71, 87n34; *see also* worldsteel
ILO (International Labour Organization) 70, 87n32; IOE and 27, 28, 34, 173
IMF (International Monetary Fund) 9, 80
IMO (International Maritime Organization) 63, 75, 76

188 Index

industry association 13, 55–6, 168–9, 176; challenges 57; civil society and 57, 64, 73; collective action 57, 58, 65, 67, 73, 75, 80, 169–70; competition and cooperation 58, 59–60, 61, 65, 78, 83, 173; diversity 13, 83–4, 168; governance 61, 168–9; IGOs/other actors and 13, 56, 60, 63–4, 68, 70, 72, 74, 76, 83, 84, 169, 173; membership 58, 60–2, 70, 83; MNCs and 56, 64, 67, 73; national associations 58–9, 60–1, 64, 67; niches 48, 58, 84, 96, 173; overlapping 58, 84; participation 63; policies and services 62–3, 83; population 55, 57–9, 83, 168; public regulation 13, 56, 57, 63–4, 67, 73, 74, 81; secretariats 61–2; self-regulation 56, 64, 66, 68, 70, 72, 74, 78, 81, 82, 84; specialization 48, 64–82, 84; stability 48, 83; *see also* advertising industry; airline industry; chemical industry; finance industry; food industry; pharmaceutical industry; shipping industry; steel industry; textile industry
INGO (international non-governmental organization) 9, 175
Intel 101
International Food & Beverage Association 86n24
international relations 7, 9, 129, 175, 177n2
internationalization 5, 6, 17n11, 19n26
INTERTANKO (International Association of Independent Tanker Owners) 75
IO (international organization) 9
IOE (International Organization of Employers) 24, 34–6, 100; collective action 35, 36; direct-membership model 35; IGOs/other actors and 27, 34–5; ILO and 27, 28, 34, 173; IOE Partner Company Initiative 35; Management Board 35–6; market orientation 24–5; membership 24, 25, 30, 35; origins 34; policy field 25–6; role 34; secretariat 36, 52n30; service provision 27, 35; unions and 29
IPE (international political economy) 8–9, 175
ISDA (International Swaps and Derivatives Association) 79
ISF (International Shipping Federation) 75, 87n45
ISIC (International Standard Industrial Classification of All Activities) 84n2
ISO (International Organization for Standardization) 70, 162n12
ITMF (International Textile Manufacturers Federation) 68–71; Guideline for Standardized Instrument Testing of Cotton 70; International Federation of Master Cotton Spinners' and Manufacturers' Association 69, *69*; membership 69; service provision 70

JCIA (Japan Chemical Industry Association) 73

KPMG *153*, 155

law firm 141, 144, 149–50, 152, 163n21; *see also* facilitator
LCIA (London Court of International Arbitration) 148
League of Nations 32, 34
Lenovo 104
Lex Mundi 150

market 15; alliances, state/market-related 97–8, 110; global business associations and 14, 15; market facilitation 141, 142; peak associations and 23, 24–5
Mastercard 104
McDonald's 108
McKinsey & Company 101, 152–3, *153*, 154
MEDEF (Mouvement des Entreprises de France) 45
Michelin Guide 157
Microsoft 104

Index 189

mining and mineral industry 65–6; *see also* industry association
MNC (multinational corporation) 1, 7, 165, 175; clubs and 120; industry association and 56, 64, 67, 73; research on 7, 18n18; *see also* alliance of corporations and associations
MNE (multinational enterprise) 7; *see also* MNC
Moody's Investors Service 156
MSC (Marine Stewardship Council) 147

Nestlé 67, 108
NGO (non-governmental organization) 19n23, 114n33, 134; *see also* civil society
niche 12, 16n7, 85n4, 124, 173; alliance of corporations and associations 92, 96, 109, 111, 169; industry association 48, 58, 84, 96, 173; *see also* division of labor domain

OECD (Organisation for Economic Co-operation and Development) 9, 28, 74, 80, 175; *see also* BIAC
Open Society Foundations 117, **127**, 132–3
overlapping 12, 149, 167, 173; alliance of corporations and associations 111; facilitator 144, 149, 152, 156; industry association 58, 84; peak association 22, 25, 168; related private entities 170; think tank 118, 134, 135; *see also* division of labor; niche

PayPal 104
PCI SCC (Payment Card Industry Security Standards Council) 113n25
peak association 6, 10, 12–13, 21–3, 47–9, 168, 176; civil society and 27, 31; collective action 24, 35, 36, 40, 42, 44, 48, 49n1, 169–70; competition between 13, 23, 25, 48, 49, 168, 173; direct-membership model 24, 35; division of labor 25, 26, 48; federation 24, 44, 49n1; global peak association 29, 30, 47–8; IGOs/other actors and 27–9, 31, 48, 168, 173; indirect-membership model 24; market and 23, 24–5; membership 22, 23, 24, 25, 28, 29, *30*, 48, 50–1n16, 168, 173; national association 22, 24, 48, 50–1n16; overlapping 22, 25, 168; policy fields and service provision 25–7, 31, 48, 173; profiles 29–31, 48; specialization 12–13, 23, 25, 29–30, 31, 48, 168; stability 48; tasks and roles 11, 22, 23, 168, 172–3; territorial domain 23–4, 172; trans-industry character of 21, 41, 47
pharmaceutical industry 60, 73, 134; *see also* chemical industry; industry association
philanthropy 101, 126, 131, 133, 138n37
Pinkerton 152
PMA (Produce Marketing Association) 67–8
political science 7, 9, 10, 175
population ecology approach 16n4, 176–7, 177n7
PricewaterhouseCoopers 152–3, *153*, 155
public affairs and public relations bureaus 141, 144, 145–6, 160; *see also* facilitator
public regulation 165; alliance of corporations and associations 108, 109, 110; banking 80; facilitator and 14, 141, 142, 143, 150, 155, 159; IACC 107, 108; IGOs and 147; industry association and 13, 56, 57, 63–4, 67, 73, 74, 81; *see also* self-regulation
public sector 19n30, 137n6, 163n28; *see also* IGO; state
PWBLF (The Prince of Wales Business Leaders Forum) 137n19

rating agency 141, 156–8, 160; *see also* facilitator
regulation *see* public regulation
related private entities 3, 167, 170–2; associations/related entities competition 12, 173–4; overlapping

170; *see also* club; facilitator; think tank
Rockefeller, David 122
Rotary International 119–20; UN and 120
Rothschild, E.L. 125
RT (Round Table of International Shipping Associations) 76, 87n48
Rutgers University, *Conference Report* 84n1

SAC (Sustainable Apparel Coalition) 87n33, 111n2
Samsung 104
security and crime protection 142, 150–2; *see also* facilitator
self-regulation 10, 147; alliance of corporations and associations 92, 98, 100, 107, 108, 109; civil society 147; ICC 25, 34; industry association 56, 64, 66, 68, 70, 72, 74, 78, 81, 82, 84; *see also* public regulation
self-regulator 141, 142, 147–8, 156, 160; *see also* facilitator
shipping industry 72, 74–6, 141, 169; Cyber Security Onboard Ships 76, 77; piracy 76, 151; security problems 151–2; *see also* industry association
Siemens 58
SME (small and medium-sized enterprise) 37, 50n7
SNAC International 67
social class 1, 7–8, 10
sociology 7, 10, 175; economic sociology 10, 17n17, 142, 175; international political sociology 175
Soros, George 132, 133
Standard & Poor's 156
state 175, 176; alliances, state/market-related 97–8, 110; business and 9, 19n30, 166; global business associations and 14, 15; *see also* IGO
steel industry 71–4; *see also* industry association
sustainability 72, 99–100, 114n31; ICC 53n46; ICMM 66; 'Transforming our World: The 2030 Agenda for

Sustainable Development' 99; WBCSD 28, 41–3

TABD (TransAtlantic Business Dialogue) 137n12
TBC (Transatlantic Business Coalition) 120, 137n12
textile industry 68–71, 169; *see also* industry association
think tank 13, 115–17, 126, 134–6, 171; agenda-setting 3, 13, 116, 126, 135, 136n1, 139n40; association-like features 115–16, 136, 136n1, 171; business-based and -oriented think tanks 126–34; civil society and 128; clubs/think tanks common features 116, 118, 123; diversity 116, 126, 135; donor 116, 126, 135; facilitators/think tanks common features 128, 135, 136; globalization of 126, 128, 130, 132, 134; IGOs and 130, 135; location of think tank offices and entities **127**; overlapping 118, 134, 135; political issues 117, 128, 171; research/knowledge-based tasks 123, 128, 131, 135, 171; role of 128, 135, 136
Thomson Reuters and Bloomberg L.P. 158–9
TNC (transnational corporation) 7; *see also* MNC; MNE
Transparency International 157
Trilateral Commission 117, 122–3; research task 123
Tyler, Tony 78

UIA (International Association of Lawyers) 163n21
UN (United Nations) 40, 108; 1992 UN Rio Conference 74; ICC and 51n19; Rotary International 120; 'Transforming our World: The 2030 Agenda for Sustainable Development' 99
UN Global Compact 124
UNEP (UN Environment Programme) 74

Index   191

UNESCO (UN Educational, Scientific and Cultural Organization) 120
UNFCCC (UN Framework Convention on Climate Change) 74
UNICEF (UN Children's Fund) 120
Unilever 67
UNITAR (UN Institute for Training and Research) 74
university 120, 134
UNWTO (UN World Tourism Organization) 63

WBCSD (World Business Council for Sustainable Development) 17n16, 24, 41–3, 49n2, 100; collective action 42; Council 43; Executive Committee 42, 43; headquarters 43; IGOs/other actors and 28, 29, 43; market orientation 25; membership 30, 42, 51n16; origins 41–2, 53n46; policy field 25, 26, 42–3; portfolio 28; secretariat 43, 114n31; service provision 27, 43; sustainability agenda 28, 41–3
WCF (World Chambers Federation) 24, 27, 29; chambers of commerce and industry 37, 51n16; General Council 37; IBCC 52n31; ICC 36–7; IGOs/other actors and 28–9; IIBCC 52n31; market orientation 25; membership 30, 50n7; origins 36; policy field 25, 26; secretariat 37; SMEs 37, 50n7

WEF (World Economic Forum) 17n16, 24, 39–41; Board of Trustees and Managing Board 41, 53n42; club features 125, 137n6; collective action 40; Davos 40; hybrid character 40; IGOs/other actors and 28, 29, 41; market orientation 25; membership 30, 40–1, 51n16; mimicry 52n39; origins 39–40; policy field 25, 26; portfolio 28; resources 41; secretariat 41; service provision 27; think tank features 40, 128
Western Union 101
WFA (World Federation of Advertisers) 81–2, 89n67
WHO (World Health Organization) 63, 108, 120
WIPO (World Intellectual Property Organization) 151
Wolfsberg Group 88n57
World Bank 9, 80; World Bank Group 80
World War I 31, 38
World War II 6
worldsteel (World Steel Association) 71–2; 'Antitrust Compliance Guidelines' 72; as IISI 71, 87n34
WSC (World Shipping Council) 74–5
WTO (World Trade Organization) 9, 50n13, 70, 72, 74, 175
WTTC (World Travel & Tourism Council) 63